浙江省社科联社科普及立项课题成果

◎王雅平 著

In the Name of Bridges:
Chinese Cultural Codes on the Grand Canal（Chinese-English Bilingual）

以桥之名

——大运河上的中国文化密码

中英双语

浙江工商大学出版社
ZHEJIANG GONGSHANG UNIVERSITY PRESS
·杭州·

图书在版编目（CIP）数据

以桥之名：大运河上的中国文化密码：汉、英 ／
王雅平著．— 杭州：浙江工商大学出版社，2023.6
ISBN 978-7-5178-5498-2

Ⅰ．①以… Ⅱ．①王… Ⅲ．①大运河－文化－中国－
汉、英 Ⅳ．① K928.42

中国国家版本馆 CIP 数据核字（2023）第 102231 号

以桥之名——大运河上的中国文化密码（中英双语）
YI QIAO ZHI MING—DAYUNHE SHANG DE ZHONGGUO WENHUA MIMA
(ZHONG-YING SHUANG YU)

王雅平 著

责任编辑	王　英
责任校对	李远东
封面设计	观止堂
责任印制	包建辉
出版发行	浙江工商大学出版社
	（杭州市教工路 198 号　邮政编码 310012）
	（E-mail：zjgsupress@163.com）
	（网址：http://www.zjgsupress.com）
	电话：0571-88904980，88831806（传真）
排　　版	杭州彩地电脑图文有限公司
印　　刷	杭州宏雅印刷有限公司
开　　本	710 mm×1000 mm　1/16
印　　张	16.25
字　　数	263 千
版印次	2023 年 6 月第 1 版　2023 年 6 月第 1 次印刷
书　　号	ISBN 978-7-5178-5498-2
定　　价	88.00 元

王雅平同志历时 4 年创作的文化科普作品《以桥之名——大运河上的中国文化密码（中英双语）》即将付梓，面对这部 26 万多字的有关大运河文化的中英双语著作，我为她感到高兴。

京杭大运河与我校有千丝万缕的联系。我校位于良渚，毗邻大运河，正如校歌开篇所言"运河流远，良渚曙光"。我校有得天独厚的世界自然遗产区域地理优势，因此更负有利用大运河做好文化育人工作的责任。交通职业教育是我校的立校之本，与桥梁、水上运输相关的专业均是我校的重点专业板块。我校一直重视校园文化培育，以"书香育人，阅读领航"为重要抓手，致力于为工科院校学生的人文综合素养和可持续发展夯实基础。成为国家"双高计划"建设单位以来，我校进一步加强对校园文化品牌的培育，加大对教师学术研究与著作出版的扶持，加强对学生爱国情怀的培植，为有质量、有特色的社会文化服务赋能，体现我校为党育人、为国育才的大学担当。

《以桥之名——大运河上的中国文化密码（中英双语）》正是这样一部著作。该书立足大运河文化交流，以京杭大运河杭州段与浙东运河段上的重要桥梁为骨架，以相关中国传统文化为血肉，以桥梁为点，以大运河为线，以中国传统文化为面，穿珠成链，由此及彼，将中国故事娓娓道来，建构了可亲、可敬、可爱的中国形象。相信这本书能够使有兴趣了解中国文化、致力于讲好中国故事的广大读者有所受益。

　　我了解到王雅平同志为创作此书，多年来利用假期自费去实地考察、调研运河文化，足迹车辙遍布杭州、绍兴、湖州、宁波等地。在工作之余，她笔耕不辍，几经打磨，终于完成了这部沉甸甸的作品。这种求真务实的精神，是教书育人的职责所系，也是当前社会环境下的一种难能可贵的精神。此外，我校屠群峰同志、陈星月同学手绘了部分相关图片，从这个角度来说，这本书也是我校师生凝心聚力良好风貌的一个印证。

　　"服务交通强国建设，彰显中国职教特色，创建世界水平学校"是我校的建设目标，"立德树人，德技并修，提供优质教育服务"是我校的质量方针。希望有更多的教师能加入创造智力成果、谱写文化新篇章的事业中，有更多的同志能凝心聚力、身体力行，实践以文化人，为引领新时代职业教育高质量发展而共同努力。

浙江交通职业技术学院党委书记　孙校伟

2023 年 5 月

　　2019 年 2 月，中共中央办公厅、国务院办公厅印发了《大运河文化保护传承利用规划纲要》，强调要深入挖掘和丰富大运河文化内涵，充分展现大运河遗存承载的文化，活化大运河流淌伴生的文化，弘扬大运河历史凝练的文化。2021 年 6 月，习近平总书记在中央政治局第三十次集体学习时强调："要更好推动中华文化走出去，以文载道、以文传声、以文化人，向世界阐释推介更多具有中国特色、体现中国精神、蕴藏中国智慧的优秀文化。"本书的创作正是中华文化"走出去"的一次探索与实践，旨在挖掘大运河在浙江承载的历史文化资源，加大大运河文化因子的提炼力度，推动中国形象的国际构建。

　　自中国大运河"申遗"以来，与大运河相关的研究、出版工作成为重要内容。浙江人民美术出版社、杭州出版社等相继出版了与运河文化相关的丛书。以王国平主持的"杭州全书·运河（河道）丛书"为代表，顾希佳等编写的《运河村落的蚕丝情结》对运河的桥船码头和沿岸风俗进行了介绍。任轩的《遇见：一个人的大运河》侧重对运河杭州段史料的深度挖掘。列入世界文化遗产名录之后，以大运河为载体的虚构类写作增加，如徐则臣的小说《北上》，夏坚勇的《大运河传》《湮没的辉煌》，黄亚洲的诗集《我在运河南端歌唱》，浙江话剧院的话剧《运河 1937》，等等。在运河专业研究方面，有学者就运河漕运制度等进行了研究并出版专著，而聊城大学运河文化研究中心发起并推动出版了运河研究论文集，这些为运河研究的发展提供了重要佐证。多种多样的运河文艺与专业创作体现了文化主管部门对弘扬运河文化的高度重视，也印证了运河书写是一座可待多角度挖掘的富矿。

为贯彻落实习近平总书记关于"保护好、传承好、利用好大运河"的重要指示精神，打造展示中华文明的大运河文化这张"金名片"，亟须加强运河文化的国际化推广。在实践层面，需要通过大运河讲好中国故事，让大运河蕴含的中国文化易于为外国读者接受，在国际社会得以传播。但是，前述已有的与运河相关的作品，特别是科普类图书，主要以中文为创作语言，面向的是中文读者和国内人群，制约了运河文化的国际化推广。

以英文或者中英双语撰写，适用于中西文化交流且能直接为运河文化国际化推广服务的运河文化读本，少之又少。有关部门意识到运河文化英语读物的缺失现状，邀请了浙江大学外籍教师撰写了 *Postcards from China: Travels Along the Grand Canal* 一书。该书作者记叙了他在日常生活与工作中所接触到的与运河相关的数位人士，为我们了解"外国人怎样看运河边的人"提供了一个视角。但是该书全篇以英语写就，作者的学者身份和英语母语者身份，使得该书的阅读、传播有一定难度和专业度，这给希望直接借鉴此书，向外国人讲好中国运河故事的读者与从业人员造成了阅读和理解的障碍。

笔者自 2013 年开始进行运河文化对外宣传与交流方面的研究与实践，完成了"景区旅游文本的翻译策略""'中国文化走出去'背景下的运河旅游文化翻译""运河旅游文化的美学翻译策略""馆地协同开展运河文化国际化推广"等课题的研究；在应用方面，完成了运河文化美学、运河水上旅游英文导游词的翻译工作，以及中国大运河拱宸桥桥西历史文化馆、小河直街历史文化长廊、拱墅区民俗记忆馆等的与运河相关文献的翻译实践。这些工作加深了笔者对大运河的认识和感情，也发现了运河文化的国际化推广在出版物方面的缺失。

基于上述考虑，笔者创作了《以桥之名——大运河上的中国文化密码（中英双语）》一书，并在内容、形式上进行了创新。本书梳理大运河（浙江段）代表性古桥背后的文化含义，穿珠成链，借桥说文，并非照搬百度百科类的史实介绍，也不是艰深难懂的高头讲章，不拘于桥的形制，而是以桥的名义，挖掘和凸显大运河作为交通之河、文化之河、民族之河的丰富内涵。本书以中英双语写就，在一定意义上是对已有的运河文化出版物的一种补白。

在动笔创作之前，笔者实地考察了大运河杭州段、绍兴段、宁波段等多处桥梁和运河文化遗存，积累了大量实地图片。在此过程中，笔者发现同一处运河文化旅游景点的英文介绍或参差不齐，或各执一词，深感有必要创作一本面向国内外读者的以运河桥梁为链的有关中国传统文化的图书。

本书聚焦京杭大运河杭州段和浙东运河段上的代表性桥梁，以各桥生发的相关中国传统文化为血肉，结合史实、民俗、工艺，展开基于中国传统文化特质的文本创作，使桥梁事实描述与文化故事虚构相融合，使内容既有文化科普性，又有文学可读性。为提高站位，本书从构建中国"可亲、可敬、可爱"国际形象的国家战略出发，一方面将中国故事娓娓道来，另一方面考虑中国文化国际传播的要求，在典型桥梁选择、文化因子提炼、中英双语转化等方面，力求达到专家肯定、读者喜爱、文旅企业可用、国际友人愿读的目标。历经 4 年的创作与打磨，本书即将付梓，26 万多字的内容主要讲述了什么呢？

从广济桥到太平桥，从登云桥到城东桥，读者可以对京杭大运河杭州段与浙东段上的重要桥梁，形成自北向南再向东的整体印象。在一个个桥梁故事中，形象地了解中国人民造桥修桥的勠力同心、传统科举制度的深刻影响、维系大国命脉的仓储体系、民间市集呈现的繁华商贸、桥梁艺术蕴含的传统审美、运河促进的文化交融、保家卫国的感人情怀、民族工业的"吉光片羽"……此外，本书收录的实景照片、手绘的精美插图，都能让读者获得有关桥梁文化的直观感知。阅读是最好的体验，通过阅读本书，读者能够和作者一起进行运河文化的深度体验，加深对大运河蕴含的文化密码的理解，加强中华传统文化对外输出的能力。

本书作为以桥梁为点、大运河为线、中国文化为面的双语文化科普图书，较为系统地介绍了大运河（浙江段）代表性桥梁的文史知识及其蕴含的文化故事，适用于致力"中国文化走出去"的教育、宣传等部门与系统的从业人士，也可作为中高等教育的通识读本。中国文化部分的英语书写，可以作为英语四、六级/A、B级等全国性考试中文化翻译类题型的素材库。本书可用于运河管理机构、旅游企事业单位等的员工培训教材，还可以作为共同富裕建设的抓手，推广全民阅读。适逢第19届亚运会召开之年，国际友人和媒体将会来到杭州。本书可投放于大运河遗产点和相关旅游文化机构，也可赠予外国游客和对中国文化感兴趣的人士，直接产生运河文化国际推广的社会效益。通过阅读，了解乡土文化，厚植爱国情怀，讲好中国故事，开展文化交流。

本书得以创作完成，离不开众多学者和友人的帮助。多卷本、万花筒式的"杭州全书·运河（河道）丛书"，促发了笔者创作本书的初心。深耕杭州地方运河文化研究的任轩老师的多篇文章，给予本书事实方面的佐证。杭州江南古桥文化研究会的史官云老师、杭州市运河集团郑彬铨先生等为我的实践调研提供了便利。全国交通运输职业教育教学指导委员会秘书长屠群峰教授为本书提供了手绘桥梁图片。我的同事朱旻老师对部分英文章节提出了修改意见。我的大学老师郭国良教授亲自为本书后记润色。杭州市京杭运河（杭州段）综合保护委员会及拱墅区运河官微、杭州市运河集团建设的运河文化带的实地场景，开阔了我的视野并提供了创作的依凭。我所供职的浙江交通职业技术学院，更是推动本书从个人创作走到公开出版的重要力量。学院图书馆的运河专题文献与桥梁文献，为我查阅图书资料提供了极大的便利；学院"双高"建设将本书纳入子项目，不但为本书的出版解决了经济上的后顾之忧，更为本书的文化传播与文化育人打开了可能的路径。还要感谢本书的责任编辑王英，她在出版的过程中，以极大的耐心和专业精神，促成了此书的最终完稿。我的朋友、同行、师长听闻我在尝试这项"大胆"的创作工程后所给予的鼓励同样是本书得以完成的精神源泉。而我的家人得知书稿缓慢推进，从不质疑，而是不吝于点赞支持，他们为本书的最终完成所做的贡献是不言而喻的。需要感谢的机构和个人不能枚举，唯有铭记在心。

虽然笔者汲汲数年，有心创作一本精品著作，但囿于水平，如史料掌握不足、非母语写作，本书瑕疵在所难免，欢迎方家指正。运河文化的国际推广，任重道远，唯愿笔者的斗胆尝试，能抛砖引玉，吸引更多的有学之士投入运河文化作品的双语创作中，共同为构建"可亲、可敬、可爱"的当代中国形象而尽绵薄之力。

王雅平

于杭州流云轩

2023 年 4 月

天下大势，浩浩汤汤。运河流远，贯通京杭。大江大河向来都与国家命运相连，与社会变迁同频，与人民福祉攸关。

中国大运河，以其工程的浩大、历史的久远、流域的辽阔、影响的深广，而举世罕见。放眼世界，重要的运河不止一条，如国际上的巴拿马运河、苏伊士运河，服务于一国内部交通的伊利运河（美国）、阿尔贝特运河（比利时），而名中带"大"者，唯中国大运河。这个"大"字在国际上通用的英语专名为"grand"，而根据牛津词典的解释，"grand"不仅意味着物理空间的"广大"，还意味着作用和意义的"重大"，更意味着给人带来强烈视觉与情感冲击的形态意义上的"大美"。中国大运河由隋唐大运河、京杭大运河和浙东运河组成，全长约 2700 千米。其中，京杭大运河是南北通津的大动脉。流经北京、天津、河北、山东、江苏和浙江 6 个省市，全长近 1800 千米的京杭大运河，是交通要道、经济动脉、文化"汇流"，是自然之河也是民生之河，是古老之河也是新生之河。从春秋战国到清末，再到民国至当代，大运河象征着一部生生不息而跌宕起伏的历史传奇，是古代中国人胼手胝足缔造的世界级工程，也是当代儿女描绘的新时代画卷。

2014 年 6 月 22 日，在第 38 届世界遗产大会上，由隋唐大运河、京杭大运河、浙东运河组成的中国大运河项目成功入选世界文化遗产名录。从这一刻起，作为京杭大运河南端的城市杭州就拥有了除西湖之外的第二个世界级文化遗产。而大运河杭州段成为一颗"硕大且俨"的文化旅游明珠，赋予杭州作为历史文化名城和国际著名旅游城市新的内涵。

那么，一个步履匆匆初到杭州的游客，怎样尽可能多地领略京杭大运河的风貌呢？答案是览一河、一桥、一仓。

上塘河——开京杭大运河地理和文化之先河

一说到和大运河有关的朝代，人们脱口而出的就是隋朝。这个不足百年的封建王朝帝祚之短暂，曾被归咎于劳民伤财的大运河的开凿。要使唐朝诗人皮日休的客观评价"尽道隋亡为此河，至今千里赖通波。若无水殿龙舟事，共禹论功不较多"真正深入人心，则须人们不再囿于统治阶级的视角，回归对大运河经济文化价值的探究，才能实现。京杭大运河亘古伟业，绵延近 1800 千米，追根溯源，则须从小小的一段上塘河开始。

实际上这一旷世工程的开端还要上溯至秦始皇时期。这位首次统一中国的政治家巡察庞大帝国的东南郡县时，命人疏通河道（据《越绝书》，秦始皇治陵水道到钱塘越地，通浙江），时称秦河（今上塘河）。之后，隋炀帝对它进行了疏浚，使之成为江南运河南端。由唐至宋，税赋粮米仰赖东南，上塘河成为重要的运输通道。特别是宋室南迁定都临安（今杭州）之后，宋高宗赵构重视贸易。上塘河以其通达钱塘江、连接东海之利，越发"舟船辐辏、昼夜喧沓"，河两岸商铺林立，赤岸古埠由此设立。还有官驿"班荆馆"，外国使者觐见南宋皇帝时须在此等候、听诏。1359 年，张士诚新开江南运河之后，上塘河不再作为主要的运输官道，但它连接东海的独特地位并未消失。相传康熙、乾隆南巡，乾隆看望海宁陈阁老，都是经由上塘河前往的。

交通，既意味着地理概念上的接近、物资上的传递，也和人员的流动、文化的交融密不可分。今天的人们仍可以从古人的诗句中感知古上塘河的风貌，如"水塍新筑稻秧畦"，唐代诗人张祜记录了上塘河畔的稻田风景。又如"烟雨桃花夹岸栽，低低浑欲傍船来"，宋代诗人范成大描绘了上塘河两岸的春色。陆游暂住班荆馆时写道："二日……过赤岸班荆馆，小休前亭。班荆者，北使宿顿及赐燕之地，距临安三十六里。"元朝诗人方回写下了日常生活中的一个温馨片段：天刚刚亮的时候，去桂芳桥边买新鲜鱼虾，沾沾这户因出了3名进士而造桥纪念的人家的"书香之气"——"记取五更霜显白，桂芳桥买小鱼鲜"。

上塘河不仅仅是文人笔下的柔美江南，它还听闻过吴越争霸的鸣镝，感受过岳飞抗金的胆魄（打铁关、岳帅桥），见证过韩世忠将军荡寇平叛的忠勇（得胜桥）。宋皇室在金人大军压境的恐惧之中颠沛流离，撇下繁华都城东京（今开封），一路向东。赵构在父兄均被金军掳走之后，更加迫切地向东南泽国避祸，虽然逃亡十分仓促，但必须说这是一个危急关头的理性决策——长驱直入的北方游牧民族，到了水乡遍布的江南，就失去了马背上的优势。在大片水荡之中，韩世忠率领将士们与金军展开激战，不谙水性的金军最后铩羽而归。

韩世忠因为夫人梁红玉的击鼓励兵而获得了更具传奇的色彩。韩世忠和梁红玉，与其说是英雄爱美人，不如说是女伯乐慧眼识英才。酒席上陪宴的歌伎梁红玉，遇到落魄不得志的下级青年军官韩世忠，激励他何不振作建功。没有什么比来自一名年轻女子的真诚期待更能激励一名青年男子的了。数年后韩世忠立了军功升了职，他履约纳梁红玉为妾。妾者，半仆半妻也。一般来说，女子一旦为妾，人生也就看到头了。但是梁红玉不是普通女子。莺歌燕舞，只是她的生存技能，内在的心志让她有别于一般女子。出身于习武之家的梁红玉，胆气、英气和志气是与生俱来的。在韩世忠带领将士和金军在嘉兴附近的黄天荡展开拉锯战的48天里，梁红玉没有像普通妇女那样战战兢兢、足不出户，而是来到战士之中，挽起袖子，跃上高台，于江南飘摇的细雨之中，擂响震天战鼓。女子尚且如此勇猛，何况男儿哉？铿锵玫瑰，当从红玉始。南宋初，苗、刘二将兵变，在赵构被困于大内的危急时刻，也是梁红玉，以一己之身，一匹快马，连夜逃出报信，搬来救兵。如果说苏东坡和朝云是士大夫与侍妾相知的佳话代表，那么韩世忠和梁红玉，则是夫妻并肩战斗的励志故事。

父兄的遭遇历历在目，赵构既不敢班师中原，也不敢择一大城定居。他在浙江沿海漂流了数月，惶惶不可终日。幸而得到儒家忠君思想浸淫的文臣武将的勠力护卫，赵构这个原本耽于享乐的皇子不得不接受大臣们义正词严的"国不可一日无君"的劝谏，被架上皇位，不得不肩负起家国大任，最终定都临安。上塘河作为临安城内可通舟楫的大河，见证了南宋皇室最初的仓皇，也很快成为南宋发展内外贸易的窗口。内外贸易带来的繁华，落入了近 150 年后经上塘河而来的意大利人马可·波罗的眼中，令他发出了"世界上最华美的天城"的惊叹，由此在遥远的欧洲掀起了"东方热"。

这条河流，迎来过女词人李清照，迎来过科学家沈括，也迎来过大学士苏东坡。就连许仙白娘子的传奇，也离不开上塘河。这条不足 50 千米的人工河，一端是第一个统一的封建国家，另一端是发达的对外贸易王朝；一端是巩固内部统治实行"车同轨，书同文"的皇权，另一端是开放的海上丝绸之路；一端是焚书坑儒的思想钳制，另一端是群星璀璨的文化大观……它连接着赓续 2000 多年的文化传统，从经世致用到古代科学，从吟诗作画到海外贸易，从忠勇之义到民间传奇，上塘河开京杭大运河地理和文化之先河。

进入 21 世纪的上塘河，经历了发黑发臭的时期，而后经过持续不懈的"五水共治"，重新呈现出夹岸杨柳新、春水涨碧桃的美丽景象。旅游综合管理机构在上塘河沿岸打造了多个公园，种下了木芙蓉、红紫荆、鸡爪槭等，设计了景观雕塑，重开了香积古寺，建造了亭榭游廊，凿刻了佳句楹联……上塘河畔，绿水人家，风起翠幕；河上烟波画船，白鹭翻飞，正是一派江南好景象。

现在的上塘河，继往开来，除了延续古镇风貌，还成为全民健身的重要地域文化带。在上塘河绍兴路一带，有规模宏大的城北体育公园，各类专业运动场馆不一而足。而上塘河本身，则成为龙舟竞渡的绝佳场所。在 2022 年端午佳节之际，来自陕西、北京等多个地区的龙舟队在上塘河进行龙舟赛，吸引了许多市民走出家门，在河边树下或在河埠头站数小时，切身感受龙舟竞渡的现场情景。龙舟赛将传统文化和现代体育结合起来，十分有观赏性。器宇轩昂、威风凛凛的龙头，金光闪闪、装饰考究的龙舟，从来都是中华民族的精神图腾。从潜龙在渊到虎踞龙盘，从龙凤呈祥到鱼跃龙门，中国的文化在很大程度上就是龙的文化。龙舟竞渡是对孤高清贵的屈原的纪念，后来则演变成春末夏初端午时节人们所展现的对生活之热爱的一种仪式。 不妨看一首唐人展现龙舟竞渡的诗作：

　　　　五月五日天晴明，杨花绕江啼晓莺。

　　　　使君未出郡斋外，江上早闻齐和声。

　　　　使君出时皆有准，马前已被红旗引。

　　　　两岸罗衣破鼻香，银钗照日如霜刃。

　　　　鼓声三下红旗开，两龙跃出浮水来。

　　　　棹影斡波飞万剑，鼓声劈浪鸣千雷。

　　　　鼓声渐急标将近，两龙望标目如瞬。

　　　　波上人呼霹雳惊，竿头彩挂虹蜺晕。

　　　　…………①

这首诗完整地描绘了龙舟竞渡的时间、天气、风物，观看的官员、

---

①［唐］刘禹锡：《竞渡歌》，选自《刘禹锡集》，中华书局 1990 年版，第 634 页。

百姓，两艘龙舟的行动，以及鼓声、人声、水声等。也有表达在群情激昂的龙舟竞赛中好整以暇的，如"画鼓红旗送彩舟，健儿八百竞中流。谁知有个停桡者，闲倚江山第一楼"[1]。别人都在奋力划船，偏有一位停了桨，悠闲地把船停靠在水边的一处高楼下，物我两忘了。

拱宸桥——300 多年前"浙江精神"的实证

如果说上塘河见证的是王朝兴替和中国文脉，那么拱宸桥则是亲民的桥、经济的桥。这座三孔薄墩拱桥，东西横跨大运河，形制宏伟而不失江南灵秀，是京杭大运河进入杭州地界的首座大桥。在 2014 年 6 月的世界遗产大会上，拱宸桥的影像多次出现。此后，拱宸桥成为大运河杭州段公认的代表性建筑。

拱宸桥桥面宽阔，中间铺陈的是纵向条石，条石两侧横向排列麻石台阶，台阶外围为护栏，护栏以望柱相隔。在桥梁两侧，放置了两张窄长石凳。坐在石凳上伸直双腿小憩时，运河上带着些微泥沙味的风迎面吹来。此时极目北望皋亭山，遥想当年赵构为躲避金军在山中显宁寺逗留，岳家军忠勇抗金；惜乎皇帝后来失去抗金的决心，大好河山落入敌手。皋亭山下，上塘河畔的繁华商埠灯火零落，至南宋末年文天祥在此被金军扣押，桩桩件件纷涌而来……却看眼前，大河宁静沉稳，货船川流不息，靠近此桥时纷纷鸣笛示意，桥头鲜艳的五星红旗猎猎招展。抚今追昔，怎能不叫人思绪纷飞，"欣逢盛世"之感油然而生呢？！

从桥上向南望，在不远处的开阔河道东侧，整饬出了一大片平整墙面，上书红色大字"北新关"。当然，这只是遗址。明清时期，随着商业的繁荣，政府设立了类似于收费站的钞关，北新关即其中之一。

---

①［明］张弼：《端阳竞渡》。摘自古诗文网，参见 https://www.shiwens.com/search.html?k=%E7%AB%AF%E9%98%B3%E7%AB%9E%E6%B8%A1。

今天，人口稠密的大型居住区"大关"由此得名。业务繁忙的北新关，催生了北关夜市。明人高得旸《北关夜市》描绘道：

> 北城晚集市如林，上国流传直至今。
>
> 青苎受风摇月影，绛纱笼火照春阴。
>
> 楼前饮伴联游袂，湖上归人散醉襟。
>
> 阛阓喧阗如昼日，禁钟未动夜将深。

有意思的是，北新关和拱宸桥一样由官家主导，大利民生。用今天的话来说，拱宸桥鲜明地体现了交通基础性、先导性的地位。漕粮、丝绸、茶叶、竹木等大宗商品经运河北上，或者继续向南经西兴镇入钱塘江出海。拱宸桥一带的运河是民生之河。漕粮、竹木等的装卸需要大量的力工，因此拱宸桥畔设有装卸工人公会——一个行业自治组织，带有工会雏形的色彩。这一公会必然有漕帮参加。漕帮者，运漕粮的船夫力工是也。以康熙皇帝为榜样的乾隆皇帝六下江南，留下了上万首诗词，也留下了诸多与漕帮相关的韵事传说。

不过与影视剧中将乾隆下江南娱乐化不同的是，皇帝一再南巡，并非只贪恋江南风光、儿女情长。《清史稿》记载，康熙初登大宝，日夜不忘三件大事，奋笔书之，挂于殿中大柱。三件大事，漕运居其一。漕运不通则米粮盐布断绝，饥荒起而盗贼生，或民变或官腐。运河，是王朝的经济要道，也是政权根基。运河通畅，则货畅其流，人民安居。

再说回拱宸桥和北新关。不同于临安城南河坊街为达官贵族的享乐之地，北关夜市主要是平民聚会的欢乐之所。北新关因收钞而设，运河繁忙，不能即刻通关的船只滞留于此；通关会钞了的，要进行一番商场上的社交游乐宴请；力工得了工钱自然也要花钱买点快活，而长年出门在外的人也会买点临安城的新奇玩意儿给家乡老少。运河及其附属设施的交通基础功能刺激了民间经济的发展，继而促进了文化的交融，促发了市民阶层的兴起。

北新关的繁忙与拱宸桥息息相关，拱宸桥的修造就是市民阶层孕育的结果。

据传，明崇祯四年（1631），举人祝华峰感叹运河两岸人们往来不便，毁家捐资，建拱宸桥。另一说是它由明末商人夏木江所倡建。[①]虽然修拱宸桥的第一人究竟是祝举人还是夏商人并无定论，但是有一点是一样的，即民间募资修造。在奄奄一息的明王朝没有财力满足人民迫切需求的时候，市民阶层承担起了民建民享公共交通的职责。

民间的捐资行为也促发了官员的作为。顺治八年（1651），拱宸桥桥身坍塌。康熙五十三年（1714），浙江布政使段志熙倡率捐筑。也就是说，修桥的费用绝大部分仍然来自市民阶层。又过了12年，雍正朝的浙江巡抚李卫将拱宸桥的修造向前推进了一大步，他带头捐出俸禄，商户和市民受到感召，再次聚集银两，拱宸桥被加厚加宽。当然，李卫捐出的俸禄相比修桥资金来说九牛一毛，但是他作为地方最高行政官的态度和行为，起到了四两拨千斤的效果。可以说，拱宸桥巍巍之象，在于市民和官员的共同努力，是一种"不等不靠朝廷拨款"的地方民众自力更生的积极实践。今天，我们说"浙江精神"其来有自，300多年前的拱宸桥修建史正是一处生动的例证。

然而，乱世桥梁易毁。同治二年（1863）秋，左宗棠与太平军在拱宸桥激战，桥芯因设有太平军的堡垒而成为战火焦点，这座大桥再次倒塌。之后，它的恢复又一次依赖民间力量。光绪十一年（1885），杭州士绅丁丙主持重修拱宸桥。丁丙家族经营布业，富于资财，他本人无心仕途，而是热心公益，潜心藏书，骨子里是个传统意义上的士人。

拱宸桥，这座美丽、宏伟兼具的大桥，是大运河南端的标志，也是杭州城北的地标，而它曲折往复的修造过程还隐含着大运河作为交通要道与其培育的市民阶层的内在关系：大河需大桥，大桥利民生，

---

① 据《古今图书集成·杭州桥梁考》和康熙《杭州府志》。

桥复而民富，民富而桥坚。

站在拱宸桥顶转身向东，映入眼帘的是雄伟的青石牌坊，正中四个大字"南北通津"，坊柱的楹联为"牌屹东隅万缕丹曦迎璀璨；坊邻西子一轮皓月共婵娟"。沿着宽阔的麻石台阶下桥，转到石牌坊另一面，则是"利泽千秋"，两侧楹联为"吴沟隋柳元河三朝伟迹；一水五江六省千里通衢"。这两组楹联精要地概括了京杭大运河的历史、流域、作用，并把大运河与西湖联系起来，提醒人们大运河和西湖一样，是杭州市的世界文化遗产双姝——当时的人们还不能预测到仅仅在几年之后，良渚成为杭州的第三张世遗文化名片。

从拱宸桥西侧下来，再向北走数步是抄手游廊，时常有一个微型的民间越剧团在吹拉弹唱。从体现杭嘉湖平原桑田风貌的《桑园访妻》到越剧《红楼梦》名段《天上掉下个林妹妹》，或柔美婉转，或响遏行云。水助曲声，曲助游兴，传统艺术焕发了新生。桥堍南侧是一排"美人靠"，这一临水而置的木构造是江南人天才的发明。它向水面倾斜出契合人体脊背需要的弧度，在亭廊柱子之间延伸出适合人体放松的宽度和适合人们社交的距离，无声而亲切地邀请人们到此歇脚。人们沐浴在河岸凉风之中，在拍岸水声和货船鸣笛中感受相得益彰的韵律之美，偶然一两声搭配着竹板的嗒嗒吆喝"甜酒酿——甜酒酿哎——"创造出一小节变奏……这一刻，没有人会感受不到内心的宁静。

沿着拱宸桥西侧向西五六步，可以看到一座民国风格的以青砖为主体、红泥线勾勒的两层小楼。这是通益公纱厂旧址。运河上来往穿梭的运丝船，促发了中国最早的一批民族工业。拱宸桥以其货运和客流的便利，被民族资本家选址建造纱厂。杭嘉湖一带心灵手巧、素有桑蚕业传统手艺的妇女，成为第一批纱厂女工。行业的发展亟须适合的职业培训学校，女子蚕桑学校便在这一带应运而生。著名的文化学者资中筠先生的母亲在接受了完整的传统教育后，就被其身为银行家的外公送至女子蚕桑学校学习。可以说，拱宸桥畔既是民族工业的萌芽地，也是职业教育的萌发地，还是妇女解放的首发地。而这一切追根溯源，都要归功于大运河的交通之便。

富义仓——近代物流的遗存

过了拱宸桥向南，在大运河与胜利河的交汇处，有一处较为开阔的河埠头。沿着梯形河埠头拾级而上，"富义仓"三个大字就在眼前。推开三开木门，迈过门槛，迎面是一片青色地砖铺就的广场，广场上七口大水缸纵列。绕着广场的是一间间木屋，乍一看，以为是明清官衙的朴素庑房；再一看则心生疑惑，木屋外为何专门设了数级台阶——宛如一架微型楼梯？

丁丙曾写过一首关于富义仓的诗：

> 惯习櫺槌卅尺强，让他瓦白足春粮。
>
> 商量转运临河便，预备新增富义仓。

富义仓的读法，严格说来应当是"富/义仓"。"手里有粮，心中不慌。"为了应对自然气候引发的粮食供应不足的问题，中国自汉文帝时期起就开始探索国家储备粮食的制度，找到的办法是——仓储。粮仓主要分为常平仓和义仓，前者利用官府的资金进行粮食和实物的囤积，后者则是在官府的组织下，按人头和田亩抽成进行征收和采购，是一种官方倡议、民间运营的仓储方式。无论是常平仓还是义仓，它们的基本目的和运作方式都是一样的，就是调节米价，以利民生。丰年时籴粮，防止谷贱伤农；荒年时平粜，以对冲贵粮，赈济流民。

仓储和运输的关系是密不可分的。仓储的前提是大量的粮食得以运送，没有便利的交通则粮仓"无粮可储"；仓储的目的是调节粮价，存储的粮如果不能便利地运送出去，则会造成巨大的浪费。清政府对负责管理粮仓的官员要求十分严格："州县仓谷霉烂者革职留任，限一年赔完复职；逾年不完，解任；三年外不完，定罪，著落家产追赔。"① 粮食储存、管理不好，轻则革职、赔付，重则坐牢抄家。多部影视剧对此有过生动的呈现：上级开仓查粮，发现粮谷霉烂，粮官不堪压力而自杀谢罪。粮官可谓品级虽低，但责任重大。

由此，前文所述的木屋外的微型楼梯之谜就可以解开了：登上三级楼梯，推门而入，地面齐平，也就是说，屋内地面比屋外广场地面高出将近 60 厘米。这高差用什么来补齐呢？地板下是一根根木档，将地面架空。江南多雨，这一设计构造可以尽可能地隔离地表潮气，加强通风透气功能，减少谷子霉变。

开凿运河的最初目的是运送粮食，唐朝称之为"漕粮"。3600 多里漫漫航程，谷仓就成为必不可少的配套设施。运河与谷仓，正是中国古代物流的一体两面，兹事体大。从隋代起中央就在淮安设立漕运专署；到明清两代，专门设立了漕运总督衙门，中央部级大臣督办漕事。今天我们熟悉的诸多肱股之臣，如范仲淹、史可法、施世纶、恩铭等，都曾担负过漕运大任。

关于富义仓，有句话广为天下知，即"北有南新仓，南有富义仓"，此二仓并称天下粮仓。在中国大运河首批 58 处遗产点中，富义仓是元、明、清三代运河中罕见的仓储设施遗存。

作为南宋国都，杭州的仓储制度此时相当完善，从运输、储存、装卸、搬运，到包装、加工、配送、数据分析等，整条物流链分工明确，管理严格。经由大运河运来的米谷在码头卸下，经过筛选、定级，分类存储，由行头定价，然后批发给城内外的商户。中国京杭大运河博物馆展陈的文物中有一个小小的碾子，手掌大小，运来的谷子放入其中，上下两层一转一压，谷壳脱落，米粒出现，验粮师一眼就能够知道这批粮食的等级。杭州城北现仍有多处地名，如仓基新村、米市巷、东粮泊巷等，能让人怀想当年米业储运的盛景。据《杭州市粮食志》

---

① ［清］赵尔巽等：《清史稿》（卷八四～卷一三〇），天津古籍出版社 2000 年版。

（1994）数据，1934年富义仓一带的米店有10余家。而装卸的脚夫也有自己专门的行会组织，甚至还有专门出租装米的"叉袋"的商家。

如今的富义仓，摇身一变，成为时尚创意空间，咖啡馆、书茶馆、研习社，不一而足，各有趣味。无论是在朗朗晴空下凌霄花开的盛夏，还是在天地茫茫白雪纷飞的隆冬，在富义仓文化园品茗读书、抚琴听雪，或看院内七星大水缸里，春雨数点缀新荷；或看廊下马槽中，菖蒲几丛伴云栽……人和天地自然融为一体，物我两忘，岂不快哉！

富义仓内有一家书院，横批不同于常见的4字，而是6个字：奇茶妙墨俱香。楹联为："问茶哪得香如许；惟有韵和妙墨来。"

这倒令人想起一句古话"仓廪实而知礼节"，当人们不必再为生计发愁的时候，就会关注精神层面的需求。

昔日的富义仓是大运河国之命脉所系的见证；近代的富义仓折射出杭州人务实诚恳、居安思危的精神；今天的富义仓则优雅转身，从"物质粮仓"转变为"精神粮仓"，成为浙江建设共同富裕示范区的文化惠民地标。

京杭大运河在杭州有11处世界文化遗产点，更有几十个文化记忆点和旅游文化体验点，从北端"落雨天不打伞"的塘栖古镇，到中段接待过G20杭州峰会首脑夫人们的手工业活态体验馆，再到南端与钱塘江相连的三堡船闸，林林总总，不一而足。随着国家《大运河文化保护传承利用规划纲要》的颁布、杭州运河文化带建设的持续推进，大运河还有更多的风景等待人们去揭开面纱，还有更多的人文故事有待讲述。保护、传承、利用大运河的中国人的精神，也将和这条运河一起，悠悠2000多年而不衰，从过去走向未来。

中文部分

英文部分

中文部分

　　意大利旅行家马可·波罗描述道：行在城（今杭州）有一万两千座石桥。行在城内河道众多，由桥梁相连。有的石桥十分高大，竖着高高桅杆的大船都可以穿行。桥面也相当宽阔，桥上行车马，桥下行船。"一万两千"这个数字也许是他被这座华美之城深深折服后的夸张之言，不过，作为数个王朝（其中又以南宋最广为人知）的都城，同时又作为繁华的商业枢纽、热门的旅游胜地，杭州确实是一座桥之城。有一点马可·波罗描述得没错——杭州似乎是立在水中，被水环绕的——这就需要建造大量的桥以便人们自由通行。

　　杭州，这座曾经的皇都，后来的交通、文化和商业中心，见证了京杭大运河的发展。河上的桥梁连接了大运河①东西两岸的人民，其自身也是有趣而重要的文化符号。沿着大运河杭州段，有数十座桥，如广济桥、拱宸桥、登云桥、大关桥、江涨桥、德胜桥、潮王桥、朝晖桥、青园桥、西湖文化广场桥、中北桥、建北桥、艮山桥、衍家桥、

---

① 本书所言桥梁或与运河相关建筑，除太平桥和题扇桥之外，均在京杭大运河上或其附近。为行文简洁，一般写作"大运河"；在涉及隋唐大运河和浙东运河时，文中另行说明。英文亦做相应处理。

皋塘桥、顾家桥、城东桥、昙花庵路桥、景御桥等；在大运河杭州段的支流上，则有半山桥、衣锦桥、祥符桥、长征桥、坝子桥、屋子桥、古星桥等。有延续千百年风貌的古桥，也有应当代交通需要而造的新桥。这些桥梁的周边，则有与桥密切相关的地名，如北新关、卖鱼桥、富义仓等。

流经绍兴的浙东运河及其支流上的桥梁也很多，如柯桥、八字桥、题扇桥、融光桥、太平桥等。

各式各样、或古或新的桥梁，宛如一串珠链，串起了长长的大运河，串起了运河沿岸的兴衰，串起了运河人家的生活，也串起了源远流长的中国传统文化。其中有诗情画意，也有战火纷飞；有科举之路艰难往复，也有皇帝南巡意在言外；有商埠繁华灯火，也有纤夫满面风霜；有农家小院温馨日常，也有织锦作坊机杼声声……大运河上的桥，从遥远的京城走来，从历史的深处走来，见证了世事变迁。千年运河水赋予它们多样的故事，值得今天的我们去探寻。

现在，请和我一起，与这些桥梁相遇，与中国的传统文化相识吧。

广济桥——大运河畔的乡愁

广济桥（如图 1-1 所示）是京杭大运河上唯一的七孔桥。在汉语中，"广济"的意思是给予广泛的救济和帮助，或有利于世人。广济桥形制高大，全长约 80 米，共 160 个台阶，建成于 1489 年。广济桥的修建可以说历尽艰辛。史料记载，塘栖一带水阔而深，原有的通济桥崩塌，之后造桥屡屡不成。人们通行依靠舟船，疾风骤雨时水流湍急，船覆人亡，这样的惨剧每年都要发生数次。宁波鄞县（今鄞州区）商人陈守清有一天到塘栖，经历了此番险境，发愿修桥。为此他抛家舍业，以道士身份游走四方募捐。数年过去，募捐所得依然不够，但陈守清初衷不改，他想方设法躲在漕粮船中，沿着运河北上，终于到达北京城。在京城闹市，陈守清自缚铁锁，恳请募捐。

毕竟是天子脚下，这样不同寻常的为苍生而毁家自苦的行为，机缘巧合下被深宫里的太皇太后周氏得知。她捐助白银 420 两，她的曾孙、当时的太子也捐助了 30 两，并赠送一卷无量寿佛画卷，钤印太子宝印。太皇太后和皇储的捐助即刻起到了四两拨千斤的作用，从后宫妃嫔到满堂朝臣无不捐银资助。至此，陈守清一人的修桥利民愿望成为皇家大内爱民护民的样板工程。不到一年，雄伟的广济桥完工，人们往来如履平地，再无颠覆之虞。当时的状元、翰林院国史修撰钱福撰《重建长桥记》，感慨世上有比陈守清更有能力、更负职责的人，却没有谁能像他一样有哪怕毁了自己也要坚守建桥宏愿的善念和决心。①

广济桥最初名为"通济桥"，"通"的意思是连接，而"济"的意思是帮助。"济"又作"周济"，意为在水边而相助。所以中国的许多桥梁名中都有"济"字，桥以"济"为名，自然而然。

图 1-1 广济桥
（绘图：屠群峰）

这座七孔桥十分宏伟，除中间最大的桥拱外，其他六个桥拱向两边从大到小对称排列。七个桥拱倒映在水面构成了七个完整的圆，十分秀美。

大桥令塘栖人民受益颇多。塘栖最早是负责疏浚河流连通运河的元朝士兵的驻扎地，它的字面意思是人们围绕着水塘而居住。《唐栖志》中有这样的记载："迨元以后，河开矣，桥筑矣，市聚矣……"

广济桥犹如一道长虹连接着宽阔的大运河南北两岸。北岸糕饼铺和饭馆鳞次栉比，香味吸引着乘客、船家和船工。这是萦绕广济桥的

---

① 顾志兴：《运河文化名镇塘栖》，杭州出版社 2015 年版。

独有香味，大运河浙江段的其他桥梁附近都没有如此这般能令人流连忘返而饥肠辘辘的香味。

这与塘栖的地理位置密切相关。

塘栖是沿着京杭大运河进行漫长旅行的倒数第二站。尽管航行有时候被描述得诗情画意，但是如此耗费时间又耗费体力的旅行实际上是艰苦的。在狭窄逼仄的船上生活一两个月或者更久的时间，经受风吹日晒、雨打雪欺，再提心吊胆地经过激流险滩，无论是船工还是乘客都非常渴望一次彻底的休整。此外，在和家人相见之前，也需要刮胡净面，沐浴清洁。作为一种礼数，还应当买些礼物带给家人。塘栖距杭州北新关 50 里，船行大半天就可以到。[①] 于是，塘栖就成了一个理想的地方，船主和商人在此休整，也为到杭州后的货物检查和报税缴税做好准备。杭嘉湖平原充沛的水汽和肥沃的土壤非常有利于蚕桑和稻谷的生长，这使此地成为朝廷贡赋重地，而塘栖恰好位于杭嘉湖平原的中心地带。在塘栖附近，丝织业和稻谷业大亨建立了他们的别墅美宅，一同建立的当然还有他们丰富的社会关系。

所有这些都使得大运河塘栖段成为繁忙的水上要道，而来往穿梭的船只又使塘栖成为繁华的枢纽。

哪里有人群聚集，哪里就有商业。而塘栖为什么以点心店出名呢？

想想吧，对于筋疲力尽的乘客和船工来说，还有什么比一份香甜的点心更能抚慰人心的呢？那些点心——鲜红的、大红的、淡红的、翠绿的、深绿的、浅绿的、橄榄绿的，金色的、蛋黄的、土黄的、姜黄的，雪白的、玉白的、米白的，褐色的、灰色的、墨色的、黑白分明的；圆的、方的、椭圆的、三角的，或者桃子形的、小狗形状的、小兔形状的——里面填着甜的馅儿或者咸的馅儿……它们尽情地铺陈着自己，好像巨大的五彩缤纷的调色板，又像一个个温暖香甜的梦中乐园——任何人都难以抵抗的神奇世界。

---

① 《天下水陆路程》载："北五里至唐栖。南五十里至北新关，二十里至杭州府。"

以桥之名 In the Name of Bridges: The Chinese Cultural Codes on the Grand Canal (Chinese-English Bilingual) —— 大运河上的中国文化密码（中英双语）

06

塘栖，以其秀丽的风景和令人难忘的食肆之味，唤起了乘客的乡愁，也激发着他们的渴望。

他们远离家乡，勤奋工作，在与家人分离数月乃至数年之后，终于踏上了回家的路。他们掏出小心藏好的或充盈或半瘪的荷包，走进一家点心铺，尝一尝样品，在点心的浩大集合中挑选一两样，慷慨地取出一些碎银， 吩咐店伙计包上几包。而热情的店伙计一边麻利地包着点心，一边不忘和刚进来的客人寒暄，邀请他尝一尝，仿佛客人是他的近亲。店伙计一边招呼客人，一边打包点心，也绝不会忘记在点心包上覆一张喜气洋洋的红纸，红纸上面印着店家的名号。 心满意足的客人走出点心店，抬头望望蓝天，然后回到船上。

再过一天，他就可以看到他深爱的孩子们了，离家时他曾经对孩子们许下甜蜜的诺言。而对他的妻子，尽管他从未开口说过"我爱你"（中国的男人似乎把对妻子说"我爱你"看作是一件缺乏男子气概的事情）， 但是他深深感激她的忠贞，他知道在没有他陪伴的日子里，妻子的坚持与不易。

他还要给妹妹准备一份礼物。不久之后，妹妹将会和 30 里外的一个年轻人成亲。出嫁的姑娘一年能回家看望父母的机会只有两三次，而一旦远嫁，回家看望父母几乎就成了一个遥不可及的梦。

他不会让他们失望的。

点心蕴含着美好生活的滋味
广济桥畔的点心铺
汇集着对亲人的思念
治愈着行旅的乡愁

拱宸桥——杭州历史的地标

2014 年 6 月 22 日，中国大运河世界遗产申报工作小组在卡塔尔首都多哈向联合国教科文组织世界遗产委员会介绍大运河的文化和历史价值。当看到展示出的一组横跨在流淌的大运河上的拱宸桥（如图2-1所示）的图片时，大家被深深地吸引了：这座秀美高大的三孔拱桥，沉静端庄；桥下河水缓缓流淌，繁忙的船只往来穿梭——显示出庄敬自强的气魄。

图 2-1　拱宸桥
（绘图：屠群峰）

评审组专家一致同意：在世界遗产名录上，中国大运河应当拥有一席之地。

从那时起，拱宸桥就成为大运河的象征，出现在旅游地图、纪念品上，也出现在博物馆的小手册里、媒体机构的电子屏上，还出现在航空杂志上……

拱宸桥享誉世界之前，已经存在了几百年，不过这并不意味着它是默默无闻的。

拱宸桥初建于 1631 年，于 1651 年坍塌。1714 年，清康熙年间，重建拱宸桥。12 年后，李卫主持了拱宸桥的大修工程，之后，此桥成为大运河上的巍巍大桥。遗憾的是，1863 年秋，这座大桥毁于清政府军和太平军的炮火。1885 年，清光绪年间，杭州人丁丙主持重建该大桥。几十年后日军侵占杭州，拱宸桥又一次遭到毁坏。今天的拱宸桥是杭州市政府于 2005 年按照"修旧如旧"的文物保护原则彻底重修的。

回望历史，是什么造成了拱宸桥跌宕起伏的命运？背后的原因又是什么呢？答案很可能在于两点：一是它的地理位置，二是它的巨大形制。

在汉语中，"拱"的意思是双手相合（向比自己年长或地位高的人表示尊敬）。"宸"指代北极星所在，也用来指代皇帝居住的宫殿。"拱宸"合在一起的意思是向尊贵的客人表示敬意。

拱宸桥位于杭州，而杭州是长达 1794 千米的京杭大运河的南端，拱宸桥就成了进入杭州的水上门户。筋疲力尽的船工和乘客看到拱宸桥就知道漫长的艰辛旅程即将结束，迎接他们的就是杭州这座城市的温柔与繁华。

拱宸桥由 3 个高大的圆形桥拱组成，就像富有中国传统审美趣味的圆洞门建筑，门户大开迎接来到杭州的客人。拱宸桥之于杭州的意义，就如凯旋门之于巴黎、伦敦眼之于伦敦，是因其特殊魅力而无法被忽视的文化地标。

拱宸桥常遭炮火袭击的另一个原因在于它的巨大形制。拱宸桥是清代京杭大运河上最壮丽的大桥之一。它的宏伟增添了运河的荣光，但其高度上的明显优势又使它很容易成为军事攻击的目标。

1863 年，由一名落第秀才洪秀全领导的太平军和由左宗棠将军指挥的政府军展开了激战。作为一名忠诚于朝廷的高级官员，左宗棠将军陷入了矛盾：是保护杭州城免于落入太平军的控制，还是保护拱宸桥免于炮火的袭击？在他率领将士抵达杭州之前，太平军已经占据了拱宸桥，并把这座桥改为一个要塞。如前所述，大运河是清朝的经济动脉，而拱宸桥是其中繁忙的一个站点，所有的货船都要先经过拱宸桥才能到达税关。太平军控制了拱宸桥，就等于扼住了经济动脉。左宗棠将军十分清楚拱宸桥的历史，他也知道明朝末年最早提议修造拱宸桥的举人祝华封为修桥耗尽家财，也十分了解之前的官员为修造这座大桥付出的巨大心血，他深知这座大桥对于清王朝的意义。

拱宸桥的修缮和重建大都与朝廷官员紧密相关，而后者通过修桥赢得了赞誉。

修造大桥耗资巨大。清康熙年间，浙江布政使段志熙启动了拱宸桥重修工程。由于缺少资金和劳动力，当时的拱宸桥修得比较简陋。12 年后，浙江巡抚李卫决定重新修缮拱宸桥，他带头捐出薪资修桥，也希望以此感召富裕的商人和普通百姓。

是的，拱宸桥绝不仅仅是一项建筑工程或者水利工程，它更是孔子倡导的"仁"的象征，即统治者要施仁政，改善民生。这座桥不仅连接了运河两岸的人们，也连接了陋室中的普通百姓、身居高位的政府官员，以及金銮殿上的皇帝。

主持拱宸桥修造工程的人应当既能力出众又老于世故，既能获得皇帝的信任又善于维护与同事的关系，还精于财务事务。

修桥往往需要持续多年。因此，有些主持修桥的人借用诸葛亮（三国时期广受尊敬的战略家、蜀汉丞相）的话来勉励自己，他们反复吟诵：

非淡泊无以明志，非宁静无以致远。

作为浙江总督，左宗棠久经官场。他目睹过被贬官员的艰难时日，对他们怀有同情，同时也有他自己的失望、失败和耻辱。左宗棠十分明白命运的无常。如果他不能成功地将太平军镇压下去，那么一来作为赋税重地的浙江就难以向朝廷如常纳贡，二来大清朝也会颜面无存。而此刻太平军占据着进入杭州城的制高点和水上交通要塞——拱宸桥。

尽管左宗棠是得到皇帝信任的高官，但是他的工作面临着重重困难：冗员处处，贪腐横行，上下渔利，骄奢淫逸。所有这些都加重了他作为剿灭叛军的总指挥官的负担。

他向拱宸桥望去，原本秀美流畅的桥梁线条被中间的突起破坏了，就好像美人的背上长了一个痈疽。那是太平军在桥芯建的堡垒——为将东西南北尽收眼底。原本桥下商船往来不歇，现在也了无踪迹，只有浑黄的河水一如既往地流淌。

左宗棠下了决心。

史载，1863年秋，左宗棠率兵攻垒，战火洗劫后，桥梁损毁严重，后于光绪年间坍塌。光绪十一年（1885），杭州士绅丁丙感叹此桥之重要性和朝廷财力之匮乏，重修大桥。当时修缮后的大桥就是今天看

到的三孔拱宸桥的基本形态。^①

从明末至清末，拱宸桥的修造、坍塌和重建，历经数百年。其间，它的首次和末次修建，都由地方士绅发起，中间的数次修建则由地方官员带头。它是地方士绅参与社会治理的成果，也是地方官员履行保境安民职责的例证。

拱宸桥的多舛命运并未到此结束。中日甲午战争后，杭州被列为通商口岸。觊觎大运河繁华商贸带来的丰厚利润，日本人在拱宸桥堍设海关，占据桥东为日租界。光绪二十三年（1897），日军在桥面中间铺筑约 2.5 米宽的混凝土斜面，以通汽车和人力车。美丽的拱宸桥失去了传统审美韵味，因国难而蒙羞。

一座拱宸桥，半部杭州史。拱宸桥对于杭州来说不仅是一座便利交通的石桥，还承载着特别的记忆与情感。作为京杭大运河南端的标志，拱宸桥迎接过康熙、乾隆南巡的浩浩荡荡的船队，见证过漕运、商贸的兴衰，也见证了近现代民族纺织工业的萌芽。文化和娱乐事业也在这里勃兴，杭州的第一家报社、邮局都在拱宸桥开端。

1949 年中华人民共和国成立后，拱宸桥迎来了新生命。2005 年拱宸桥被确定为省级文物保护单位，受法规保护。同年，杭州市政府对拱宸桥进行全面修缮，以"修旧如旧"的原则，保留了拱宸桥巍峨雄伟、古朴沧桑的历史景观特征。这次重修，考虑到桥下航运繁忙，为避免航船碰撞，在主孔墩侧设置 4 个防撞墩，每个防撞墩上均雕有蚣蝮——中国古代神话中能够避水保安的神兽（如图 2-2 所示）。

拱宸桥经风历雨数百年，阅尽沧桑。如今的拱宸桥，作为世界文化遗产的中国大运河的标志之一，除经济功能之外，还承载着丰富的

---

① 《重建拱宸桥记》载："桥长二十一丈四尺，广一丈三尺，桥下三洞，中洞广四丈六尺，左右洞广二丈六尺。"

以桥之名
In the Name of Bridges:
The Chinese Cultural Codes on the Grand Canal (Chinese-English Bilingual)
——大运河上的中国文化密码（中英双语）

图 2-2　防撞墩上的蚣蝮①

文化和旅游价值。时过境迁，朝代更迭，航运业兴衰起伏，但拱宸桥一次又一次被架起。它的故事反映了大运河对中国人民的日常生活和祖国统一的重要性。如今，拱宸桥作为世界文化遗产点，承载着丰富的文化和历史内涵，将不断续写它的辉煌和传奇。

---

① 本书中的实景图片由作者王雅平拍摄，后不再标注。

③ 祥符桥——运河支流的说书人

作为 21 世纪之前中国最重要的水上交通线之一，大运河一路汇集了诸多支流，连接了河流、溪涧、水塘、湖泊。大运河是人工开凿的航道，从诞生之初就积极地寻找最短的路径，最大限度地利用天然水系。自然而然，就有许多桥梁横跨在这些支流和大运河上。

祥符桥（如图 3-1 所示）就是其中之一。祥符桥架在杭州祥符镇的宦塘河上，这条小河向东汇入大运河。祥符桥是一座五孔石梁桥，南北向跨过宦塘河，长 28 米，宽 3.6 米。桥栏板有素面和须弥座两种形式，望柱柱头雕覆莲或石狮。祥符镇境内有纵横交错的河汊，西塘河和宦塘河从镇中穿过。自南宋起，苏、湖、常、秀、润诸州的漕粮及米船，都经过祥符镇抵达杭州。祥符桥作为镇内的主要桥梁，发挥过重要的运输功能。

周边地区的船只不仅给祥符镇带来了大量的货物，还带来了人气。除了商人、小贩、船工外，还有木匠、漆匠、理发匠、苦力脚夫也聚集在此，依赖船运业谋生。 最有意思的是，娱乐业也发展成一道独特的风景。在没有电力和互联网的年月，人们怎样经济实惠地打发空余的时间呢？ 不同于英国人结伴去剧院观看戏剧，中国人创造了另一种独特的民间艺术——说书。

清朝和民国时期典型的说书人形象是怎样的呢？他们通常穿着灰

图 3-1　祥符桥
（绘图：屠群峰）

色或者浅蓝色的长袍，松松的袖管挽起一截，露出洁白的内衬。长袍剪裁宽松，下摆长至脚踝，轻轻拂过白底黑面布鞋。一句话，说书人看上去整洁、体面、聪明，招人喜欢。

　　说书人通常站在一张朴素的桌子后面，桌子高度恰好在垂手的位置。桌上有一块长方形的硬木，叫作惊堂木，这是说书人最重要的工具。这块硬木不大，没有雕饰，但是远不止看上去的那样平平无奇。虽然说书人善于讲故事，但在"漫长"的讲述中，听众也会走神或者昏昏欲睡。于是说书人就要用惊堂木在桌上重重一拍，制造出惊雷一般的响声，这时听众就会被惊醒，收回漫游思绪，集中注意力，看说书人卖力的表演。

　　说书人得善于制造"诱饵"，也就是悬念。他一边观察听众面部的细微表情，一边引导他们跟着他描述的情节走，让他们深深沉浸在浪漫或冒险的故事之中。此外，说书人还必须精通"暂停"的艺术。在一两个小时的说书过程中，听众都伸长了脖子，抬着头，紧盯着说书人。这时说书人抛出一个问题，比如"这位英雄好汉会被暗杀吗？"，或者"这对私奔的情人会被抓回来吗？"，然后，停住，环视台下的观众，心中暗暗满意于自己的功力。当所有的听众都紧张地期待着答案的时候，他才继续带着礼貌又温和的微笑说："且听下回分解。"人们带着略有遗憾的满足走出说书人的书场，彼此交换着对故事中的主角的看法，在叹息或者兴奋中，各自回家。"明天见！一定要准时哦！"他们互相约定第二天再来书场，而说书人则接过茶馆老板殷勤送上来的润嗓茶水，体味一个"艺术家"的骄傲。

说书人很难在某个地方定居。花费许多精力和时间准备好的"大书"（也就是故事），在一地讲完之后，他们就得前往下一个地方，重新开始说书生意。他们有点像行吟艺术家，而大部分单身上路的民间艺术家，最好是去找一个搭档，这样既经济又安全。

幸好找个搭档不算太难。

茶馆老板会邀请说书人进行表演。茶馆，顾名思义，是人们喝茶聚会的地方。但是喝茶作为日常生活的一部分，是可以在家进行的。因此茶馆就必须有些特别之处来招徕顾客，让他们愿意额外地破费，专程到茶馆去喝。富有语言艺术和悬念设置技巧的说书人，就会为茶馆赢得"回头客"。于是茶馆老板就会和说书人达成协议：说书人可以把茶馆作为场租低廉的表演场，而茶馆则可以吸引更多被说书人的故事勾住的人日复一日地来喝茶。当然，作为一种双赢的商业行为，说书人和茶馆老板都会衡量收益和支出，若说书人技艺高超，引来源源不断的茶客时，茶馆老板就要给说书人利润分成了。这时候的说书人，与其说是语言艺术家，倒不如说是超级销售员。说书人和茶馆形成了一种事实上的共生关系，用现在的例子类比，就如同驻场歌手和酒吧。

以桥之名
In the Name of Bridges:
The Chinese Cultural Codes on the Grand Canal (Chinese-English Bilingual)
——大运河上的中国文化密码（中英双语）

贵族和大亨有实力供养自己的戏班或者聘请名角到他们美轮美奂的私家宅院表演，比如《红楼梦》就有相当篇幅描写世家贵族贾府的戏班。这个贵族家庭有一个私家昆曲戏班，包括12名年轻的专业女演员，此外还有乐师、乐工、管理人员。昆曲的流行，就和富裕的扬州盐商大有关系。普罗大众则难以望其项背，他们既没有充足的金钱，也没有充裕的时间，因此更需要经济实惠的娱乐活动。而茶馆不仅实惠，还是商人约见客户，和决策者一起探讨与拓展商业关系的好地方——时至今日，茶馆及其相应的文化，如茶礼、茶宴和茶馆里的民间艺术，在中国仍然生机勃勃，流派纷呈。

听"大书"因此成了大多数人的理想选择。票价不贵，环境也还不错。入馆喝茶听书的门票也分好几个档次：荷包充盈的可以拥有二楼的私人包厢，或者买雅座；囊中羞涩的只花很少一部分，就可以入座；最便宜的，就是站在茶馆的后排，同样可以度过一段愉快的时光。无论贫富贵贱，说书人的表演给他们提供了一个平等的机会感受听书的快乐。

但是，听书不仅仅是一种娱乐方式。在大多数人难以获得正规教育的时候，听说书人讲那些浪漫故事或英雄传奇，在某种程度上可以说是一种有效的受教育途径。一个有经验的说书人通常会一边说书，一边给出他富有智慧的评论，借事说理，借古喻今。把说书人比作受到普通百姓尊敬的教书先生，绝不为过。就像《三国演义》《水浒传》《玉簪记》《西厢记》《窦娥冤》《金瓶梅》等，这些优秀的中国传统文学作品正是通过说书人，从城镇的书场走向了广袤的乡村。而好的话本自身带有明显的道德教化功能，通过说书、听书，中国的传统道义得以口口相传，深入人心。

古希腊人在祭祀活动的狂欢中发明了戏剧，中国的传统民间艺术也是在人口稠密的城镇生发出来的。大运河的水流到哪里，哪里就有舞台下欢呼和喝彩的声音。运河沿岸的娱乐活动丰富多彩。华屋美厦中衣着体面、欣赏沉吟的士绅贵妇，路边杂耍场边随意站着、时时叫好的老人、孩童，演艺场大舞台的买票观众，他们和艺人一起奏响了中国传统演艺的交响乐。

便利的水上交通和频繁的商贸往来带来了娱乐业的繁荣。说书仅仅是其中的一个篇章。戏曲界历来有"水路即戏路"的说法。"戏路"指戏班演出路线与活动区域。"水路"指重要的交通水道。水路带动经济文化的发展，也使得戏曲表演沿水路聚集。

"祥符"的意思是"吉祥的符号"。中国人在命名街道、里巷、桥梁时，常常会选一个表达美好希冀或期待的词。祥符桥的命名就是一个典型的例子。祥符桥始建年代不详，现存石桥为明代建筑，于明嘉靖二十二年（1543）重建。

嘉靖皇帝可以说是一个富有传奇色彩的皇帝。说他富有传奇色彩并不是因为他取得过伟大的胜利，而是说他一边神秘地生活，一边牢牢掌握着帝国的权柄长达 45 年之久。

嘉靖登上皇位时才不过 15 岁，此前他和皇帝的联系仅在于：他的父亲是皇帝众多兄弟中的一个。也就是说，他只不过是皇帝的一个侄子。孩童时期的他远离皇储（太子）之位，也并未充分接受过未来皇帝所需要的权谋教育。总之，嘉靖皇帝对于成为大明朝的天子，既缺乏准备，也没有期待。在某种程度上，他害怕登上那个巨大的雕刻着猛龙的金色皇位，他害怕要对这个庞大的国家及其人民负责。

这使得他的统治方式与古代中国的其他皇帝大相径庭。他不像他的"前辈"那样，严肃地端坐在朝堂最高处，等着高级官员谨慎地报告事务，评判他们，嘉许那些政绩不错的官员，斥责那些履职不力的庸官。

他不穿龙袍，不临朝，不与大多数的官员会面，整整 20 年，嘉靖皇帝未亲理朝政。那么他做了些什么呢？

他痴迷于道教。他穿着深青色的长袍，披散着长发，在朝堂边的房间内修炼道家之术。大多数时候他沉浸在深深的冥想之中，盘腿而坐，眼睛微微地闭着，一声不出。轻烟从铜制香炉中袅袅而出，香炉后供奉的是太上老君神像。

但是，在他"无为而治"的表象之下，是内阁制度的登峰造极。在民间，对朝堂斗争不明的老百姓，还是单纯地将对美好生活的期望寄托于当朝天子，乃至在给桥梁命名时也想着天降祥瑞、庇佑众生。

长征桥——三河汇出繁华商贸

大运河穿过雄伟的拱宸桥，向南约数百米，能看到河西岸一排排黑瓦白墙的木构民居。此处水域明显变宽了。在这里大运河挽起了两条支流，一条是小河，另一条是余杭塘河。小河是西塘河的一段，从南宋时起就是漕运复线。这里的人们更爱叫它"小河"，好像呼唤家门口的邻居那样亲切。

三河汇流之处（如图4-1所示），形成了一片人口稠密的民居，其繁华延续了几个世纪。在余杭塘河宽阔的水面上建起的康家桥，是湖墅北路的尽头。在康家桥的东北方向，有一座小巧的石拱桥，这就是会安桥（又称"惠安桥"），只可步行。走过会安桥，向北折入小河直街，就能看到跨在小河上的长征桥。这三座桥形态各异，相距不远，连接着三河汇流之地，便利了当地人们的生活。在长征桥上凭栏而立，我们可以欣赏水乡人家的大致图景。

住宅和商铺鳞次栉比，黑瓦屋檐下小巧的纸灯笼好像是江南少女灵秀的睫毛，灯光流淌在绸缎般的水面上，鲜艳的店招飘摇着，空气中混合着花的清香、饭菜的浓香，这一切使得小河宛如一幅传统的中国画卷，徐徐展开，展示着数百年来小河人家繁忙的商埠生活。

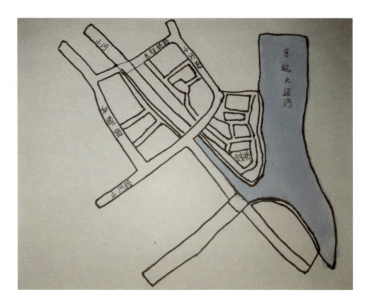

图 4-1 三河汇流
（绘图：陈星月）

　　早在南宋时期，小河一带就是转运和货物集散储备的中心。到了清朝中后期，这一带发展成了繁华的商埠，除了有物资集散功能以外，消遣娱乐功能兼备，饭铺、酒肆、茶馆林立。

　　小河的居民在建造住宅时充分考虑了商业的需求。一座典型的民宅有二层楼：楼上是卧室，楼下则分成两部分——面朝主街的那一半作为店面，后半部分则是制作货物的作坊。小河民居集中了店铺、作坊和住家功用，真正做到了三合一。那么店伙计睡在哪里呢？青年伙计通常在打烊之后睡在店铺里，承担起店铺的部分安保职责。为了尽可能多地获得光照和吸引客流，临街的门面是由可以拆卸的木板组成的，营业时卸掉，打烊时再装上。小河的早晨是从卸门板时的咔咔声、伙计之间的招呼声和河埠头各家的洗菜淘米声组成的奏鸣曲开始的。淡金色的阳光洒在黑瓦屋顶上，小河民居浸润在河流上浮起的水汽之中，有了朦胧的韵致。布制的店招就像半梦半醒的少年，直到太阳赶走了水汽才彻底有了精神。有时候，小河晨曲中还有另外一个演奏者——挑货郎。他们挑着大竹筐，边走边吆喝：透亮的水晶甜糕、翠绿的莲蓬、刚采的水红菱……在繁忙的小河，小吃担子的吆喝声是平静叙事曲中的变奏。其中最受欢迎的是甜酒酿。挑货郎把甜酒酿装在一个个粗瓷碗里，吆喝着，鼓动店里的伙计和东家的孩子们花几个小钱来上一碗。这种用大米发酵的酸甜可口的传统美食也是码头工人和船工的理想点心，它独特的酸甜滋味还蕴含着淡淡酒香，可以给这些劳动者带来体力上的补充和精神上的愉悦。

有时候豆腐担儿会来。竹筐上放着一个木制扁盒，莹白的豆腐满满地铺着。有人扬手招呼：来一块豆腐！再递过去零钱，更多的则是递过去一只粗瓷碗，里头装着大半碗黄豆。豆腐大概是保留时间最长的、门槛较低的易货货物。不过在小河的商街上，最常见的还是枇杷担子。从河埠头坐船，沿着运河往北大约半小时，就是塘栖镇。塘栖镇正是盛产枇杷的地方。6月初，枇杷挂满枝头，农人坐着船来到小河这个繁华的商埠。在这里，枇杷可以卖个好价钱。

每逢庙会，小河就更繁忙了。人们从四面八方赶来，祈求生意兴隆，家宅平安，之后少不了要买些吃的犒赏自己。清晨6点不到，点心铺老板把第一锅生煎包子一只一只密密地码进大平锅，盖上木锅盖，几分钟后打开锅盖，沿着锅沿洒下小半勺水。瞬间，锅里升腾起一片水汽，生煎包在水汽里鼓胀了脸，嘟着嘴，憨态可掬。老板眼明手快地在白白胖胖的包子上撒一把黑芝麻，再撒上碧绿的碎葱。浓郁的混合香味似乎在招呼人们："快来吃！快来吃！"隔壁的馄饨店点燃炉火，架上巨大的汤锅，把猪肉剁成细细的肉馅，手指翻飞，眨眼就变出一排排小巧玲珑的馄饨。阳光闯过香樟树，在街上洒下一指宽的光影。挑糖担儿的手艺人不是在卖甜甜的糖画，而是在卖工艺品。两根细竹棍在琥珀色的糖浆里搅和上浆，在手腕翻飞之间，活灵活现的孙悟空、兔子、老虎、蝴蝶就变出来了。这甜蜜的戏法牢牢勾住了孩子们，就连走过的大人也都停下脚步欣赏赞叹一番。 在小河，生活的节奏不疾不徐，就像一幅画卷要耐心地展开，慢慢地把玩。

小河地区也是杭州木材业的一个中心。在众多的木材行中，永达木行因其外观惹人注目。这是一栋二层青砖小楼，占地约 400 平方米。永达木行面朝小河，设有自家的码头，这对于装卸木材是必不可少的。从山里砍伐下来的树干沿着河顺流而下，在小河汇集。永达木行把原木进行粗加工后制成木材。它同时也是原木商和其他木材行之间的中介，向双方收取佣金。木材行需要官发批文才可以经营。永达木行除了缴纳自家的税金之外，还承担着督促原木买卖双方及时缴税的责任。

永达木行通过"买山"逐渐发展为木业领袖。"买山"的意思是在交易季节之前就买下某座山头的原木，有点类似于现代金融的"期货"。这当然有一定的风险——虫害、气候和生意本身是否景气，以及大额资金的注入，使得"买山"成为只有少数商家有胆子参与的"游戏"。永达木行正是由于成功"买山"，从小木材行逐渐成为拥有市场定价权的大批发商。人们说永达木行的创立者姚鑫淼天生就是做木材生意的料，他的名字中的"三个金"和"三个水"就是个证明。实际上这只不过是人们自作聪明的附会，因为给姚鑫淼取名的人何曾想到他会成为木材业的大亨呢？

还有木材特殊的运输方式。为了减少运输费用，姚鑫淼命人将圆木捆扎成木排，顺着山里的河流出山，然后并入大运河，最后到达这趟特殊旅程的终点——小河。这种经济实惠而又天才的木材运输方式只有在春季雨水丰沛、河流宽阔的时候才可以进行。想象一下这样的场景吧！源源不断的木排从崇山峻岭中顺流而下，时不时撞上河中的礁石，弹开之后又被水流推着向前，但是长长的木头仍然有可能被卡住，前半截已经探头向下，后半截还动弹不得。它需要等待下一次水流的力量借势发力，才能继续旅程。为了防止木排在水势复杂之处堆积，运排人应运而生。一个精壮有力的汉子站在水中大石上，手中的竹篙如同长了眼睛，对准眼看要卡住的木排轻轻一点或者一推——此时，木排受了恰到好处的力，得以避开卡口，继续前行。在河里漂过几百里之后，木材最终会到达终点——永达木行。只有幸运儿可以完成这趟水上旅行——有的一直被卡住，随着年月慢慢地腐烂了。

大部分木材来自杭州以西的山区，通过天目溪、苕溪和钱塘江运送到杭州城。一旦发洪水（连续大雨之后洪水是大概率事件），木排破裂，木材行就会遭受巨大的损失。高额利润从来不是独自前行的，高风险总是如影随形。有经验的扎排工和熟练的放排人在木材行业务中占有重要的位置。

这里除了永达木行，还有其他的木材行。木材行业公会由此成立，制定交易规则，评估木材质量，协调各方关系（包括工人公会），为集体利益代言。行业公会实际上是非官方的自治组织，由小河繁华的商业催生而来，又反过来促进了小河的商业文明。

今天，我们可以在小河直街以北数百米的桥西历史文化街区看到木材行业公会的旧址。

⑤ 登云桥——夏时正的科举路

"漫漫科举路，一朝登云去。"一位名叫夏时正的杭州人十年寒窗，终于被授予进士头衔，之后成为一名清官，得到百姓爱戴。他的科举之路，就是从登云桥附近开始的，他的塑像立于登云桥畔。夏时正的科举之路和登云桥的命名可以看作是中国古代科举制度的一个缩影。

通往进士之路漫漫，耗时耗神，只有极少数学子能够迈过终点线。这是一场挑战时间、精力和金钱的马拉松。

参加科举考试的学子，从童年开始就沉浸在学习经典、写作文策之中。他们参加地方政府和朝廷举办的各级考试，这次单向的旅程从他们大约七岁就开始了，日夜不辍。但是，花在这漫长旅程中的大量时间和金钱并不意味着一定能获得参加最终考试的入场券。在朝堂之上举行的最终考试，谓之殿试，由皇帝作为主考官。

中国古代的科举制度可以上溯到隋朝时期。隋文帝杨坚（541—604）需要从普通民众而不是名门世族之中选拔人才，因为后者已经强大到足以成为他政治上的对手。事实上，杨坚在夺取帝位之前，就是豪强大族，作为成功的上位者，他可不希望成为昔日同侪的效仿对象。大业元年（605），隋朝首开进士科，这被视为科举制度的开始。这一制度随后在唐、宋、元、明各朝逐步发展成一套相当复杂的体系，在 1905 年唱响了终曲。运行了 1300 多年的科举制度，毫无疑问是历史上对中国影响最大的人才选拔制度。明朝科举简表如表 5-1 所示。

表 5-1　明朝科举简表

考试名称	童子试	院试	乡试 / 秋闱	会试 / 春闱	殿试
考试性质	预科考试	选拔性	选拔性	选拔性	荣誉性
参加者	童生	生员（秀才）	科举生员	举人	贡士
主考人	知县知府	各省学政	中央特派官员	礼部	皇帝
地点	县学府学	学政巡回案临考场	省城	京城贡院	皇宫
胜出者名号	生员（秀才）	科举生员	举人	贡士	进士 •进士及第 •进士出身 •同进士出身
时间	每年	三年两考	三年一次农历八月	乡试次年农历二月	会试之后农历三月

备注：（1）农历八月和二月正值秋季和春季；

　　　　（2）作者根据综合资料择要绘制

现在让我们回到夏时正这里，跟随他的脚步，去了解这一影响深远而又举步维艰的科举制度。

少年夏时正已经在村塾里完成了学前教育，去县学参加童生录取考试。他天资聪颖，又早做准备，一考而中。之后参加童子试，斩获头名。小小年纪的他，自此拥有了"秀才"的称号。

他在学业上的优异表现对于他的母亲来说是个巨大的好消息。对于普通人家的子弟来说，"朝为田舍郎，暮登天子堂"承载着通过科举考试获得阶层跃升的巨大梦想。中国古代的科举制度是国家的人才选拔制度，而贫寒人家的子弟学习优秀不仅意味着可以获得人才选拔的机会，还意味着对家庭经济的贡献。

通过童子试只是科举考试中的其中一步，接下来府学组织了难度更大的科试，即选拔科举生员的院试。秀才夏时正又一次名列前茅，自此获得"廪生"的头衔。"廪"的意思是"米仓"，顾名思义，廪生的衣食住宿由州、府等承担。清朝沿袭明朝科举制度，清顺治九年（1652）的《御制晓示生员条教》卧碑记载了对生员的补贴和期望："……免其丁粮，厚以廪膳……各衙门官，以礼相待，全要养成贤才，以供朝廷之用……"成绩比他差一档的学生，称为"附生"。附生需要自己负担食宿开支。可见，"奖学金"这一说法并非西方大学独有，在古代中国的初中等教育中就已经存在了。总的来说，所有通过院试的男孩们都足够聪明，并且都有一个官方的头衔，即"科举生员"。科举生员身份是这套完备的人才选拔考试的入门资格，也是"学而优则仕"这条普通人走向社会高级阶层之路的起点。

选拔科举生员的院试仅仅是科举制度的"预科"考试。从此时起，夏时正和他的同伴们还将参加三次重要的科举考试，只有很少的同伴才能和他一起走到最后。

首先是乡试，由若干地方政府联合举办，在各地贡院举行，每三年一次。乡试，通常在八月份举行，因此又被称为"秋闱"。"闱"最初的意思是皇宫的小门，这里被用来指代考生参加考试的小小的房间，也暗示了科举之路的窄小、科举成功之后通向皇宫的荣耀。

夏时正这年十二三岁，全身心地投入准备之中。与参加同场考试的同伴相比，他并没有太大的压力。他还是翩翩少年，而大多数生员已经二十出头了，有的生员因为屡试不中，已近中年。乡试是一条分水岭，未能通过乡试的生员，被叫作秀才，意思是有潜力的人才；而通过乡试的被称为举人，意思是有为官的资格。"学而优则仕"，就是从举人起步的。成为举人，即具备担任实职官员的资格，乡试可以说是明清科举中最重要也最艰巨的一关。

乡试把普通人和官员分隔开来。一个富人如果没有科举上的名望，就难以获得真正的尊重，甚至在讲究门当户对的婚姻市场上也低于书香世家。而一个穷人如果能够在乡试中脱颖而出，则会一举翻身获得尊重。举人身份确实能带来一种声望，因为举人的头衔是通往仕途的第一道门槛。成语"一举高中"也暗示了"举人"和"高升""高门"

之间的联系。

　　未能通过乡试的秀才，其生活是怎样的呢？从某种程度上来说是一种悲剧。他们年复一年地学习经史子集，认为"万般皆下品，唯有读书高"，将自己困在寒酸的小屋里，满心希望有朝一日能够通过乡试，但是希望之光越来越渺茫。最终，他们会被嘲笑："百无一用是书生。"

　　吴敬梓的小说《儒林外史》，以犀利的笔触无情鞭挞了积重难返的封建科举制度对知识分子心灵的戕害，刻画了一系列深受科举毒害的迂腐的读书人、虚伪的假名士。其中的名篇《范进中举》就讲述了这样一个故事：秀才范进多年不中，突然得知中举之后，各种奉承纷至沓来，这与他之前的窘迫境况迥然不同，巨大的反差和狂喜使这个可怜的读书人发了疯。艺术来源于生活。吴敬梓能够塑造出范进中举前后其生活状态的巨大变化，正是因为作者本人多年来屡试不中所遭受的折磨：虽然通晓诗文、富有才华，却始终不能跨过举人的门槛而长期处于贫困并遭受冷遇。

　　无独有偶，中国最优秀的古典小说《红楼梦》的作者曹雪芹，也是科举制度的受害者。科举制度逐渐变成一套严酷而僵硬的体系，中断了许多饱学之士报效国家、实现抱负的梦想和雄心。不能中举入仕，对吴敬梓、曹雪芹及其家族是切实的不幸，但是，科举道路上的艰难磋磨，又使他们转向了更能彰显才能的文学创作，使其作品成为中华民族古典文学的瑰宝。

　　让我们重新回到明朝的读书少年夏时正。他第一次参加乡试失败了。虽受到打击，但他并没有失去信心。一条消息鼓舞了他：一个十二岁的男孩成功通过了乡试，获得了举人身份。这意味着这个十二岁的男孩有了担任地方官的资格。继续读书，继续科考，这是天下读书人的正途。

　　功夫不负有心人。在桂花飘香的季节，三十二岁的夏时正听到了

以桥之名
——大运河上的中国文化密码（中英双语）
In the Name of Bridges:
The Chinese Cultural Codes on the Grand Canal (Chinese-English Bilingual)

28

高中报捷的锣鼓声。① 我们可以想象这条路对于他来说是何其艰难！官方发榜是和桂花香气结伴而来的，因此录取名单又被称为"桂榜"。幸运上榜的考生被描述为"折桂"。这和西方诗歌中的桂冠诗人有相通之处，不是吗？

夏时正并没有太多的时间来庆贺乡试的胜利，因为他必须马上投入次年春天举行的会试备考。会试是由礼部组织的，参加者是乡试的胜出者，即各地的举人。会试在都城举行，因此举人在备考之余，还需要筹备资金，以应付迢迢之路上的花费。有些家境不宽裕的举人只能接受资助。赶考举人的清贫很好理解，毕竟大多数人在中举之前经历了漫长的收入菲薄的秀才时期。 这一点在文学作品中多有体现。例如，《红楼梦》中的重要人物贾雨村进京赶考，就有赖于富户甄士隐的资助——甄士隐给他的资助相当于普通农户两年的生活费②，可见进京赶考的开销之巨大。他人的资助当然是一种善举，不过这也可以看作一种投资。毕竟，一旦举人在会试中高中，成为进士，那么在他面前将打开一扇大门，欢迎这位前途光明的国之精英。

1445 年初冬，夏时正告别了妻子、孩子和母亲，踏上了前往北京参加翌年春季会试的旅程。他不能待在家里过除夕和春节——这是中国人最重要的节日，因为这趟进京赶考之旅需要至少两个半月的时间。夏时正在杭州城北登船，沿着京杭大运河一路北上。

水路对于夏时正来说是非常自然的选择。乘船也许比骑马或坐车要慢，但更加经济。 宝马雕车，从来都是富家子弟的专属。大运河的开凿，舟船出行的便利，方便了普通人的出行、求学、求业。京杭大运河到明朝已经发展为一条非常繁忙的水上运输路线，从东南各地征集的谷物、丝绸、布匹、茶叶，还有奇珍异宝通过大运河源源不断

---

① 夏时正（1412—1499），明正统十年（1445）中进士，时年三十三岁。中举在中进士前一年秋季。

② 《红楼梦》中，刘姥姥得知一顿螃蟹宴要花费二十余两银子，感叹这够得上庄户人家一年的嚼谷。甄士隐赠贾雨村五十两银子，并两套冬衣。

运到都城，皇帝将把这些物资分配下去，借此维系庞大帝国的运转。

正月，夏时正抵达了北京。都城此刻正沉浸在迎接新年的欢乐气氛里，夏时正不由得想起他远在南方的家人。尽管邮路效率不高，他还是写了一封信报平安。整个家族，无论亲疏，都在祈祷他能够在这场决定命运的考试中有好运相伴。之后他参加了会试的第一场。在分隔成一个个小间、仅供考生答题的逼仄小棚里，夏时正在凳子上坐了一整天。他仔细思考题目，搓着手取暖。北京的冬天非常寒冷，而考棚又没有门，甚至连门帘也没有，这样看守的士兵能够对考生的小动作一目了然。作弊是非常危险的，但"回报"也十分巨大，因而严密的监考是非常有必要的。这场三年才组织一次的考试太重要了，一旦通过，不仅对考生本人，而且对他的整个家族乃至整个村、整个县都有重要的意义。在出过进士的村庄，家族祠堂多修建得气派堂皇，既显示家风优良能出俊才，也意味着有弟子在朝为官，从而昭告四邻：我乃望族，不容小觑。

农历二月十二日和二月十五日，夏时正又参加了会试的后续两场。他发挥得很好，通过了考试。现在他有了一个新的科举头衔——贡士。但是他还不能踏上回家的路，告诉家人这个好消息，因为还有一场名为殿试的荣誉性考试在等着他。

殿试，顾名思义，是在皇帝和高级官员们商议大事的朝廷大殿上举行的，由皇帝亲自主持。在朝堂上举行考试有一种特别的意义：考生不再是平凡之辈，而是皇帝亲自选拔的弟子，是国家的精英，是肩负社稷之未来的栋梁。

这种骄傲盘旋在每一个考生的心中，有的获得了强大的心理动力，而有的则在巨大的心理压力下患得患失，不能正常发挥。

夏时正再一次显示出他作为万里挑一的知识分子的才能，在殿试中他获得了第十二名，从而获得了荣誉性的身份——进士出身。新科进士有的被任命为地方官，有的被纳入翰林院作为储备人才。总之，夏时正从儿童时期就开始的科举之路，直到二十余年后人到中年才算修成正果，而他已经是寥若晨星的幸运儿之一了。

在漫长的科举道路上，夏时正是极少数能走到最后并越过终点线的人。 这是一场巨大的胜利，是被其他读书人所艳羡的巨大胜利，是多年刻苦攻读的必然之中偶然获得的胜利。

他高中进士的好消息由快马一路发往家乡。夏时正后来被皇帝任命为高级官员。作为明朝的一名负责任的法官（刑部主事和刑部郎中，之后是大理寺卿）， 夏时正工作勤勉，政声颇佳。

为了纪念和赞颂他，同时也为了显示这位高官起步于杭州，人们在他当年登船赴京的地方造了一座桥，将桥命名为"登云"。这个词的字面意思是登上云端，是对夏时正"学而优则仕"的肯定。登云桥也承载着普通老百姓对有更多的优秀官员来保护他们的期待，因为真正能够给他们带来繁荣安宁生活的不仅是远在朝堂的皇帝，还有地方上的执政者。从这个意义上来说，中国的科举制度，确实行之有效，选拔出了一批优秀的人才来治理这个庞大的帝国。

6 卖鱼桥——市井生活的趣味

假设你生活在南宋的临安（今杭州），那时还没有智能手机可以定位和导航，你想买些日用品， 怎样才能迅速地找到这些隐藏在拥挤建筑中的窄巷里弄上的店铺呢？ 聪明的杭州人找到了一个简单的办法，那就是根据商业类别和行业来给街巷命名，这是在没有智能手机的年代里极大地便利人们生活的大智慧。

例如，卖鱼桥，表示这儿有个鱼市。 米市巷，告诉你可以在这里交易粮食。 还有皮市巷、菜市桥、马市街。 中文里的"市"有两层含义，作为名词的"市场"和作为动词的"买卖，交易"。 所以皮市巷是交易皮货的地方，菜市桥则是菜担子云集之处，在马市街你可以买马，给它配上漂亮的马鞍和马蹄铁。 猜猜看，清晨你会在哪里遇到南宋的高官呢？ 直接去城南，找到一个名叫官巷口的地方（官员居住的巷子，就像英国的唐宁街）， 那里距离朝廷不远。

让我们回到卖鱼桥，这个大运河杭州段的热门地。来自杭州以北水乡泽国的渔船，都在这里聚集，使这里成为一个热闹的鱼市。

回到1163年，急欲振作朝纲的皇帝赵昚起用了陆游，赐进士出身，任命其为枢密院编修官。消息由宫中传到家里，阖家大喜。中国人庆贺喜事最常见的方式就是设宴吃顿好的。陆游家的仆妇夏妈起了个大早，特意来到城北的卖鱼桥，所谓无鱼不成席。江南人家，鱼货易得，但是天气炎热，要买到新鲜又肥美的好鱼，还是得到汇聚周边鱼货的卖鱼桥来。

河边聚集了不少船只，渔民多操着德清、瓶窑一带的口音。有的渔民就在船上摆开，也有的来路远，又不善于做生意，就把整船鱼货批发给鱼铺。

河边近桥塈的地方，小贩们把鱼干、虾干堆在竹盘里。小贩的脚边有几个桶，草鱼和河鳗在里面挨挨挤挤。这些河鲜是从小河及其支流中钓起来的，很少来自运河，运河太繁忙了，渔夫们找不到平静的水面静静等待灵敏的鱼儿入网。

虾干和活鱼都没有入夏妈的眼。看到小贩们失望的目光，她安慰性地敷衍着"好的好的，下次下次"，然后朝一家比较大的鱼铺走去。她刚在店门口停下，店伙计就非常热情地迎了上来。"您来了！夏妈妈！气色真好！您肯定有喜事儿！啊，您家老爷高中进士了！这可得好好摆上两桌！"经过一大串喜气洋洋的寒暄，年轻人抛出了他真正想问的问题："今天买条什么鱼？"

店伙计非常热情，夏妈要是不买点儿什么，是离不开这店铺了。"和气生财"，是中国商人信奉的实用真理。

伙计名叫阿辉，一个常见的中国年轻人的名字。他已经在这家远房亲戚开的鱼铺里待了5年，成了一个有经验的伙计。头3年他的工作是没有薪水的，这是约定俗成的学徒规矩，管吃住，兼看店（安保）、打杂。听上去是件被盘剥的苦差事，但比起看天吃饭、侍弄庄稼，经商有"钱途"多了。临安城自被赵构定为国都以来，商业日盛。宋高宗赵构虽然在抗金方面被史学家诟病，但他倡导"市商"的意识和政策，为东南各省的商业发展打下了良好基础。

13岁那年，阿辉辞别父母，离开水乡小镇。中国以农业立国，农业为国之根本。每年开春，一国之君前往农田亲自扶犁，以倡导农耕。但是，阿辉的父母觉得，比起在庄稼地里刨食，做点儿小买卖是更能挣钱的营生。他的父母相信，到皇族高官和士绅富户云集的繁华国都做生意会给他带来第一桶金。3年后，阿辉的报酬包括每月很少的一笔津贴，以及年底发的一笔奖金——这是大头。店老板，和其他精明的生意人一样，会根据伙计的业绩表现来分配奖金。老板们有的慷慨有的吝啬，有的慈善有的贪婪，但是他们都知道一个好伙计的价值。为了减少员工的流失和降低用人的成本，老板们通常不会给员工放长假，因为长假除了意味着要协调用工之外，还意味着员工跳槽的可能性增加了。所以，不到年底这个人人都要回家团聚的时候，伙计们是拿不到奖金的。

新的一年阿辉迎来了19岁。对他来说，即将到来的春节不仅仅是如往年一样和家人团聚的假期，还要和他16岁的未婚妻完婚，订婚礼是2年前办的。娶亲得花上一大笔钱是民间共识，攒钱、娶妻、生子，是年轻男子普遍要完成的人生大事，顶门立户要从娶亲开始。所以订婚后的阿辉一直勤奋有加，娶新娘子过门就是他最大的动力，而这种动力也使得他的勤奋带有一些欢乐的色彩。

他的真诚和欢乐成功地感染了客人。夏妈愉快地挑挑拣拣，最终选了两条红鲤鱼。在中国文化里，红鲤鱼是幸运和财富的象征，尤其代表着漫长科考之后的阶级跃升，所谓"鲤鱼跃龙门"。获得进士头衔是从普通百姓跃入高等级阶层的重要保证。鲤鱼味道一般，但是不可替代，就是因为它承载着对好运的期待。时至今日，鲤鱼仍然是年画和新年剪纸凸显的重要元素，明晃晃、红艳艳、胖乎乎的一尾红鲤鱼，占据着客堂的最显眼处，这就是传统文化的力量。

鱼在汉语中与"余"同音，因此又成为富裕、富足的指代。中国人的除夕宴上一定会有一条全鱼，而且，这条鱼始终不会被分而食之，始终完完整整。全鱼是中国人餐桌上的幸运图腾。现在，亲爱的读者，你知道为什么夏妈要买两条鱼了吧？

7 北新关——见证运河繁华的钞关

大运河是帝国的经济动脉，明朝在大运河沿岸设立了 7 大钞关，向过往船只征税，上缴国库。清朝延续了这一系统。大运河杭州段的北新关，就是其中一处典型的钞关。通过北新关，我们可以一瞥明清时期税务的情况。

康熙二十五年（1686），北新关征集的税收为一年 1 万两白银，达到整个国家收入的 8.8% 左右；在光绪皇帝统治时期超过了 12 万两，这意味着北新关在国家税收中占的分量越来越重。

北新关距杭州武林门码头约 5000 米，建于 1450 年，时值明朝景泰元年。北新关由一座桥、一个官衙和一对水门组成。贩夫走卒缴纳过桥税，而水门则是为向过往船只收税而建造的。等待缴税放行的大小船只挨挨挤挤，给北新关带来了繁华，但也造成了拥堵，逐渐演变成腐败的温床。时间就是金钱，而金钱可以推动时间跑得更快。焦躁的船主和商人深知这一点，所以他们不得不"打点"守关的官员，以求尽快完成缴税通关手续。特别是江南水乡盛产的河鲜，无法抵抗炎热或多雨的天气，即便通关慢 1 个小时也会给货主造成相当大的损失。明朝沿着大运河建造了 7 大钞关，每一处钞关都用上了"钱"这个特殊的疏通剂。讽刺的是，掌管关务的官员通常都自称是孔子门生，对他们而言，正直廉洁是应有之义。船主与商人明白官员的担忧，于是送书画、瓷器等看上去十分风雅的文人物件。

粮食和货物的税金是根据品质来定的。这条规定听上去很合理，在实际操作中却滋生了腐败。精心制定税收政策的初衷是为庞大帝国获取基本财富，但是政策制定者们可能预见不到，此中的漏洞正是由精明的守关人自己挖掘的，他们神不知鬼不觉地成为帝国财富的小偷。比如在给稻谷定级的过程中，不同于现代社会有明确的质量管理体系，如"ISO 9000"或者其他标准，明清两代虽然确立了质量标准，但主要依靠检测官的个人品德。大多数人并不能遵守初入官场时的誓言——作为孔子门生要秉持公道、廉正。

税务官从中渔利有多种路径：指鹿为马、贬低货物等级、延迟通关，甚至谎称分量不足。货物的标准在哪儿？在他们的嘴上。测量设备是什么？是他们的眼睛。一旦税务官的心失去了平衡，也就没有公平了。

腐败的另一个源头是对船只用途进行的分类。根据明朝的律令，大运河首要的功能是承担国家的粮食运输，即以漕运为主，因此漕船享有优先通关权。在通关繁忙的时候，民船需要为漕船让路。此外，漕船在缴纳税金上还享有优惠，有时甚至是免税的。这对于商家来说不是秘密，因此他们会想方设法雇佣漕船，在船头挂上官旗，趾高气扬地宣称此船拥有的特权。当然，商家要获得这种利益是需要付出代价的。

商家不是唯一"打点"税务官员的人。事实上有的负责征收漕粮的地方官也会参与其中，尽管他们的初衷并非如此。

堆放在船上的粮食如果暴露在连续的阴雨带来的水汽之中，很容易变色、发芽、霉变、减重。无论是数量上的减少还是质量上的损毁，都会给主事官员带去风险，从严厉的申饬到贬职，有时甚至会丢了性命。为了自保，这些官员会采取错误但可行的办法：一是贿买通关的优先权，二是想法子提高漕粮的认定等级。

于是一张腐败网就织成了，包括漕船把头、地方官、税务官，没有一个人是无辜的，似乎也没有一个人有罪。

即使皇帝本人也对这种桌子底下的交易睁只眼闭只眼。据记载，有一次康熙皇帝查问河工，发现河道总督办事很得力，在征收漕粮和主管水利工程方面都办得不错。皇帝对他的工作很满意，心情大好之下突然抛出一个问题："你有没有贪污公款，报假账？"皇帝意味深长，虽然微笑着，但眼睛发出锐利的光。他盯着他的下属，这个下属担负着国家很大一部分的税收工作。

三藩、河务、漕运，是康熙皇帝最操心的三件事。他把这三件事题写在宫中的廊柱上，日日去看，时时自省。作为长年在草原上纵横驰骋的游牧民族的后代，康熙皇帝牢牢掌控着军队，取得了西南边境和西北边境的军事胜利，但是他并没有在水乡生活的经验，对治理国家的河务缺乏信心。尽管他被后世看作是一位伟大的帝王，但在执政时他不能确定自己的旨意能否被完整地执行，不能确定他的皇权能否真正到达帝国的每一寸土地，不能确定臣子们的忠诚和廉正。

河道总督大吃一惊，吓了一跳。不过，从最初的惊惧中镇定下来后，这个官员做出了一个大胆的决定。他跪了下来，回答道："陛下，我承认，为了便利漕粮运输，这些事情是有的。"

他的应对证明了他确实是富于经验的老练官员。康熙对他的坦白交代很满意，确认这个臣子对他是忠诚的。这一段突如其来而惊心动魄的对话在皇帝的大笑中结束，既体现了皇帝对臣子的体谅，也是一次看似温和的警告。毕竟，皇帝深知，就漕粮运输的腐败而言，他自己也不是完全没有责任。

清道光年间因多种原因，漕粮运输凋敝。几番争议之后，随着海运的兴起，光绪皇帝于 1901 年下诏正式废止漕运。

今天的北新关遗址能让我们一瞥五百多年前大运河畔的税务机构，但是北新关的详细构造只能到学者的论文里找寻。明清时期的北新关建筑群对称排列，沿着中轴线设置五进，两侧为关员办事房、内书房等附属设施。北新关的最前方矗立着一座十米高的鼓楼。栏杆后是牌坊，面朝运河，表明关界。前厅为三开间，入内后能看到正厅，同样为三开间。正厅后有一间小厅为会客室。紧挨着会客室的是书房和藏书室。正厅后有五座阁楼，俯瞰着小池塘。正厅左侧是主官的起居室，以及助手和仆人的房间。正厅右侧为仓房，用于堆放未完税的粮食。还有五间吏员的办公用房，没有办完税务的吏员是不可以随意离开关衙的。书吏办理粮食税务登记的办公房间有两间，称为庑房。[①]

有意思的是，仪门外建有一座土地庙，常年烟火缭绕，接受着官员的祭拜。明清两朝的官员基本上是通过严格的科举考试，获得"出身"之后走入仕途的，所谓学而优则仕。尽管官员们饱受儒家教育，并且熟背至圣先师的教导"子不语怪、力、乱、神"，但是他们在泥塑的土地公公面前深深地弯下腰去，向这个所谓的神灵祈求好运。这种公开的对神灵的敬拜，与其说是违背儒家教义的信仰，不如说是在巨大的现实压力之下的灵活变通。不发达的农业社会的粮食生产在很大程度上依赖天气，艰辛劳作后收获的粮食被征收为漕粮，就成为国家级战略物资。作为处理漕粮税收的钞关官员们，责任重大。仓储不当或者天气不利，都会导致漕粮的重大损失。儒家出身的官员们公开举行土地公公祭拜仪式，既是作为事务负责人诚恳期望神灵护佑的体现，更是借此昭告全体官员：兹事体大，小心行事。从某种意义上来说，对神灵的信仰和对律法的忌惮是一体两面的管理制度。

---

① 转引自唐力行：《江南社会历史评论（第三期）》，商务印书馆 2011 年版。

8 富义仓——运河仓储体系的遗存

　　让我们离开北新关沿着大运河继续向南，很快，宽阔的河面东侧出现了一座特别的白色圆柱状建筑，墙上两个大字笔墨淋漓——富义。这就是拥有"天下粮仓"美名的富义仓，是大运河漕粮运输与仓储体系的重要遗存。

　　作为人工开凿的河流，大运河从设计之初就是为了承担粮食运输的任务，即南粮北运。古代中国的皇权最早出现在北方，并选择在黄河流域定都。大多数的封建统一政权，如最早的秦朝、最后的清朝，都将国都定于广袤的北方土地上。秦朝的咸阳、隋朝的大兴和洛阳、唐朝的长安、宋朝的汴京、元朝的大都、明清两朝的北京，这些都城无一例外都是地理和文化概念上的北方城市。

　　定都北方的传统使得北方逐渐成为国家的政治中心，由此庞大的王朝管理机构也在北方城市建立起来，更繁复庞杂的附属机构也一并建立。于是，管理这套庞大机构的人，包括皇帝和他的大臣，侍奉皇族的仆从，以及中央各级部门的工作人员、皇家军队等，需要大量的粮食供养。粮食还被用作薪资。战国时期，各国普遍采用以粮食为官吏俸禄的制度，后续朝代延续并发展了这一制度。

　　尽管北方地区拥有政治上的优势，但是它必须依赖南方以获得充足的粮食。民以食为天，国以粮为本。满足不断增长的粮食需求成为一个王朝最重要的工作之一。如何才能获得充足的粮食？从何处获取充足的粮食？隋朝的两位皇帝，杨坚和他的儿子杨广，将目光投向了长江以南的广大地区。由于雨水丰沛、土壤肥沃，南方成为人口密集区，在发展渔业和丝织业之外，还发展了稻作农业。

贯通已有水系修建大运河的念头由此在杨坚心中萌芽。建立隋朝后不久，他要求杰出的大臣宇文恺主持设计一条运河，用来连接国都大兴（今西安）与军事重镇潼关。这一运河被命名为广通渠，它的修建是为了降低干旱带来的影响，提高粮食产量。

隋朝的第二位皇帝（同时也是末代皇帝）杨广继承了父亲要建造一套完整的内陆水道的宏愿。这位年轻而又野心勃勃的皇帝，曾经在长江流域的港口城市江都（今扬州）担任总督长达 10 年，之后在邻近地区又治理了 9 年。他的妻子萧氏是南北朝时期梁朝的皇族后裔，成长于江南地区，给予他很深的江南文化的影响。杨广喜爱江南的文化和文明，对江南地区的生产力有直观的感受，而江南的富饶给了他深刻的印象。605 年，当他从二皇子成为执掌国家权柄的皇帝的时候，直通江南繁华的心愿得以成为国家意志。他下诏贯通一条由长江南下的运河，连接钱塘江，起点和终点分别是长江北岸的江都和钱塘江畔的杭州，这就是江南运河。由此，隋唐大运河基本形成。

隋唐大运河以隋朝的东都洛阳为中心，由此，广袤国土的南北方得以通过水路连接，这使得通过河流进行大宗货物的运输成为可能。隋朝开启了修建大运河这一伟大工程，但是这一举世无双的水利工程并未成为隋帝国长治久安的保证，而隋朝也没有来得及充分享用这一创造人类历史的水利工程的成果。取代隋朝的唐朝延续了隋朝的运河开凿工程，并将其发展为一套全国性的水上交通系统。晚唐诗人皮日休对隋朝大运河的功能有过公允的评价："尽道隋亡为此河，至今千里赖通波。若无水殿龙舟事，共禹论功不较多。"

开凿运河代价巨大，在一定程度上加速了隋朝政权的灭亡；而唐朝繁盛的水上商贸往来，有赖于运河的畅通。杨广兴建运河的功绩可媲美中国古代大禹的治水功绩。

至唐朝中叶，隋唐大运河每年从南方运到都城长安的谷物多达300万石①②，这类谷物被称作漕粮。漕粮就是指通过水路运往京师供应官、军的粮食。

漕粮的数量持续增长，运河的建设也进一步得到完善。围绕着大运河，唐朝不断开凿周边小运河，将运河各段逐渐连接起来。元朝不再让大运河以洛阳为中心，而是直通京杭，即"截弯取直"。从此，全长约2700千米的隋唐大运河缩短为约1800千米的京杭大运河，今天也常常被简称为大运河。到了元朝末年，大运河终于成为流经中国东部大部分疆域的完整的水上交通体系。后世的明朝和清朝，随着人口的增长，对大运河更为依赖。

明朝时通过大运河运输的漕粮平均每年约400万担。在清朝于1901年废止漕运之前，京杭大运河毫无疑问是这个庞大帝国的经济大动脉。

沿着近1800千米的京杭大运河，形态各异、功能不同的谷仓得以建立，它们是中国古代存储粮食和调节米价的重要设施。

建立粮食仓储系统是为了管理粮价、备灾备荒、缓解粮荒，使得政权能够长治久安。意大利旅行家马可·波罗在他的游记中这样称赞：皇帝在粮食丰收、供大于求、价格便宜的年份，存储粮食，保存3—4年。当粮价高昂时，则开仓放粮，以较低的价格出售。③

数千年来，人们都祈望风调雨顺，人寿年丰。备荒谷仓可追溯到春秋时期，正式出现是在西汉。仓储体系在隋唐时进一步完善，史料

---

① 张显运：《运河浮沉：唐宋时期的漕运与古都洛阳兴衰》。选自光明网，参见 https://news.gmw.cn/2022-08/27/content_35981895.htm。
② 在唐代，1石约为今天的79.32千克。
③ 见杭州塘栖谷仓博物馆。

记载是"天下之粮悉数储之"。根据位置和功能的不同，谷仓包括正仓、转运仓、太仓、常平仓、义仓等。正仓是最主要的谷仓，转运仓是临时存储粮食用于转运的仓库，太仓专储存皇家粮食，常平仓用于储存粮食、调节粮价，义仓则是慈善仓库。除义仓通常由地方士绅捐资建造维护以外，其他谷仓都由中央或地方政府建造和管理。

官方谷仓体系的有效运转，一方面支撑国家机构的运转，另一方面有助于缓解季节性饥馑，从而使得政权能够有效维持下去。

整套谷仓体系是如何分工的呢？

正仓是国家的中央仓库，通常设立在主要产粮区，承担着战略储备的功能。转运仓，顾名思义，用于转运谷物。转运仓通常沿着大运河而建。太仓，位于都城，供皇家储存粮食。常平仓是一个了不起的创举。西汉设立常平仓，通过调节粮价来达到供需平衡。当供大于求、粮价走低时，常平仓就大量购买谷物并储存起来；在自然灾害导致歉收、粮价高企时，谷仓的储备粮食就进入流通市场，从而平抑谷价。通过丰年积谷、灾年粜粮的方法，常平仓既保护了农民的利益，也有助于社会的稳定、安宁。

义仓的出现可以追溯到隋朝。由于洪涝等灾害，人民时遭饥馑，这促成了慈善性质的义仓的出现。义仓并非由官方设立，而是由城镇居民发起的。义仓中的粮食只有在饥荒发生的时候才会向地方百姓发放，尤其是当极端天气导致庄稼绝收时，义仓就会发挥很大的作用。到了南宋，著名学者朱熹提议在乡村设立义仓。这一尝试被证明是成功的，由此，农村义仓在全国推广开来，使得偏远农村的穷苦百姓免于挨饿。

明朝有天津、临清、德州、徐州、淮安五大转运仓。至清代，临、德二仓为存在时间最长、发挥作用最大的转运仓。大运河漕粮的运输与城市的发展息息相关。以临清为例，它的繁荣在很大程度上仰赖漕粮的运输与仓储需要。当时，位于临清的临清闸和会通闸启闭时，一些漕运船只就把粮食卸下，储存在临清仓。通过卫河运过来的河南地区的粮食，通过会通河运来的江浙一带的粮食大都储存在临清粮仓，以备京城调用。[1]漕粮船除了运输谷物，也装载供马匹食用的豆类，此外还有各地特产，名为"土宜"，这是朝廷给长途运粮的漕军的特殊补贴，而这一措施促进了南北物资的流通。

明朝永乐至宣德年间（1403—1435），临清粮仓达到鼎盛，时称"天下第一仓"。临清仓的货物吞吐量、运输量和战略地位都远高于大运河沿岸其他谷仓。随着漕粮存储和转运量的不断增加，临清也从一个小镇发展为繁华城市。新的市民阶层出现了，而他们的精神文化需求促成了文化娱乐业的繁荣。许多著名的长篇小说和戏曲话本就有丰富的临清元素，如《金瓶梅》大量的故事情节是以临清为背景展开的，《醒世姻缘传》《聊斋志异》《老残游记》等均有大量来自临清的人物。生动的场景以临清为背景，地点从酒肆到商铺，人物从歌女到商人、从急公好义的侠士到觥筹往来的巨富，这些显示出临清因运河而兴盛，也显示出基层仓官的独木难支和同流合污，呈现出人性在利益面前的多样性。

京杭大运河边有一个著名的谷仓，南临江涨桥，北望拱宸桥，这座慈善谷仓叫富义仓，建于清光绪年间。富义仓由当时的浙江巡抚谭钟麟发起督造，而仓中粮食由本地商人捐资购买。富义仓占地总面积约8000平方米，建筑面积约3000平方米，是一座包含谷仓和附属设施的仓储综合体。包括迎客厅、晒谷场、办事庑房，50余个分列4行的谷仓，每个约20平方米，以及数间稻谷加工房。

谷仓发明之初，并非为运河而生。但是大运河开凿成功、担负起运输粮食的重任之后，谷仓成了关乎民生和社会稳定的重要设施。大

---

[1] 转引自郑民德：《明清京杭运河沿线漕运仓储系统研究》，中国社会科学出版社2015年版。

运河赐予谷仓以特殊的战略地位，谷仓则在大运河发展为国家经济命脉的过程中成为不可或缺的一部分。没有谷仓，漕粮的转运和存储无从谈起。此外，粮食的有效储存，使得人们不再困守于劳作的田野，得以从事其他营生。谷仓催生了城镇，催生了相关的商业活动和消费行为，也催生了城市群落和市民阶层。从这个意义上来说，谷仓孕育了人类多彩绚烂的文明之花。

江涨桥——皇帝南巡的秘密

　　江涨桥，其字面意思是江水涨到和桥面一样的高度。江涨桥位于大运河杭州段的中心位置。桥长约 95 米，宽约 20 米，东连大兜路，西接湖墅北路和信义坊。传说，东海和钱塘江的潮水会一直涨到这里，江涨桥由此得名。

　　桥底部左右两侧的支撑墙面（桥台）刻着康熙皇帝和他的孙子乾隆皇帝的半身浮雕像。这祖孙俩也是目前为止中国当代老百姓最熟悉的两位皇帝。他们的传奇故事多次被写成小说，改编成热播影视剧。

　　1911 年以前，中国一共有 494 位皇帝，他们中的大多数对于老百姓来说都是仅存于史书的陌生人，那为什么康乾两帝能够被普罗大众所熟知呢？ 康熙、乾隆不仅仅是两个皇帝年号、天之子，不仅仅是肃穆朝堂上的皇权符号，他们还活在老百姓口口相传的生动故事里，有的老百姓甚至能骄傲地指着一块刻有康熙或者乾隆落款的大石头，娓娓道来。

　　两位皇帝在杭州留下了许多书法作品，题诗、作文，或者铭文。他们的墨宝或刻于巨大匾额上，鬏以金漆，高挂于亭台楼阁；或刻于大石上，立于泉边、林下。 他们的书法作品真的具有很高的艺术价值吗？答案并不重要，重要的是皇帝的作品通常因为他们的身份而受到赞美——当然从客观上说作为皇室成员，他们确实受到了很好的教育，有良好的审美和文学欣赏水平。据说乾隆皇帝一生写了 4 万多首诗，其中不少跟杭州有关。

地方主政官员非常渴望得到皇帝的手书，不论长短，不论是诗词还是四字箴言，他们都如获至宝。皇帝赐墨毫无疑问意味着一种极高的赞赏，而且将会在普通百姓的口口相传中逐渐演变为一段传奇。

皇帝很清楚他的手书的价值。这是一个有趣的悖论：不珍贵的珍贵。与珍宝华屋、良田美舍相比，题几个字成本极低。然而，从声名和荣耀来说，他的墨宝对于官员乃至其家族来说又具有永恒的价值，值得代代相传。

为什么康熙和乾隆这两位皇帝会在杭州留下这么多书法作品呢？这与他们俩先后共 12 次南巡到达杭州不无关系。

今天我们乘船游览大运河，可以看到江涨桥下的支撑墙面上记录的康、乾巡察杭州的事迹。西墙上刻着康熙的五言绝句，赞美了浙江的风光，也表达了他受到浙江人民爱戴的喜悦之情；还刻着一尊身着皇袍的康熙半身像，正对着东面刻载的故事——他的孙子乾隆皇帝 6 次从首都北京沿着大运河乘船南下到达杭州——京杭大运河最南端的城市。江涨桥的建筑师和设计师一定读懂了康熙皇帝的心思，据说乾隆在孩提时代就被爷爷康熙作为皇权的接班人着意培养。

为什么两位皇帝不顾长途跋涉的艰辛和巨大的花费多次南巡呢？乾隆对 6 次南巡做了总结："予临御五十年凡举二大事，一曰西师，一曰南巡……"[①]

乾隆在江南的美丽与繁华中流连忘返的说法不全是错的。但是要说他整日沉溺在奢华享乐中，那对这位皇帝来说有失公允。据史书记载，乾隆励精图治，勤勉治国。例如，他减免地方税赋（塘栖桥御碑亭载，减免浙江税赋 30 万两），巡察水利，了解民生，考察地方官政绩，笼络地方士绅贤达，视察军队，参加满汉先贤的祭祀大典（尽

---

① 李景屏：《乾隆王朝真相》，农村读物出版社 2003 年版，第 216 页。

管他本人是满族血统）。有趣的是，他对士绅贤达的笼络大部分是以写诗、作文、赐墨的形式进行的。要知道这些江南士族并不缺钱，而是缺声名。对于皇帝来说，题字与赋诗是怡情养性的优雅消遣，但是当万乘之尊的皇帝离开朝廷时，怡情养性的消遣也就成了工作的一部分。

为什么乾隆皇帝要写这么多字、作这么多诗？

在漫长的封建社会，汉族控制了广大疆域，确立了统治地位。得天下易，得人心难。清朝皇帝从明朝皇帝手中夺去大片江山后，认识到要吸取元朝的教训。元朝，这个由蒙古族建立的王朝存在时间不长，原因之一是其蔑视汉族文化和儒家思想，而后者自秦始皇以来就被奉为圭臬。江南士族深深奉行儒家思想，有许多士绅坚持认为儒家思想的优越性无可比拟。他们斥责清朝的统治，认为其的统治是对儒家思想这一中国人的思想共核的彻底背叛。

这些士族的文章、观点当然会动摇政权。儒家信徒们最珍视、最在意的是什么呢？不是财富，而是声名——秉持儒家思想的声名，被皇帝看重、尊重的声名，作为孔子的坚定追随者而被皇帝倚重的名声。因此，皇帝找到了最有效又最经济的安抚士族的方式：将他的手书赐予少数几个深孚众望的士族。他们会迫不及待将皇帝的墨宝刻在牌匾上，高高悬挂于客堂中央。对皇帝来说，这方法很简单，却很有效，不是吗？尽管在今人眼里，多少有一点讽刺的意味。

南巡远不止是观光旅行这么简单。作为当时世界上的大国之一，清朝在康熙时走向繁荣，而他的孙子乾隆皇帝延续了这个封建帝国的荣光并使之达到鼎盛。他们的 12 次南巡，在改善吏治、改善民生和巩固中央统治方面起到了不可替代的作用。

南巡花费巨大，劳民伤财。乾隆在回忆中自我问责："朕临御六十年并无失德，惟六次南巡，劳民伤财……"[①]他要求他的大臣：

---

① 李景屏：《乾隆王朝真相》，农村读物出版社 2003 年版，第 228 页。

若后世再有皇帝要南巡的，必须加以阻止。在乾隆退位（1795）后的100多年里，继任的6位皇帝无一南巡。

一次南巡通常耗时3—5个月。史料记载了某次南巡：浩浩荡荡的皇家船队约500艘船、6000匹马、3000名军士。船队于正月从北京出发，沿着大运河，于三月初到达运河南端之城杭州。在此地，船队掉头，再经过几个月的航行返回北京。如此漫长和奢华的旅行毫无疑问耗费颇巨，对于地方政府来说尤甚。他们会竞相奉献祥瑞，作为皇帝万寿无疆或国泰民安的证明。而官员的野心也毫无疑问会转嫁到汲汲百姓身上。

将一个大国治理得井井有条的皇帝，可以被称作明君、圣主而载入史册，传唱于百姓之中。但是在笔者看来，更值得记录的，是皇帝的自我批评的精神。

⑩ 德胜桥——爱情与胜利的传奇

　　"德胜"的意思是"美德与胜利"。"德胜"的同音词是"得胜"，意思是取得胜利。德胜桥的命名意在提醒人们铭记南宋初年政府军战胜叛军的传奇战斗。

　　中国古代封建王朝的不正常更替基本上出于两种原因：一是本国强大的政治家的叛乱，二是非汉族的其他民族对本朝的征服。南宋的建立就属于第二种情况。

　　南宋的建立是针对北宋大部分领土落入北方女真部落之手这一境况的制度性救济。宋朝皇帝宋徽宗和他的儿子宋钦宗被金军俘获后，金军打算把这个富裕国家的领导者作为筹码，用来交换大片的土地和巨额的财富。朝廷中的主战派反对向侵略者投降。国不可一日无君，非常时期，他们建议推举宋钦宗的弟弟康王赵构继承皇位。于是赵构坐上了金色的龙椅，史称宋高宗（1127—1162）。

　　宋高宗害怕女真人的侵略，更害怕被俘获后带来的耻辱，最终，在逃亡数年后，偏安于南方的临安，史称南宋。

　　宋高宗统治国家的合法性也令人生疑，因为宋钦宗还活着。建炎三年（1129），赵构继承皇权的合法性遭到了公开的质疑。他被批评说缺乏强有力的意志力，领导无能，缺乏军事战略眼光。他宠信宦官，给他们委以重任，这伤害了冒着生命危险拥戴他的将军们。皇家卫队御营司的将领——苗傅和刘彦正，就是其中的两位。

苗、刘二人发动了一场军事行动。他们包围了皇宫，首先斩杀了祸国殃民的大臣王渊和宦官康履等[1]，之后要求赵构把皇位交给他的侄儿——宋钦宗三岁的儿子。赵构害怕被这些愤怒的将军砍头，回复得十分谦卑：我确实没有资格坐在这龙椅上。

苗、刘二人并没有残暴地砍掉这位皇帝的脑袋。他们争辩说这不是叛乱，而是拥立明主的行动。尽管如此，但他们仍害怕被其他将军攻击，其中有一名猛将叫韩世忠。时任宰相朱胜非建议把韩世忠将军争取过来。

韩世忠出生在中国陕西农村。他十几岁就当了兵，作战英勇，可是论功行赏时他只得到一个小小的头衔，这让他相当失望。在随后的庆功宴上，韩世忠遇到了年轻的歌伎梁红玉[2]。她向韩世忠表达了爱慕之情，并且相信他必成大器，英名远播。对于一个雄心勃勃却失意的年轻男人来说，没有什么比一个美丽的年轻姑娘的爱慕更能安慰他的了。韩世忠的心弦被悄然拨动了。之后他得知梁姑娘原本是将军之女，父亲战败被处死之后，她从富裕之家的千金小姐沦为卖唱的营妓。在年轻男子的英雄气概和爱情的共同作用之下，韩世忠把她带回家，充作侍妾，丝毫不理会风言风语。几年后，梁红玉生了一个儿子，母子俩深得韩世忠的喜爱。苗、刘二人也听说过这段罗曼史，认为梁红玉能够劝降韩世忠，于是同意了朱胜非的计划。

听完劝降计划的梁红玉没有犹豫。她亲吻和拥抱了年幼的儿子，轻声告诉他：妈妈会回来接你的。

快马奔驰了整整一夜，梁红玉来到了杭州以北约数百里的秀州（今嘉兴），她的丈夫韩世忠率军驻扎在这里。但是，她没有请求韩世忠和叛军站到一起。相反，她解除了韩世忠的疑虑，鼓励他与苗、刘大

---

① 虞云国：《南渡君臣：宋高宗及其时代》，上海人民出版社 2019 年版。
② 姓名不详，"红玉"是其去世后各类野史和话本中的名字。

以桥之名
In the Name of Bridges:
The Chinese Cultural Codes on the Grand Canal (Chinese-English Bilingual)
——大运河上的中国文化密码（中英双语）

50

战一场。梁红玉冒着失去儿子的危险，对丈夫晓以大义。苗、刘的兵变很快以失败告终。

韩世忠被高宗授予"忠勇"二字。梁夫人则被授予"安国夫人"的头衔。

后来梁夫人参加了韩世忠的军队，两人一同作战。1130 年，在金军又一次来犯时，梁红玉亲自来到阵前鼓舞士气。在杭州以北约 200 千米的水乡泽国黄天荡，这场战役整整持续了 48 天。梁红玉身披铠甲，跳上高台，挥舞手臂，擂响战鼓，鼓舞将士们战斗到底。获得胜利后，朝廷加封她为"杨国夫人"。她的形象正如法国圣女贞德的形象，是一个保家卫国的女英雄，也像古希腊神话中的胜利女神尼姬。

值得一提的是，梁红玉是以一个独立勇敢的女战士的形象被人们传颂的，而不仅仅是成功丈夫背后的女人。在古代封建社会贬低女性的文化里，梁红玉的努力和成就打破了对女性的认知，塑造了古代中国一个不朽的女性传奇。

对于韩世忠来说，梁红玉不仅仅是一个女人、一个妻子，更是和他荣辱与共、并肩战斗的伙伴。他们是灵魂伴侣。梁红玉成长在武官之家，受过良好的教育，又能舞枪弄棒，还有对朝廷的忠诚。虽遭逢巨大变故，从官宦之家的千金小姐沦落为军营歌伎，但梁红玉从未向命运低头。韩世忠和梁红玉的爱情故事，冲破世俗的藩篱，在民族大义中闪耀着宝贵的光芒。夫妇俩并肩作战，其事迹可见于《说岳全传》：

百战功名四海钦，贤哉内助智谋深。

而今风浪金焦过，犹作夫人击鼓音。①

另一个有趣的问题是官员们对皇帝的忠心。

① [清] 钱彩、金丰：《说岳全传》，团结出版社 2017 年版，第 377 页。

宰相朱胜非其实是诈降。在危急时刻，他宁愿冒着生命危险也要扶持被围困的皇帝，而不是听从已将大内团团包围的叛军的命令，扶持年仅3岁的孩子当傀儡皇帝。他同样很清楚梁红玉和韩世忠对朝廷的忠诚。

"世忠"，意思是世代忠良，韩世忠是深受数万士兵爱戴的统帅。他宁愿冒着失去儿子的危险，也不愿意背叛皇帝，尽管赵构做皇帝并不称职。

事实上赵构从他戴上皇冠的那一天起就不称职。在大宋王朝的危机中，他因为皇子的身份而被匆匆推上皇位，从一开始就充满了对皇帝所担负的职责的恐惧。入侵者已经俘获了他的父亲和兄长，但是他们对这一结果仍不满足。野蛮的入侵者没有喝止他们的战马，也没有将武器收入行囊。当朝中的文臣武将绞尽脑汁想着抵御外侮的时候，至高无上的皇帝赵构却日夜沉溺于酒色之中。尽管忠臣们对此日益不满，但他们还是容忍了皇帝的这种生活方式，因为根据他们习惯的"教义"，皇帝就是天选之子，享有特权是他凌驾于普通人之上的标志之一。

赵构沉迷于酒色，对政事没有兴趣，他把朝政交给宦官。在逃难的路上，贪官污吏搜刮了巨量的金银财宝和古董，强行命令数十艘船承运，却对无法上船的百姓的哭声充耳不闻，任由他们在金军日益迫近的马蹄声中陷入被杀害和被侮辱的恐惧之中。

苗、刘二人宣称兵变的目的不是要推翻赵家对宋朝的统治，而是要把皇权交到他们认可的真正的继承人手里。他们质疑赵构称帝的合法性，认为他的哥哥（被俘获的宋钦宗）的亲生儿子才是龙椅的真正主人。这里有必要指出的是，两位叛军将领似乎从未试图抢夺皇帝的权杖。

此次兵变被定性为苗、刘二人的军事行动，是对皇帝和朝廷的叛乱。对于大多数官员来说，压倒性的思想仍然是对皇帝效忠，无论这位皇帝是否勤政爱民。他们认可孔子的教导"君君，臣臣"。 但是中国古代另一位著名的哲学家孟子则持相反的观点，他认为"民为贵，社稷次之，君为轻"，百姓的利益应该放在君王的利益之前。当然，对于统治阶级的代表——君王来说，孟子的这套理论并不利于他们的统治。不过，孟子的仁政思想仍然有其追随者，其中最著名的一位就是初唐宰相魏征。他把百姓和皇帝比作水和舟，认为"水能载舟，亦能覆舟"。唐太宗接受了魏征的这一谏言，在不断地努力下，开创了唐朝的繁荣时代。

苗、刘二人对赵构的挑战，尽管是由对赵构抗金不利、治政不勤的失望引起的，但无法赢得大臣和将领的公开支持。他们的失败是官员群体对皇权效忠的结果。

在民间话语中，梁红玉和韩世忠这对勇敢而忠诚的夫妇成为传奇，在故事和戏曲中被代代相传。现在，人们通过德胜桥歌颂他们的胜利和美德。

⑪ 潮王桥——治水英雄与民间的神

"潮王"的意思是潮水之王，京杭大运河杭州段的潮王是由唐朝的一位皇帝唐穆宗授予一个老百姓的称号。就像大不列颠女王授予她勇敢忠诚的大臣贵族头衔一样，古代中国的皇帝们封他们的近亲和高官为"王"，让他们享有很高的社会地位，仅次于皇帝。王作为封地的主人，是封地的领导者。除了批准关于民生的建议和提议外，王还是军队的统帅，要保护封地上的子民。黎民百姓也期望王能够护佑其平安。考虑到民众给皇室缴纳的大量赋税，他们有这样一种期待是十分合理的。

遗憾的是，王并不是万能的神。在洪水来临的时候，王并不比街头的市民或在田间劳作的农人更具应对能力，他的财富和权力并不能赋予他超能力。

好在这一点对于他恭顺的子民来说并不是秘密。即便是"天之子"，当洪水肆虐时，他也无能为力。因此，王和子民都需要一种信仰，相信某个人能够控制和征服洪水，阻止洪水摧毁家园、夺走孩子。而这个人，比王或者皇帝更强大，就像古希腊神话中的海神波塞冬。

好了，我们在介绍潮王之前已经说得够多了。

如前所述，潮王是由皇帝授予的荣誉性的称号。通常来说，和皇帝有近亲血缘关系的人才有可能被封为王，而潮王本人并没有皇族血统。在他一次又一次地跳入汹涌的洪水救起濒临绝境的人们，最终失去自己的性命之后，皇帝才追封给他这一封号。

故事的主人公名叫石奎，身体健壮，助人为乐。有一次洪水肆虐，他奋不顾身跳进水中救人，最后筋疲力尽，被洪水吞没。人们看到他一直拼到最后一口气，深受感动，于是把他的英勇事迹报告给当地官员，之后当地政府又上奏朝廷。皇帝正迫切需要一个鼓舞人心的典范来激励人们和洪水做斗争，因此他非常乐于见到普通百姓之中能够有这样一位英雄，于是就封这位死去的英雄为潮王，号令老百姓祭祀、敬拜。

我的猜想是，通过给普通老百姓授予其能够梦想到的最高荣誉，皇帝意在鼓励官员和百姓向石奎学习，言外之意是：你们可以自己抗洪救灾保护自己，而不是仅仅指望朝廷和天子。

石奎是在身死之后才被封为潮王的。古代中国人相信神灵，相信超能力。人们会为那些有超能力的人建立祠堂，例如三国时期勇敢无畏而无比忠诚的将军关羽，关帝庙就是为他而建的。但是如果再想一想，我们就会困惑：为什么英雄活着的时候没有被大力颂扬？

这可能是皇帝的另一个秘密了——只有他本人可以作为现实中的人而被普通民众敬拜。皇帝和潮王之间的区别在于权力的属性：皇帝的权力实实在在，是可以支配的；而潮王的呢，只是接受供奉而已。即便是这些供奉，作为泥塑之身，潮王也显然无法品尝。这些美味去哪儿了呢？一部分可能会留在潮王塑像前的陶盘里，而另一部分则被蝙蝠、乌鸦、野猫、黄鼠狼等生灵享用。一定也有遭受洪灾的胆大少年，冒着遭"天谴"的危险，大快朵颐。在难挨的饥饿面前，与其依赖神灵，不如抓取实实在在的吃食。

读者朋友，你觉得这些肚子里塞满了敬献给潮王的餐食的大胆的人，能够获得抵抗洪水的勇气吗？

城东桥——听闻机杼声声

京杭大运河从北京一路向南至杭州，进入杭州后在武林门转了一个弯，由南北向转成东西向。在这段由西向东的运河上修建了多座现代化大桥，城东桥便是其中之一。城东桥乍一看造型简单，平平无奇，与常见的当代公路桥别无二致，但这座桥独具审美韵味，乘车过桥的人发现不了，行船的人则绝不会错过桥栏上的"五彩缤纷"（如图12-1所示）。桥栏上的篆体大字引人注目，对于当代人来说，这种中国古代早期的字体难以辨认；而对于生长在杭州和浙江东北地区的人来说，这几个大字都是熟悉的老友，一望而知。为什么呢？因为这几个字都和丝绸有关，而丝绸是杭州1700多年来的重要特产。

图 12-1　城东桥侧丝绸图案（摄于 2021 年）

杭州的丝绸与纺织业历史悠久。相关研究表明，早在春秋吴越争霸时期，杭州的蚕桑业就得到了大力发展。随着西晋末年永嘉南渡，精工巧匠大量南迁，杭州的丝织业有了质的提升。据马可·波罗的游记，当时杭州的普通市民因为得天独厚的便利条件，能穿精致的丝绸衣裳，而无须像西方贵族那样进口这种舒适的衣料。城东桥的艺术设计，显示出此地与丝织业的深厚渊源。

城东桥附近有个小区名叫机神新村，因原先建有杭州最大的机神庙而得名。旧时机神庙供奉着三大机神：得到蚕神献丝的轩辕帝、巧手裁帛制衣的伯余、传授机制工艺的唐朝名臣褚载。回望历史，城东织机遍布受益于两条大河，即钱塘江和大运河。钱塘江带来的富含钙质的大片土壤有利于种植蚕桑。在杭州城东的三堡船闸，大运河向南连接了钱塘江，后者流入东海（如图 12-2 所示）。由此，大运河、钱塘江、东海共同组成的综合水上交通，为丝织品的运输与国内外贸易提供了便利。

图 12-2　三堡船闸

"红袖织绫夸柿蒂"——唐朝诗人、担任过杭州刺史的白居易记录了杭州女子织绫斗艺的生动图景。①杭州自唐末以来丝织业就十分发达，吴越王钱镠重视蚕桑，并设置了官营织造工场——织室，这是杭州设立官府织造机构的开端。北宋年间，官营丝织业继续发展，随着专门管理对外贸易机构市舶司的设立，杭州生产的丝织品成为重要的出口商品，远销东南亚和阿拉伯地区。宋室南渡给杭州的丝织业带来了大批能工巧匠，技艺也得到进一步发展，并使丝绸在元朝成为大宗出口货物。明朝成为杭州丝织业发展的又一个高峰——"习以工巧，衣被天下"。清朝在全国设立了3个江南织造局（南京、苏州、杭州），乾隆年间杭州织造局出产的丝织品达4683匹，占3个织造局丝织品总量的40.4%，为全国之首。②

杭州自古以来丝织业发达，从全城多处的机神庙可见一斑，《东畲杂记》称"杭州机杼甲天下"。其中民营的丝织作坊集中在东园巷、艮山门附近，可谓"机杼之声，比户相闻"。

1926年6月1日，美国费城世界博览会开幕。当时，这个古老的东方国家会在展示最先进产品的世界博览会上呈现什么呢？这个曾经的巨人，自19世纪晚期以来饱受侵蚀，现在已经虚弱不堪，无力赶上工业革命的浪潮，它能拿出什么样的产品来匹配这个光芒闪烁的世界盛会呢？

这个疑虑被证明是多余的，都锦生选送的仿古织锦画《宫妃夜游图》一举夺得金奖。而他的山水织锦更是精彩绝伦。精美的锦缎上，平静的水面徐徐展开，涟漪微动，倒映着长堤上的碧柳软枝、灼灼红桃；长堤向远处透迤而去，隐入层峦叠嶂的青山之中；翠峰之上，一座华美的宝塔高高矗立——这是其中一幅。该作品以现代工艺和传统技艺的完美融合，再现了一座城市在800多年前身为帝国都城时就享

①［唐］白居易：《杭州春望》，转引自上海辞书出版社文学鉴赏辞典编纂中心：《白居易诗文鉴赏辞典》，上海辞书出版社2014年版。柿蒂，指的是柿子蒂花纹。
②徐铮、袁宣萍：《杭州丝绸史》，中国社会科学出版社2011年版。

有的山水盛景，再现了它 20 世纪初的美丽风姿。

都锦生（1897—1943），是都锦生丝织厂的创立者。1926 年，都锦生丝织厂拥有 100 台手拉机、5 台轧花机、134 名工人。都锦生甚至高价聘请了 8 名意大利人作为丝织技术专家，这些专家对丝织品工艺的提升功不可没。可以说，都锦生丝织厂是 20 世纪 20 年代丝织业的一艘旗舰。

都锦生在丝织业上的成功是多种因素共同作用的结果，如杭嘉湖地区传统的蚕桑业提供的优质的丝绸原料，杭州丝织业发展的黄金时代造就的富有经验的技工，还有都锦生本人接受的现代丝织工艺教育，等等。都锦生在浙江省甲种工业学校专门学习机织技术，以荣誉毕业生的身份留校任教。1922 年，都锦生创办了工厂。他的第一幅织锦作品正是在教学实践中完成的。

在设立现代工业学校之前，杭州于 1907 年成立了一家蚕桑女子学堂，女孩们得以在此学习科学养蚕的技术，学校的实际管理者和教员均为女性。从这所学校走出的毕业生，则会成为那个时代令人羡慕的现代职业女性。

坝子桥——中国人的龙凤图腾

夕阳向东河投去最后的温柔一瞥，在水面上轻轻掷下她的金色面纱，摇碎了坝子桥的倒影（如图 13-1 所示）。大运河杭州段的支流上桥梁众多，而坝子桥是其中独具特色的一座拱桥。

图 13-1　坝子桥
（绘图：屠群峰）

坝子桥横跨在东河上，顾名思义，东河是杭州市东部的一条河。虽然拱宸桥普遍被看作是京杭大运河最南端的标志性建筑，但它并不是这条宏伟的人工河的终点。大运河过了拱宸桥之后继续向南，再转入钱塘江，一路上连接起了许多支流。支流上的桥比拱宸桥小许多，但仍然有其存在的意义。修建在大运河支流东河上的坝子桥，就是其中之一。

关于坝子桥最早的记载可见于南宋淳祐年间（1241—1252），称在 100 多年前，就有一座桥建于东河水坝附近，用以调节水量。 这座桥初名"坝子桥"，后几度更名，而后复称"坝子桥"，沿用至今。

尽管近千年的历史增加了这座桥的魅力，但是真正令它脱颖而出的，则是它独特的审美价值。

在西方传说中，雅典娜头戴珠冠，缪斯弹拨乐器，萨提尔头顶鹿角，维纳斯则在巨大的白色海贝中站了起来——女神们让人倾慕的原因之一在于她们独有的兼具功能性的装饰。坝子桥，也是如此，凭借美丽的桥亭而与众不同。

桥亭是以典型的中国传统审美趣味来修造的：八根柱子支撑着屋顶，四面斜屋顶攀升在中间聚拢成主屋脊，屋脊左右两侧各盘旋着一条龙。四角屋檐向上翘出优美的弧线，檐角挂着铜铃，清脆的铃声回荡在温柔的晚风之中。屋顶的侧面正如象形文字"山"，因此得名"歇山顶"。整座桥亭轻盈灵巧。斜面屋顶便于排水，而这正是适合江南湿润多雨气候的特殊设计。

在屋檐底部的木梁上，挂着一块匾，上刻"凤凰亭"三个大字。有趣的是，盘踞在屋顶的是两条龙，而不是凤凰。

熟悉中国文化的人对龙一定不陌生，从中华文明的第一缕曙光开始，龙就是最重要的图腾。龙的形象广为人知。在皇帝的龙袍上，它体态矫健，尽显威仪；在紫禁城门前高耸的华表上，它盘旋而上，彰显天子之威。在乡间祠堂的白墙上，人们用黑白两色勾勒出腾云驾雾的龙，向神仙表达敬意。有些寺庙的屋脊上也盘踞着龙。龙的眼睛炯炯有神，其盘旋的身体上覆盖着龙鳞，巨大而尖利的爪子在空中张开，这样的形象看上去确实能够让它成为普通老百姓的保护神。

在远古的传说中，龙主掌雷、雨、水、海，类似于西方神话中的海神波塞冬，但是又比波塞冬的地位尊崇得多。龙被赋予了更多的期待，承载着更多的寄托，自然而然，它被作为人间最高贵的统治者——皇帝的象征，也就是所谓的真龙天子。皇帝的各种服饰和器具上，乃至金銮殿上的龙椅上都饰有龙纹，以彰显他独一无二的天子身份。

直到今天，"龙"还是中国人给男孩取名时最常见的字之一，表达了父母对儿子拥有卓越能力、灿烂前途的希望。在第32届东京奥运会上，率领中国男子乒乓球队夺得优异成绩的队长就叫"马龙"。而女孩的名字或与女性相关的称谓中常常带有"凤"字，比如：《红楼梦》中着墨极多的当家少奶奶王熙凤，又称"凤姐"；贾府长女元春被选为皇妃后，加封为"凤藻宫尚书"，以表明元春才能卓越，堪比凤凰。凤凰是中国传统文化中对女性的最高礼赞。

凤凰是中国人心目中的一种神鸟，拖着三根长长的华美的尾羽，翱翔在天空。凤凰头顶三翎，身体和孔雀的相似，形态非常优美。凤凰是先民从鸟的形象中得到灵感而进行的艺术创作，而鸟在远古时期的很多地方被奉为神祇。至于为什么把龙和凤组成一对夫妇，并没有确切的解释，也许是因为它们都能在高高的天空中飞翔吧！

另一个原因是，龙和凤暗含着一种微妙的对等——尽管它们都拥有超自然的能力，但并不是神仙，神仙都有形如人类的样貌，动物形态的多是神仙的仆人。《西游记》里的大小神仙妖怪就反映了这一点。毕竟，神话传说是现实生活的一面镜子。统治现实世界的规则，在想象中的神仙世界里是可以通用的。中国的先民根据自己世俗生活的经验，认为龙作为一个雄性的神灵，应当有一个妻子，一个雌性的神灵。凤凰以其高贵的形貌，翱翔天际的能力，成为龙的理想伴侣。（说到这里，不禁令人发笑：为什么雄性的龙不能有一个雌性的龙作为它的配偶呢？雌性的龙一定是存在的。而当你想到在民间传说中这对龙凤夫妇从来没有孕育出任何子嗣时，就更有趣了。我猜，大概凤凰仅仅是龙的精神伴侣吧！）

让我们回到坝子桥上的这座名为"凤凰亭"的桥亭吧。正如凤凰图腾含有女性意味，凤凰亭也具有女性色彩。它轻捷地立于坝子桥芯，身形灵巧，姿态优雅，正是人们休闲的理想去处。特别是在夏天的夜晚，自告奋勇的民间歌手来到凤凰亭，一展歌喉，也不乏美声唱法。有时候一支"迷你"的乐队能为纳凉的人们奉献一场小型的户外音乐会，而乐队成员们基本都退休了。当吃饱穿暖之后，人们总会展现出艺术追求。

桥亭四面没有墙，桥下盈盈东河流淌，在凤凰亭里表演的歌手和乐队的旋律更令人心醉神迷。清晨的凤凰亭则是太极拳爱好者的理想之地，他们远离拥挤的人群和交通高峰期来回奔忙的汽车，在现实生活中寻求安静之所，也寻求内心的宁静。偶尔凤凰亭中的寂静会被过往船只的汽笛声或马达声打断，但是它内在的安宁是剥夺不了的，喧嚣一定会被宁静所取代。

传说坝子桥的桥亭得名"凤凰"是因为曾有一群神鸟飞来，栖息于桥上。这当然是想象中的图景。不过，在如今的春秋两季，这座桥亭常常会迎来热情的有巨大双翼和美丽白羽的访客，她们有时轻轻掠过水面，有时在河边傲然独立。她们有一个美丽的名字——白鹭。

与仅仅存在于传说中的神鸟凤凰相比，白鹭是美丽环境的使者，也是现实世界中人类的朋友。

14 太平桥——精美的石雕艺术

　　京杭大运河到杭州后汇入钱塘江。跨过钱塘江，就到了浙东运河水系，这使得浙东运河成为中国大运河的一部分。与京杭大运河上数座世界闻名的桥梁不同，浙东运河上的桥梁并不那么令世人熟知，但它们在交通、建筑和审美上同样具有很高的价值。

　　浙东运河主要流经现在的绍兴和宁波。立于东海之滨的宁波以天然大港为主要特征，而绍兴则是典型的江南水乡风貌，水系发达，沟渠遍布，有河、湖、塘、湾，还有河埠、码头、堤坝，不一而足。在绍兴这样一座繁华且早于杭州就成为王朝都城的城市，交通往来多赖于舟楫桥梁，从远古到清末，建桥修桥一直没有停止。桥梁数目众多，形态各异。据1993年底的统计，绍兴全市有10610座桥。持续修桥建桥不仅使得绍兴古城桥梁遍布，也大大提升了绍兴桥的工艺水准和审美价值。

　　绍兴作为国都的荣光可以追溯到2500多年前。早在公元前490年，列国之一的越国定都绍兴（时名会稽）。富有传奇色彩的越国国君勾践，在征服者吴王夫差的马厩里忍辱负重，之后成功复国。这一传奇故事充满着英雄主义、钢铁意志，无论是屈辱还是绝望，都没有阻碍勾践的复国大业。1300多年后，当杭人钱镠建立政权时，沿用"越"字，将其作为新国名"吴越国"的一部分，以此向古越国致敬。在钱镠治国期间，绍兴逐渐发展为一个人口密集、文化昌盛的繁华郡治。而当宋代皇族躲避入侵的金军时，皇帝赵构最开始指定绍兴作为他的临时御跸。

跟随皇帝一同南下的众多工匠和文人带来了建造技术和艺术志趣。而桥梁，作为在日常生活中常见的水利设施，成为审美趣味的理想载体。太平桥正是这样一座充分展现精美的石雕艺术和精巧的建造技术的桥梁。

太平桥初建于宋代，当时正是中国绘画与雕刻艺术的高峰，宋代的多位皇帝爱好艺术。宋徽宗独具天赋，创造了一种新的书法字体——瘦金体，笔画清瘦而刚劲，兼具优雅和力量之美。他本人沉迷丹青，对国画有很高的品位。他笔下的花鸟，鸟羽纤毫毕现，牡丹花瓣重叠，栩栩如生。赏画作画需要足够的耐心、足够的审慎、平静的心态，还需高超的技法。一件伟大的艺术作品既是天才创造的奇迹，也是天才长久忍受孤独的结果。

与常见的单孔或三孔拱桥不同，太平桥（如图 14-1 所示）是一座由石拱桥和石梁桥相结合的长桥。它全长约 50 米，横跨浙东运河，由单孔石拱桥和八孔石梁桥组成，是拱桥和高低石梁桥相结合的多跨桥梁。大船走高拱桥，小舢板走低梁桥。太平桥多跨融合，高低错落。桥拱拱脚内侧铺设石板纤道路，桥上行人，桥下行舟背纤，宛如运河上的立交桥。太平桥由南向北，从高高的拱桥到逐渐降低接近水面的梁桥，犹如一条矫健的游龙正要潜入水中。

太平桥展示了中国高超的传统石雕艺术。在仔细欣赏太平桥的建筑之美之前，有必要先对中国拱桥的整体样貌做一个了解。

一座典型的中式拱桥通常由四部分组成：桥中心平整的桥芯板、对称的桥侧栏板、两侧的石阶斜坡、水面上的桥拱（如图 14-2 所示）。其中，桥侧栏板平滑又有一定的宽度，成为展示石匠雕刻技艺的展板。

图 14-1　太平桥

（绘图：屠群峰）

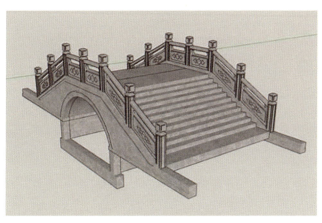

图 14-2　中式拱桥

　　太平桥最长的一块栏板上图案丰富，如图 14-3 所示。构图主体是一头大象，上面坐着一位神仙（上半部分已经湮灭），身边青松环绕，前方则是名为万年青的植物。象首上方，有一朵盛开的大莲花。这组图案整体呈六边形，以石刻双边勾线，宛如莲花花瓣。图案的两侧是连续的"卍"字花纹，在佛教中寓意为永生。

图 14-3　栏板石雕

正对面栏板上的石雕图案大体相似，区别在于在大象前方的不是万年青而是祥云，如图 14-4 所示。另一个值得注意的细节是祥云中有蝙蝠飞翔。遗憾的是，这块栏板上的骑象神仙的上半部分也难以辨认了。

图 14-4　正对面栏板上的石雕

这两块主栏板的雕刻都富有佛教元素，如莲花、连续的"卍"字纹及莲花花瓣的框架。蝠，与"福"谐音，又与"富"近音；松树和万年青象征着健康、长寿。这些图案表达了俗世中的普通人对富足和长寿的期盼。

斜坡侧栏板上的石雕图案简洁、优美。其中一块雕刻着长长的绸带，联结成 4 个连续的椭圆，整体看起来像一个中国结。在每一个椭圆中间有 4 片呈十字形的花瓣，形状常见，难以确定名称，可能是桂花，因桂花树在江南地区很常见，并和高中科举的捷报有关。如图 14-5 所示。

另一块侧栏板上是 4 个相连的圆，正中又有一个圆，比这 4 个略大。这 5 个圆形图案像中国的古制钱币。如图 14-6 所示。

图 14-5　斜坡侧栏板上的
石雕

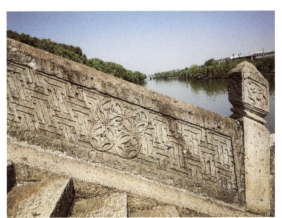

图 14-6　另一块侧栏板上的石雕

在得出太平桥的石雕是佛教图案和世俗愿望的结合这一结论后，我们再观察一番太平桥侧桥栏上的望柱。在每一个望柱顶端，有一块方石，四面雕刻着图案，如图 14-7 所示。这些精美的雕刻值得细细观赏，粗粗一瞥会忽略这些石雕的精妙之美。一眼看去它们彼此相似，但实际上是不同的，是日常生活和朝堂公务的象征。石雕图案有琵琶、长笛、笙等民间乐器，

图 14-7　望柱石雕

有两幅画轴，有一对古代官员上朝用的笏板，有装着莲花的大花篮，还有大铃铛。为什么这些看似没有关联的图案会同时出现？是出于偶然，还是有意为之？匠人在构思图案的时候想到了什么呢？

我们也许可以从道教中找到线索。不同于从印度"舶来"的佛教，道教发源于中国，而道教中的神仙也往往映射着现实生活中的人物。因此，他们的随身物品也能在日常生活中找到对应。广为流传的道教人物"八仙"，为首的是能够治病救人的铁拐李，其他 7 位分别是：须发飘飘手持拂尘的吕洞宾、吹笛的韩湘子、倒骑毛驴的张果老、穿绯色官服的曹国舅、梳着双髻的汉钟离、手持莲花的美丽妇人何仙姑，还有提着竹篮唱歌的青年蓝采和。部分人物如图 14-8 所示。

图 14-8　八仙（部分）

（绘图：陈星月）

八仙的故事在中国民间广为流传，也为剪纸、戏曲、雕刻和年画等民间艺术提供了丰富的素材。手工艺人喜爱这些谦和而善良的神仙，于是把八仙及其随身物品雕刻在太平桥的栏板上，保佑过往行人和舟船远离灾祸，平平安安。

2013 年，太平桥被列入全国重点文物保护单位。

⑮ 题扇桥——中国书法的魅力

　　题扇桥（如图15-1所示）位于浙江省绍兴市区蕺山街，为单孔半圆形石拱桥，该桥全长18.5米，高3.8米，宽4.3米，桥坡石阶约20级，保留了清道光八年（1828）重修时的形态。在光绪年间刊行的科举参考书《策府统宗》一书中，题扇桥是唯一的绍兴古桥代表。

图 15-1　题扇桥
（绘图：屠群峰）

相传此桥与大书法家王羲之有关。王羲之府邸在蕺山街，他出府邸过桥时总能看见一位老婆婆在桥头摆小摊卖六角扇。买的人很少，老婆婆总是一脸愁容。有一天，王羲之又过小桥，婆婆可怜无助的样子让他生出恻隐之心，就径直提笔在她的扇子上题了几个字。老婆婆看到赖以为生的扇子竟然被弄脏了，恼怒之下，更添绝望。王羲之笑着说，你只要对人说扇子上有王羲之题的字，必能卖出好价钱。老婆婆将信将疑，按照王羲之的嘱咐吆喝。不一会儿，扇子便被抢购一空，老婆婆又惊又喜。从此以后，这座桥就被称为题扇桥。①

普普通通的扇子一经王羲之题字就能够身价百倍，这是因为王羲之是著名的书法家，一字难求。

书法是中国传统文化的重要组成部分，是文人必备的琴棋书画四项修习之一。古代科举取士，文字书写也作为重要的考量因素。一手潇洒漂亮的字，既彰显了书写者的文化修养，也令观者赏心悦目。

汉字流变历经数千年，现在还留存于世的主要有五大类：篆书（常见于治印艺术）、隶书（官吏抄录公文时使用）、楷书（形态端方）、草书（匆匆而就，潇洒不羁）和行书（行笔顺滑，多见于日常使用）。篆书在秦朝被推广为统一的书写文字，即"书同文"。篆书行笔圆润，布局紧凑，字形典雅。但是这种风格使得字形复杂，笔画相似，辨认困难。于是篆书被简化成新的字体。这种字体便于读写，在文牍众多的官吏中广受欢迎，被称为隶书。隶书之后，至 3 世纪，楷书出现了。楷书形态方正，笔画端直。与中规中矩的楷书风格明显相反的是草书，它突破传统的笔画和布局限制，往往将上一字的最末一笔带入下一字的第一笔中，曲笔相连，从而加快了书写速度。"草"的含义是"匆匆写就"，笔画洒脱不羁，也因此难以辨读。在此基础上行书出现了。它既吸收了草书笔画的灵动之美和书写效率，又保留了楷书的精确之美和端方仪态，得以在官员和士大夫中流行，之后在日常生活中被广

①［唐］房玄龄等撰，何怀远、贾歆、孙梦魁主编：《晋书》，远方出版社 2006 年版。

泛使用。

被赞誉为"天下第一行书"的《兰亭集序》就是以行书写成的旷世杰作。《兰亭集序》这一人类文化史上的华彩乐章与一个古老的节日——上巳节有关。上巳节在每年农历三月初三。春来生暖，上至朝廷下至民间，人们聚于水滨嬉戏洗濯，以拔除不祥，祈求安康。后来上巳节成为春暖郊游的好日子。

东晋穆帝永和九年（353）上巳节，时任会稽内史的王羲之与友人、子侄等共41人，在兰亭集会。人们把觞放入弯曲的清溪中任其漂流，停在谁面前，谁就探身而取，饮觞中酒，即兴赋诗。春水带来灵感，酒兴又助诗兴。或徐行沉吟，或口占成诵。一诗既成，一二友人点评，余者点头品味。乐在其中的赋诗人谦让"过奖，过奖"，再饮一杯敬谢众人。之后，把酒杯放入河中，新的一轮曲水流觞开始。如此这般，众人饮酒赋诗，汇诗成集。雅集既考验急才，又显露文化功底，而早春的美好风光也令人愉悦。对于多在朝廷为官的知识分子来说，雅集也是表达政治抱负、一吐心声、结识友人的好机会。

聚会接近尾声时，大家已经作了数十首诗，酒杯也已空空。大家公推王羲之为之作序。酒至微酣、逸兴扬扬的王羲之欣然落笔，一气呵成。

一幅伟大的艺术作品由此诞生。

《兰亭集序》共28行，324个字（如图15-2所示），记述了当时文人雅集的情景。作者因当时天时地利人和发挥极致，据说后来再写已不能逮。其中有20多个"之"字，写法各不相同。此外，《兰亭集序》本身也是一篇优秀的韵文，用词考究、节奏优美，读起来令人身临其境。

题扇桥的故事广为人知，不过故事并未到此结束。桥附近有块大石名为"躲婆石"，又有一巷称"笔飞弄"。老婆婆知道了王羲之书法的神奇魔力之后，就做了更多的扇子，在桥边等着求王羲之题字。

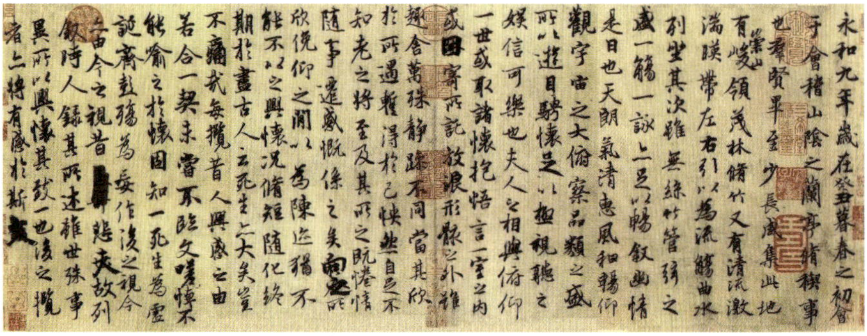

图 15-2 《兰亭集序》

王羲之一看，这不是办法，每次外出见到她，就躲到石头背后藏起来，还把笔扔到附近的巷子里。

题扇轶事可见于《晋书》，但见了老婆婆躲起来并把笔扔掉则是民间传说。"躲婆石""笔飞弄"这两个有趣的地名给题扇桥的故事增加了文学的趣味，使得这个故事让人在感受王羲之书法的魅力之外，还能产生一点对人性的思考。

民间桥俗——运河人家的朴素愿望

　　似乎全世界的人们都认为人有三世：世人所生活的当今世界、圣人所在的天堂，以及亡灵所去的地狱。有趣的是人们普遍接受的一个事实——除了极少数幸运儿或者道德特别高尚的人，大多数凡人死后只能下地狱。尽管人们常常祈祷自己死后能进天堂，但心里还是认为自己只能去地狱报到。这是中国人有趣的实用主义思想。

　　在中国神话中，一个人要通往地狱之前必须先过奈何桥。这座桥很特殊，桥上有个老婆婆姓孟，喝了她的汤之后，人的灵魂在人间就再无羁绊，可以无牵无挂地往生了。"奈何"表示没有办法，是一种叹息，意思是"我得说服自己接受自己已死的事实，我也没有别的办法"，是一种接受人总有一死这一固有命运的"随遇而安"的态度。民国时期，学贯中西的大学者辜鸿铭在他的著作《中国人的精神》里表示：中国人的生活始终是一种精神上的生活，是一种礼貌的、乐观的、富有诗意的生活。过奈何桥、喝孟婆汤的传说，似乎就是中国人乐天安命的例证。

　　在中国江南地区，妇女有在正月十五月圆之夜走三桥的习俗，即在晚饭后出门走路，要一连走过三座桥才能驻足。在封建时代，妇女走三桥是为了求子。与长子长女都可以作为家族继承人的英国不同，在古代父权制度下的中国，唯有儿子享有继承家族财产和壮大家族的特权。因此，没有生出儿子的妇女就会遭受很大的压力，会被看作是不合格的妻子，严重的还会被丈夫休弃，而这被她本人还有她的父母兄长视为莫大的耻辱。

于是，桥作为指引的象征，成了妇女们向神仙祈祷求子的信差。在元宵节的夜晚，妇女们盛装打扮，和女伴约好，或者索性由小姑子、婆婆陪同，走出将她们日夜围困的深宅大院或寒屋陋舍，去走桥。桥沐浴在无数灯笼所发出的暖黄色的光芒里，而她们的心好似被希望点燃了。

她们轻声祈求神仙送个儿子来，虔诚地走过一座又一座桥。女人们当然知道她们的祈求并不能保证来年一定能够生出儿子，但是抱有某种信念有助于减轻压力、舒缓焦虑情绪。即便来年没有儿子，至少，她们在行动上已经努力过了，向神祈求过了。而且在一起走桥求子的夜晚，女人们之间相互心照不宣的理解和共情，也是一种默默无言的安慰。元宵节晚上走桥求子的习俗缺乏科学依据，但是它也确确实实安慰了那个年代里只能将命运依附于家庭男性成员身上的女人们。从这个意义上来说，走桥的习俗倒也不失为一种特殊的慰藉。

有些地方的走桥习俗有着更宽泛的含义，并不仅仅是求子，而是去百病。在中国古典文学巨著《金瓶梅》（此书被许多研究者认为是代表中国古典小说最高峰的《红楼梦》的灵感来源）中，男主人公西门庆的妻妾们就在元宵节晚上一起去看灯、走百病。在这晚，女人们可以打扮得十分美丽。对于终年被"妇道人家，大门不出，二门不迈"所规训的女人来说，去百病固然是个动听的理由，而其更深的缘由，恐怕在于她们总算有了宝贵地走出深宅大院、呼吸自由空气的时刻吧。

如今的元宵节走三桥风俗发生了变化。它不再是妇女对于生子的卑微而渺茫的诉求，而是一次有利于健康的欢乐的运动。正月十五元宵节，水乡张灯结彩，桥在花灯的掩映下分外好看。元宵节晚上，在吃了满满一碗高糖的元宵之后，人们确实有必要进行一番低强度运动，帮助消化，以免积食。一连走完三座桥，既保证了步行的长度，消耗了足够多的卡路里，也是一次欣赏花灯的愉快旅程。鱼灯、宫灯、兔子灯、龙灯、花篮灯、仙女灯……形态各异的花灯倒映在水面上，让水乡的夜晚分外迷人。从这个角度来说，正月十五走三桥这个民俗正是中国人智慧的体现：既注重实用，又兼顾审美；既包含理性主义，又具有感性色彩。

在大运河上航行有条特殊的习俗：在经过某些桥时需要全体噤声，宛如哑巴，故这些桥又被称为哑巴桥。其中比较著名的一座就是杭州的拱宸桥，另一座是位于湖州的潮音桥。

过桥时船夫一声不出，闭口不言，以此向桥神表示敬畏，但这一习俗真正考虑的是行船安全。桥下湍急的水流，繁忙的航道，使得聊天都成为极其危险的行为。所以船夫们必须全神贯注，一心一意地行船。另一项禁忌是当桥下过船时女子不得踏上桥面。这个旧俗和走桥求子一样，是对女性的歧视，但也说明了旧时的人们相信桥能通天、地、人三界。今天的中国已经没有这样歧视妇女的旧俗了。

蚕花大会在蚕丝产区湖州很常见。湖州位于杭州以北约 90 千米。顶级的生丝被统称为"湖丝"，这足以说明此地丝织业的发达。尽管蚕花会在清明节（通常是每年的四月五日）的晚上才开始，但是人们实际上早在二月就开始筹备这场盛事了。

三月，天气转暖，万物从漫长冬天的蛰伏中苏醒，蚕就是其中之一。蚕是一种非常娇弱的生物，只能在舒适的环境里存活。舒适的环境，包括合适的室内温度和湿度、干净无尘的墙壁、没有一丝腐臭气味的清新空气等。蚕对食物的要求也很高，极度依赖新鲜的桑叶。随着身体逐渐长大，蚕对桑叶的需求也越来越大。在生命的最后几天，蚕除了一刻不停地吃桑叶外什么也不干。挑剔的生活习惯使得蚕获得了一个别名——蚕宝宝（人类的宝宝总是让妈妈筋疲力尽的）。照料蚕宝宝于是也成了村妇们的一项重要工作，她们像抚养自己的新生儿那样精心照料着这种娇气而又神奇的小虫。

与农耕相比，养蚕看上去更有利可图。大明帝国每年需要大额的贸易顺差，以弥补戍边和其他要务的巨额支出，这是颁布鼓励江南地区种桑养蚕政策的原因之一。这一政令规定蚕农可以以丝代粮，作为税赋。税丝缴足之后，蚕农可以做自己想做的其他事情。一年的蚕桑季节只有从农历三月到五月的 90 多天，因此农民有机会自主安排劳作，来改善自己的生活条件。这一政令得到了普遍的欢迎与积极的实施。

不过鼓励蚕桑的另一面是不能完成缴纳税丝任务的人会被关进监狱，甚至会掉脑袋。这样一来，养蚕对于一户农家来说就至关重要了，承担照顾蚕宝宝任务的农妇必须万分小心。

人们总是会向某个神灵祈求来获得内心的宁静，如果神灵不存在，那么就创造一个。明清时期的养蚕人当然也是如此。不然，还能做什么呢？

蚕花大会也就是蚕花节应运而生。清明节前后，人们从四面八方赶来，一起看彩妆游行。走在最前面的人敲锣打鼓，从拥挤的人群中开辟出一条道来。围观者往后退一步，又迅速聚拢，舍不得错过蚕花大会中最激动人心的一幕——近距离欣赏今年的蚕神。蚕神，或者说蚕花娘娘，可以追溯到远古时期嫘祖发现蚕丝的传说。相传劳作后在树下休息的嫘祖发现虫茧可以取丝。另一个传说"马头娘"则没有这么温情脉脉。"马头娘"的故事是：一个姑娘欺骗了勤劳的马，以至于马被姑娘的父亲打死；而姑娘背信弃义、见死不救，马皮跳起来裹住了姑娘，使之成为"马头娘"并日夜吐丝不止。显然这是一个讽刺而惊悚的故事。

与通常祭祀中的"神"———座涂抹着彩色泥巴的木制人形雕像不同，蚕衣大会上的蚕神实际上是由一名姑娘装扮的。这一罕见的女性而非男性神祇的形象，不仅仅与传说中蚕丝的发现者有关，还与她的养蚕技术有关。从事蚕桑业的人们把唯心主义和实用主义合二为一了。通过对来自现实世界的女神的尊敬和赞美，人们也获得了一个当面聆听养蚕经验的机会，获得了一个可以汲取经验的真实偶像。参加蚕花大会的人大部分是妇女，她们在蚕花大会主要祈求养蚕顺顺利利。

不过还是有一些男性参与者，青年男子或者中年男人，他们得以借此一睹女子芳容而不必冒着被斥责为登徒子的风险。事实上这对于青年女子来说也是一个难得走出家门、好好放松享乐的机会。蚕花大会在某种意义上是一个心照不宣寻觅佳偶的社交活动。借用德国贝克啤酒的广告"有多少罗曼史从一杯淡啤酒开始"，我们可以说：有多少罗曼史从蚕花大会开始。这一点并没有确切的证据，但是毫无疑问的是，这场一年一度的盛会为浙江湖州的蚕桑业带来了繁荣。在运河畔湖州新市古镇的展览馆，展现了从正月初一吃蚕宴到养蚕季的种种风俗。

鹊桥——突破藩篱的爱情传说

　　在中国文化中，桥不仅是水利工程中的一个建筑类型，还承载着民间普遍的神秘信仰——人们相信桥能连接天地，能够通神。

　　我们可以在一首宋代的著名词作中找到这方面的佐证。这首词的词牌名为"鹊桥仙"，顾名思义，喜鹊搭成一座连接天地的桥，帮助一对由凡人和仙人结合的夫妇相会。词的起句描绘了银河的灿烂景象，之后描绘了这对爱侣一年一度亲密相会的时刻。尾句两人互诉衷肠："两情若是久长时，又岂在朝朝暮暮。"这句美丽、惆怅的诗句，代代相传，已成为情人之间尤其是异地恋人之间最动听的誓言。

　　这首词描绘的场景起源于一个古老的传说。天庭仙女织女爱上了人间的牧牛人董永，嫁给了他，并且生育了一双儿女。男耕女织，儿女双全，这是很典型的人间幸福家庭的样本。可是这件事被天庭的主宰者玉帝发现了。玉帝命令天兵天将把织女捉回来。织女的母亲，天后西王母，扔出一根发簪，这根发簪瞬间变成了一条宽阔的天河。

　　大河使得这对恩爱夫妻被分开了。织女被关在织坊内，思念儿女和丈夫董永，不断地哭泣。她的哀歌蕴含着深深的悲伤，飞过的喜鹊收起了翅膀，驻足倾听。它们被织女非同凡俗的爱情深深地打动了，决心合力帮助她。天庭的禁令虽然严酷无情，但是阻止不了真挚的爱情。凡间的俗夫和天上的仙女，为什么就不能有真爱呢？

喜鹊们除了会飞还有别的本事吗？它们只不过是平凡的鸟儿罢了，并不像神鸟凤凰那样拥有神奇的法力。但是深沉的善意可以激发平凡者的内在智慧和力量。喜鹊们有了主意。

农历七月初七，成千上万的喜鹊一起飞来，扇动着翅膀，停留在空中，彼此身体相接，搭起了一座鹊桥，从天上织女的房间通向地上董永的小屋。

鹊桥一落到门前，董永就用扁担挑起一对竹筐——筐里分别坐着儿子和女儿，向天上奔去。而此时，织女已经溜出了织房，站在鹊桥中间等着，望眼欲穿。在宽阔的天河的正中间，这对苦命而又勇敢的夫妻相会了，阖家团圆。喜鹊们欢腾成一片，天上的云也全部散了，月色皎洁，似乎都在祝福这对有情人终于相会。

这番神奇的景象感动了西王母，她劝说玉帝，给这对人仙结合的夫妻一点儿怜悯。最后，玉帝允许织女在每年农历七月初七的晚上和丈夫、儿女团聚。

牛郎织女的传说在中国家喻户晓，是突破阻挠获得真爱的象征。而鹊桥代表着对真挚爱情的共情，也寄托了人们希望通过神力来获得真爱的愿望。今天，鹊桥已经成为一个众所周知的意象，用来表示恋人之间长久分离之后的重聚。

大多数中国神话故事遵循的主线是不幸的人们获得仁慈的神仙的帮助，从而过上幸福生活。织女和董永的故事也不例外。不过，使这个浪漫爱情故事与众不同的是，其与生活在中国传统农业社会中的凡人生活的紧密联系。

第一，故事的女主人公虽为天庭的仙女，其实更像一个普通的民间少女。就如"织女"的名字所表露的，她终日织布，就如人间的每一个平凡女子。第二，织女逃离华美的天庭而降落人间，是出于对凡间生活的好奇，这正是渴望到遥远的外部世界一探究竟的乡村少女的写照。第三，董永是挑着一对大竹筐（筐里坐着两个孩子），去和织女相会的。这也正是农村父亲带着孩子去远地赶集的真实反映。第四，搭桥的喜鹊不像传说中的凤凰那样神秘，它就是老百姓经常能看见的凡鸟。而其名中带有"喜"字，预示着好运。第五，即便是天庭的统治者，玉帝和西王母，这两位完全基于想象创造出来的神仙，也为故事的大团圆结局做出了贡献。开始玉帝和西王母阻挠织女的婚姻，正是人间父母对女儿"下嫁"十分不满的写照。而最后他们同意织女和丈夫、孩子相会，也正如人间的父母——怜子之心占据了上风，最终接纳了长大成人按自己的心愿我行我素的孩子。

读了鹊桥的故事，或者说织女和董永的罗曼史，我们可以发现故事中有非常多的现实世界中普通人的生活细节。由于这种与实际生活的联结带来的亲切感，所以它成为城乡祖母们讲述得最多的故事之一。它已经成为数百年来代代相传的常青树，成为中国人精神底色的一部分。除了善良、忠贞、团圆，还有让真爱突破阶级鸿沟的理想。不论今天的世界多么现代、多么智能，也不论未来会变成什么样，人类对真爱的向往和坚守，是永远不会消亡的。

翠竹——手工艺品的文化承载

竹是中国最常见的植物之一，它承载了诸多美德，谦卑又强大，丰茂而轻盈，柔软又坚韧。中国传统知识分子喜爱竹子，因为竹子的自然特性是君子品格的直观反映，例如谦恭（竹子中空）、变通（竹子易于弯曲但不易折断）、意志坚定（竹子能忍受严寒，地下根系发达），以及仪态优雅（竹子枝叶形态优美）。

在中国文人的生活中竹子随处可见。文房四宝、书房书桌，竹子都是常见的图案和材料。石桥的栏板上常常雕刻着竹子，衣饰上也常有竹子造型。文人把竹子、松树、梅花并称为"岁寒三友"。他们也经常坐在竹林中饮茶、冥想、弹琴……竹子是中国传统知识分子的精神伴侣。

竹子是中国文人雅士永恒的创作主题。唐朝诗人王维的《竹里馆》描述了文人的理想生活：

独坐幽篁里，

弹琴复长啸。

深林人不知，

明月来相照。

大多数人并不把竹子看作精神伴侣，而是经济实惠的工具、吃苦耐劳的仆人、宽容易处的朋友。竹子易于生长，质量很轻，砍伐也不费力。竹子是做成日用品的好材料。

早在杭州作为南宋（1127—1279）都城期间，杭州的竹制品业就十分发达。宋代末年，杭州人吴自牧在回忆都城风貌的《梦粱录》一书中记载：杭州的竹制品作坊能够制作各种各样的竹制品，包括竹扫帚、竹椅子、竹门帘、竹凉枕，还有竹箱、竹笠、竹扁担。由于竹子轻巧坚韧、成本低廉，所以是江南地区棚舍的常见建筑材料。它的特质还能激发建筑设计师的灵感。

初秋时节，杭州城西的农民走进竹林，砍下竹子，沿着窄路拖拽着回村。茂盛的竹叶扫在地上，扬起一路土尘。当他走进院子时，院子即刻充满绿意。从山里到院中，虽被一路拖拽，但竹子还能轻快地弹跳着，中空的弹性十足的竹子总能很好地适应环境。

对于一个熟练的手艺人来说，竹子的每个部分都是有用的。竹竿下部粗壮、质地坚硬，顶部纤细、质地柔软，可以加工成不同的物品。竹竿中空，是现成的引水管，把清澈甘甜的山泉一路接引而来，浇灌庄稼果蔬，或作家用。竹竿还是天然的炊具。砍下一截竹子，在竹子里放入米，灌进水，再用竹节做盖子。把这个盛米的竹筒放到火上烤一烤，静静等待。当淡淡乳白色的蒸汽升起来时，你得让自己再等一等。熄灭火苗，再等上几分钟，让米饭充分地吸收竹筒的香气。蒸汽散尽，竹筒饭就到了最美味的时候。莹白的大米泛着幽幽的淡绿，这是竹子的馈赠。口渴了，那就拿个竹碗，接一碗山泉。你还可以就地取材，做一双竹筷。竹子顶部纤细柔软的枝条很容易制成竹筷，而竹筷是人们日常生活中不可或缺的物件，也是物美价廉的旅游纪念品。

新鲜竹叶经济易得，可以入中药，清肺止咳。刚萌芽的竹叶气味清香，沏茶甘甜。竹的嫩根，也就是笋，味道鲜美，是不少经典杭帮菜的关键配料。即使竹子内那层膜也有利用价值。竹膜极薄，可以加工成竹纤维，做成衣服，透气凉爽，很适合江南地区燠热的天气。

现在让我们回到砍竹下山的农民家的院中。我们叫他老王，"王"是中国的一个大姓，很常见。在中国文化中，称呼中有一个"老"字，既表示尊重，又显得亲切。

老王怎么处理这些竹子呢？竹子挺多，妻子、儿子都来帮忙。老王先砍下带着许多竹叶的嫩枝，它们可以做成扫帚。他看了看去除枝叶后的竹竿，然后把竹竿砍成两段，如此这般就把竹竿分成了两批，一批柔软坚韧，另一批又粗又硬。他劈开竹竿，做成竹条，在火上烤出弧度，做了一些衣架。他又挑了两根竹竿，留了些枝杈在上面，这些枝杈正好可以做晾衣钩。再选一根竹竿，尽量削得光滑一些，做晾竿。这样，老王就做成了一套晾晒架。这样的自制晾衣组合最实用的一点是，支撑杆上的枝杈高低错落，可以方便晾竿移动到任意高度，既可以架高晒被褥，也可以放低晒小物件。冬天太阳好的时候，晾竿上就会挂上成排的咸肉、鱼干、酱鸭，这些都是江南人家过年期间的常备美味。当看到晾竿上飘动的衣服，或者整整齐齐散发出香味的腌货时，这个简朴的农家小院就充满了宝贵的家的气息。

老王妻子对丈夫的手艺很满意，那么要给宝贝儿子做个什么呢？5岁的小男孩正是爱玩的年纪。身为农民的爸爸要省出钱来去买玩具有点儿困难，但是手巧的爸爸可以想办法变出一篮子玩具。老王挑选了一根竹枝，试了试韧性，用特制的竹刀把竹枝削成极薄的竹片。他打算做个竹蜻蜓。竹蜻蜓下端是把手，上端是翼，就像一只展翅的大蜻蜓，看上去又像大写的英文字母"T"。老王先把一片竹子削成细条，在正中钻一个小洞。然后把竹条的左右两侧各削去一块，形成对称的两个斜面。最后在洞里插入细竹棍作把手。老王愉快地做着竹蜻蜓，小儿子就蹲在他身边，目不转睛地看着爸爸怎么把平平无奇的竹子变成他喜爱的玩具。他聚精会神，绝不打扰爸爸的工作。此刻在这个小男孩眼里，勤劳寡言的爸爸不啻一个魔术师。他早就想和小伙伴们比赛飞竹蜻蜓了！

现在，小男孩有了一只竹蜻蜓，但是它能不能像一只真正的蜻蜓那样，顺利地飞上天呢？男孩把竹蜻蜓的把手紧握在两只手掌中间，迅速地搓动，然后一松手——小小的竹蜻蜓一下子腾空了！它飞起来了！它在空中滑翔！兴奋的孩子等不及再试飞一次，他高高地举着竹蜻蜓，冲出了院门。他要和小伙伴们去比赛了！

竹蜻蜓是中国古人的发明，18世纪时传入欧洲。这个小男孩们的简单玩具迷住了欧洲使臣，他们把它叫作"中国螺旋"。中国竹蜻蜓启发了一位名叫乔治·凯利的英国人，他开始了直升机螺旋桨的研发，他被称为"空气动力学之父"。

孩子高高兴兴举着竹蜻蜓跑出去玩了，老王夫妇还要继续把满院的竹子利用起来。在林林总总的竹制品中，杭州竹篮广受欢迎，这是老王妻子一展手艺的时候了。不仅杭州人喜欢杭州竹篮（如图18-1所示），周边地区的人们也喜欢。老王把竹竿劈成细细长长的竹条，这些竹条柔软坚韧，适合手编。老王妻子拿了两根细竹条，编了一个十字结，然后插进一根竹条，使十字结变大。她一边编结一边加竹条，渐渐地手里出现了一个圆形，这就是竹篮的圆底。之后，她用略硬一点的竹条给圆底锁边。竹篮的主体部分需要用更细软的竹条，她把十几根柔软的细竹条插入篮底边缘，再把竹条连接起来。几个小时之后，竹篮的主体部分完工了。现在轮到老王了，他先把竹篮边缘长短不一的细竹条修剪成一样的高度，然后给竹篮安装把手。老王选了两根竹条，将四端插到篮子口，再用薄薄的竹皮把两个把手捆扎

图18-1　杭州竹篮
（绘图：陈星月）

成一个。最后他还要检查一遍竹篮有没有竹刺，要再做一遍磨光的工作。这是一个手艺人的责任心，也是他骄傲的来源。

他们打算做上十几只竹篮。杭州竹篮不仅适宜日常使用，也是受欢迎的旅游纪念品。常来杭州的游客中有一批比较特殊——女香客。她们来自周边乡、县，乘船沿着大运河来到杭州，一路观赏运河沿岸风景，还会到杭州的名寺古刹祈福。回程时带上一个杭州竹篮，作为来杭州的证明。杭州竹篮既有清秀典雅的审美韵味，又适合盛纳烧香祈福的物件。杭州竹篮轻巧耐用，简朴雅致，做工精细又经济实惠。谁能拒绝这样一个篮子呢？

以
桥
之
名

In the Name of Bridges:
The Chinese Cultural Codes on the Grand Canal（Chinese-English Bilingual）
——大运河上的中国文化密码（中英双语）

86

桥西直街——运河畔的悠悠药草香

以桥西直街为主体的桥西历史文化街区因位于拱宸桥西侧而得名，是一个以中国传统文化为特色的综合性街区，又以中医文化最为显著。在这条悠长的石板路上，有数家著名的中医馆，既因黑瓦白墙的形态而肃穆，又因中草药安神的气味而友善。

这些中医馆的名字非常有趣。"方回春堂"，字面意思是回到春天，也比喻痊愈，就像从严冬回暖到春天。"天禄号"，意思是天降福禄，好像在说这家医馆得到了上天的护佑，人们对它大可信赖。

中医馆名的神秘感是中草药文化的一部分。步入宽敞的医馆大堂，迎面而来的是一座巨大的抽屉墙。所有的抽屉形制完全一样，整齐而静默地排列着，好像宫殿里不苟言笑的卫兵。不过，这些抽屉又通过外部贴的标签释放出一种幽默感。看看这些中文名称的字面意思吧：当归——"你该回去了，别瞧病了"、王不留行——"国王没法把你留下来"、十大功劳——"十桩丰功伟绩"。有些药名听上去宛如珍宝，可是你一旦知道真相，怕是要哑然失笑。例如：夜明砂，会让你联想到珍贵的夜明珠，实际上是蝙蝠的粪便。望月砂，会让你想起"举头望明月"的美好意象，实际上是兔子的粪便——也对，传说中的月宫里不是住着兔子吗？白丁香，是洁白的丁香花吗？不不不，它是麻雀的粪便——想想吧，一群麻雀从你头顶飞过，噗，鸟粪，哦不，"白丁香"落了下来。龙涎香，是龙这种神物口中流出的有香味的口水吗？不，它是鲸鱼的排泄物。据说女士们的最爱之一——香奈儿五号——这款经典而昂贵的香水中就有龙涎香的成分。与此相似的是，在中国的传说中龙涎香也有一席之地：既因为其昂贵的价格，又因为其名中的"龙"——皇帝的化身，所以只有九五之尊的皇帝陛下才可以使用。这很有趣，不是吗？

中药的命名者清楚地知道人们厌恶一切动物的排泄物，但是中医师们又有一种说不清道不明的执念，因为这些动物的粪便在某些病症的中医处方中是不可或缺的。于是，给中药取名的人，既通医术，又成了语言修辞大师。对于这种命名的艺术我们应当持欣赏的态度，而不应苛责，毕竟，心理抚慰是医药的一部分，而语言则是处方的一部分。再说，当我们想到昂贵而流行的"猫屎咖啡"时，我们有理由相信其他国家的人们也会对中药的名称有更好的理解。

不同于现代西方医学，中医药已经发展了 5000 余年，其疗效正在被世界发现和认可。在抗击新冠疫情的过程中，中药被证明是有积极作用的。中医理论有时可能难以理解，部分原因是类似于经络穴脉等的古词语，但是在现代医学出现之前，中医药已经存在了数千年。传统中医药与其说是一门学科，不如说是对自然的尊重。从前的中医师相信，世间万物，不论大小、美丑、珍贵还是普通，都有其自身的价值，也因此在苍天之下自有其位。他们对这些自然界的存在持有淳朴而诚挚的敬畏，于是努力研究它们的内在，由此获取可以治疗疾病的成分。从某种程度上说，中医药是一种哲学——敬畏自然并在此基础上恰当地利用自然界的物质及其功效。简言之，中医药给予我们的哲学思想是道法自然。

行文至此，我们该花一点时间了解一下中国文化的重要一脉——道教。道，表达的是自然而为，并非强制性的。当把"道"作为一个动词时，它的意思是引导、指导。不必强人所难：修道之人不必强迫自己，也不必通过艰难的奋斗来争取，因为有些是自然而然就会获得的，是自然交给命运的安排。

什么是道呢？道教的倡导者老子通过把道比作水来阐释道。他说："上善若水。"水能赋形，又能附形，因势利导，自然而然。这就是"道"的核心。

在中国民间传说中，张三丰被看作道教的大师。张三丰确有其人，生活在元末明初。他创立了一个武术门派，把它命名为"武当派"。武当山就是张三丰修道的地方。张三丰的形象出现在一系列畅销武侠小说中后更广为人知。富有天分的武侠小说家把中国功夫的神乎其技和动荡时期的家国命运融合在一起。

在这些武侠小说家中，最家喻户晓的是金庸，他大胆地运用这种创意写作，取得了很高的文学成就。成千上万的读者被小说中激烈的情感冲突深深地感动：爱国主义与民族主义、真爱至上与家族世仇、仁义道德与虚伪背叛、为争名逐利而进行的嗜血屠杀与远离残暴的人文精神。通过阅读他的武侠小说，少年获得了英雄主义的第一课，少女投去了第一次爱恋的目光，中年人的心中响起了在团队责任和个人自由之间挣扎的共鸣，老年人则在传统诗词中陷入了遥远的乡愁。金庸的武侠小说，不是读罢就扔的浅薄之作，而是某种意义上的中国传统文化百科全书。他的作品在中国以外的地方也很受欢迎，有的被译成英文或其他语言，甚至搬上银幕。当张三丰创建武当派的时候，他恐怕不会想到他对长寿的追寻会演变成人们梦想的武学宗派，并以此寄托国泰民安的祈盼。

这或许可以解释为什么另一个姓张的人被人们以一种特殊的方式来纪念。在拱宸桥畔，有一座纪念道观——张大仙庙。这位张姓人是个修道之人，颇通医术，疗愈颇多而不取分文。事实上，这位张先生名叫张胜贵，确有其人。他生活在清朝末年。1878 年的某个夜晚，当他照常在拱宸桥上修道的时候，突然看到一个妇女坠河。张道士毫不犹豫，纵身入水，救起了这个妇女，但自己沉入水中。正在此时，一只大鹰疾飞而来，叼住他的头发，奋力将他拖向岸边。但张道士已无呼吸，可是其面色如常人一般。这一不可思议的景象使得人们相信张道士已经涅槃得化，成为永生的圣人。人们将他葬在拱宸桥边，坟墓上塑了一只鹰的雕像。次年乡贤上书朝廷，请造道观纪念，光绪皇帝批准了这一请求。从那以后，张胜贵被称作张大仙，以一位慈眉善目、银髯飘飘的老者的形象，在道观中接受人们的祭拜。

张大仙庙就在桥西直街，紧挨着方回春堂。

很多道士精通养生之术，其中不乏长寿者。有的因为善采药治病成了有名的医生。在一定程度上，道教和中医药有着较为密切的联系。因此，在桥西直街林立的中医馆中夹杂着一座道观就不足为奇了。心灵的安宁与身体的灵便共同构成了人体的康健。张大仙庙与中医馆比邻而居，可以说是中国人实用主义精神的又一个例证。

The Grand Canal of China: A Cultural Heritage of Human Beings

The Grand Canal of China forms a vast inland waterway system in the north-eastern and central eastern plains of China, passing through two municipality and four provinces nowadays. It runs from the capital Beijing in the north to Zhejiang Province in the south. Constructed in sections from the 5th century BC, it was conceived as a unified means of communication for the Empire for the first time in the 7th century AD (the Sui Dynasty). This led to a series of gigantic worksites, creating the largest and most extensive civil engineering project prior to the Industrial Revolution. Completed and maintained by successive dynasties, the Grand Canal formed the backbone of the Empire's inland communication system.

The Grand Canal of China reached a new peak in the 13th century (the Yuan Dynasty), providing a unified inland navigation network consisting of more than 2,000 km of artificial waterways, linking five of the most important river basins in China, including the Yellow River and the Yangtze River. Still a major means of internal communication today, it has played an important role in ensuring the economic prosperity and stability of China over the ages.

"The most splendid city in the world", written in the popular travelling book in the 13th century, the Italian author Marco Polo gave a detailed account for Hangzhou, which was called Kinsai City or the city of Kinsai in the Yuan Dynasty. Marco Polo narrated, "it stands as it is in the water and surrounded by water", and "there are twelve thousand bridges of stone, connecting many waterways in Kinsai City". In particular, he noticed the bridges—under the high bridge, big ships with tall mast could go through it. The quantity of bridges may be Marco Polo's exaggeration, nevertheless, his narration of busy and efficient water traffic in Kingsai City is rational. The prosperity of Kingsai City could date back to the Sui Dynasty when a great hydraulic project, the man-made Sui-Tang Grand Canal, put its south end at Hangzhou. Since then, Hangzhou grew into a prosperous metropolis and became the capital city of the Southern Song Dynasty, over a hundred years before Marco Polo arrived in China. Though Hangzhou didn't take the role of the capital city after the Southern Song Dynasty, it maintained significant development thanks to the Grand Canal as a main artery of economy, culture and society.

The Sui-Tang Grand Canal, based on a large number of canals dug by the previous dynasties, was launched in 605 in the Sui Dynasty. It centered at Luoyang, the east capital city of the Sui Dynasty, looked like a huge seagull whose right wing stretching to Zhuojun (today's Beijing) and the left wing to Yuhang (today's Hangzhou). In the Yuan Dynasty, the Grand

Canal turned into a generally straight waterway from Beijing to Hangzhou, with the length of about 1,800 kilometers. Shorter than its original length, the Beijing-Hangzhou Grand Canal became a more important and efficient waterway for the whole nation. The Grand Canal, seagull-form or straight waterway, has been an enormously great hydraulic project nourishing the Chinese people, not only in economy, but also in culture for more than 2,000 years.

The Grand Canal has been inscribed into the World Heritage List by UNESCO since 2014.

Where there are rivers, there are bridges. The Grand Canal as a man-made waterway system, connecting a lot of natural rivers, brooks, ponds, and pools. The south area of China has abundant water resources, which give birth to a great number of bridges.

Hangzhou, having been the south end of the Grand Canal for about 1,500 years, has built dozens of bridges above the Grand Canal. These bridges, ancient or modern, not only link people and lands along the Grand Canal, but also link the past and the future.

The Guangji Bridge: Nostalgia Along the Grand Canal

The Guangji Bridge (see Figure 1-1) is the only bridge in the form of seven arches on the Grand Canal. Guangji, in Chinese " 广 济 ", means "widely helpful" or "to benefit a vast number of people". Built in 1489, the Guangji Bridge is located in Tangqi Town, about 80 meters in length with 160 steps. The construction of the Guangji Bridge is full of hardship. According to the local archives, the hydrologic conditions of the Grand Canal going through Tangqi Town was severe that the initial try to build a bridge fell into failure. People had to go through the canal by boat, risking the overturn of boat and losing their lives. Such tragedies occurred several times a year, leaving people with endless sorrow. On a stormy night, a merchant called Chen Shouqing experienced the dangerous situation. After being rescued on the second morning, Chen made a determination to build a solid bridge for the Tangqi people and those who came here for business or went through the Grand Canal. In order to fulfil the wish as early as possible, Chen Shouqing devoted himself into collecting funds for building bridge. He made farewell to his family, converted to the Taoism and became a Taoist. He travelled on his foot all around Tangqi Town and some cities in the Jiangnan Area. Several years later, a significant sum of money was collected but it's not enough to build a big bridge. Chen Shouqing was getting old, but his original determination never unchanged. One day he got an idea when he saw the Caoliang (tribute grain) ships. He managed to hide in a Caoliang ship going northward to Beijing, and finally reached the capital city. To catch people's attention as soon as possible, he made a startling debut by tying himself with heavy iron chains in the penetrating cold of Beijing, kneeling down on the main street and yelling: We need a bridge!

Figure 1-1 The Guangji Bridge
(Painter: Tu Qunfeng)

His bold action as well as determination was heard by the Empress Dowager Zhou, a warmhearted senior lady as well as a believer of the Taoism. She donated 420 taels of silver, and her great-grandson, the crown prince, also offered 30 taels of silver. In addition, the crown prince presented a scroll printed with his personal seal. The Empress Dowager

Zhou was the most respected lady in the country, so her benevolence got followers. More donations, such as silver, gold, and jewelry went from the emperor's concubines' dressing rooms to Chen Shouqing's donation package. Then officials and local gentlemen followed. Generosity gathered so soon that by the end of that year, Chen Shouqing had collected enough fund for building bridge. In the year of 1489, a huge seven-hole stone arch bridge was completed. Thanks to the wide bridge, people and carts could walk on the bridge with sound safety, free from the fear of falling into the water. Ships could go through the biggest arch while small boats could use the smaller arches, hence the traffic got greatly improved. Tangqi Town began its prime time as an ideal venue for business and shipment along the Grand Canal.

The bridge is named after "Tongji" at first, in which "tong" means "to go through" and "ji" means "to help". "Ji" also appears in the word "zhouji" which means offering help around the water, so many bridges in China have the character in their names. The Guangji Bridge is named after "ji" naturally.

This bridge is quite a huge one over the Grand Canal due to its seven arches, whose reflections on water make up a row of six circles symmetrically from the smallest on both ends while the largest in the center.

The bridge benefited Tangqi Town a lot. Tangqi was the inhabitant site of soldiers in the Yuan Dynasty who dredged rivers to connect the Grand Canal at first. It literally means that people live around a pond. *The Archive of Tangqi* published officially in the Qing Dynasty (in the reign of Emperor Guangxu) writes: "Since the river had been dug out to connect the Grand Canal in the Yuan Dynasty, a huge bridge was built, then markets emerged, people thronged, and business thrived..."

The Guangji Bridge is like a long rainbow connecting the north and the south banks of the wide Grand Canal. On the north bank there are rows of shops of traditional pastries and restaurants, tempting passengers, ship-owners and crew with their wonderful scent. This is a unique aroma surrounding the Guangji Bridge and no other bridges over the Grand Canal in Zhejiang Province have been immersed in such a soothing and enchanting aroma.

Why are there numerous pastry shops and restaurants in Tangqi? The answer lies in its geographical condition.

Tangqi Town was the penultimate stop on the long-distance journey by ship on the Grand Canal. The journey might inspire poets to compose verses and poems, sometimes a romantic one, nevertheless, such a time- and labor-consuming journey was indeed an extremely tough task. After days of being confined within humble cabins, of being exposed into the sun, the rain, the wind and the snow, and of being risking turbulent water and bombora with the heart in throat, both crew and passengers were in a great anxiety for thorough relaxation. In addition, shaving, hair-cutting and bathing were absolutely necessary before the final destination. As a ritual routine, they would like to buy some gifts conveying love for families. Tangqi Town was 50 li① away from the Beixin Pass of Hangzhou. Usually it could be reached in half a day by ship. Hence, Tangqi became a suitable venue for ship-owners, crew and merchants to have a good rest, as well as to make preparations for inspecting goods and tax-declaration in Hangzhou. Besides, the Hangjiahu Plain, with moderate climate and fertile soil, was an ideal production base for silk and grain, which were

---

① li, a Chinese length unit. 1 li is equal to 500 meters.

annual tribute to the emperors in the capital city. Enjoying geographical advantages of the plain and the Grand Canal, Tangqi saw tycoons in silk industry and grain production set up their villas and social connections as well.

All the factors above made the Grand Canal Tangqi section a bustling water lane, bringing a thriving town that attracted various people.

Where there are crowds, there are business. But why was Tangqi in particular featured with pastry business?

Well, for exhausted passengers or crew, what else could be an instant comfort except for a sweet soft pastry? Those pastries—reddish, rubrical, pink, greenish, dark-green, light green, olive green, golden, faint yellow, earthy yellow, ginkgo-leave yellow, snow-white, lily-white, rice-white, brownish, grey, ink-black, in shapes of round, square, oval, triangle, or in shapes of peach, puppy, bunny, with sweet or salt stuffing or not, displayed themselves as huge splendid color pallets, just like a warm and sweet dreamland that no one could resist the temptation.

Tangqi with rows and lines of pastry shops demonstrated the traditional waterside architecture. Its spectacular scenery and unforgettable taste would evoke passengers' nostalgia.

They left hometown; they worked hard; they saved up every coin until they finally were on their home way. They stepped into a pastry shop, tasted some samples, picked up one or more from the collections. From the moneybag hidden cautiously, full or half-empty, they poured out several coins with generosity, and commanded the shop assistant to wrap up several pastries. The assistant greeted customers joyfully, introduced pastries by inviting them to taste a sample while engaging in small talk as if they were close relatives. Then the assistant packed pastries nicely and neatly, covering with a piece of crimson paper bearing the shop's logo on package. The shop was full of sweet and joy. Now the satisfied customer stepped out to the narrow street, looking up at the blue sky, then got back into the ships.

There would be no more than one day before he could see his beloved children to whom he had given sweet promise. As for his wife, although to whom he had never said "I love you", he was full of gratitude, knowing her difficulties, efforts and persistence. (In Chinese traditional culture, it was commonly believed that a man should hold his tongue of sweet words for his wife because these loving oaths would decrease his authority as the family leader.)

He would also prepare a special gift for his younger sister, who was going to marry a young man before long. According to the unwritten rule, a married woman would seldom return and meet her parents. If she married afar, it could be rare to return to her birthplace, plus the undeveloped transportation. He would not let them down.

> These pastries carried their dreams of good living;
> Pastry shops by the Guangji Bridge;
> These pastries conveyed their love for families;
> Heal the nostalgia of travel.

The Gongchen Bridge: A Landmark of Hangzhou's History

It was June 22nd, 2014, Doha, Qatar. An official was delivering a speech on the cultural and historical value of the Grand Canal of China to the panels of UNESCO World Intangible Cultural Heritage Committee. When he presented a series of snaps of the Gongchen Bridge (see Figure 2-1) elegantly overlooking the flowing Beijing-Hangzhou Grand Canal, the experts were deeply impressed with its glamor, glory and grace.

Figure 2-1 The Gongchen Bridge
(Painter: Tu Qunfeng)

The panel unanimously agreed that China' Grand Canal should take a seat on the World Heritage List.

Since then, the Gongchen Bridge has been wildly taken as a symbol of the Grand Canal of China. The image of the great three-arch-bridge can be found on tourism maps, souvenirs, boutiques, and guidebooks. It's also a typical pattern on handouts in the museums about the Grand Canal, huge electronic screens of authoritative news agencies, and advertisements in aviation magazines...

It has been a long journey before the Gongchen Bridge has a world-wide reputation.

The Gongchen Bridge was initially built in 1631, and collapsed in 1651. It was rebuilt in 1714 in the reign of Emperor Kangxi of the Qing Dynasty. Twelve years later, Governor Li Wei presided over the thorough renovation which finally made the bridge a gorgeously grand bridge on the Grand Canal. Unfortunately, it was destroyed during the military conflict between the government army and the rebel troop named Taiping in the autumn of 1863. In the year of 1885, the bridge had been in the reconstruction in the charge of Mr Ding Bing from Hangzhou (in the reign of Emperor Guangxu of the Qing Dynasty), but this was not the end of the Gongchen Bridge's tortuous life yet. The Gongchen Bridge clasped once again in the fire from cannons of the invading Japanese troops in the early years of 1900s. The Gongchen Bridge was completely rebuilt by Hangzhou municipal government in 2005 in accordance with the principle of cultural relics protection.

Why did the Gongchen Bridge go through so many tough times? The answer probably lies in two aspects: its location and its size.

In the bridge name "gongchen", "gong" means bending your palms to show respect, while "chen" refers to the Polaris in the northern sky and the palace where emperors live. Hence, "gongchen" is also a metaphor of expressing respect and hospitality to honorable guests.

Located in Hangzhou, the southern end of the 1794-km Beijing-Hangzhou Grand Canal, the Gongchen Bridge has been standing there as the terminal of the long journey and the entrance to the city. Seeing the bridge approaching, exhausted crew and passengers were clearly aware of the end of tough days, and the sweet and prosperity were just at the corner.

The bridge's three high and huge arches are like round gates with traditional Chinese aesthetics that are opening widely for the guests to Hangzhou. The significance of the Gongchen Bridge to Hangzhou, is similar to the Arc'de Triumph to Pairs, or the London Bridge to London. It is such an arresting culture landmark can never being neglected.

The other reason why the Gongchen Bridge suffered so much gunfire was due to its enormousness. The bridge was one of the biggest bridges on the Grand Canal in the Qing Dynasty. The huge size contributed its glory as a part of transportation project, while the obvious advantage of its height also resulted in disaster as a military target.

In the year of 1863, the Taiping troops led by a discontented literati Hong Xiuquan, battled with the government army commanded by General Zuo Zongtang. The royal and senior official, General Zuo, had an inner-conflict when he found he was in a dilemma of preventing the Hangzhou city from the control of Taiping troops or protecting the Gongchen Bridge from the gunfire. Before the government army got to Hangzhou, the Taiping troops had already occupied the Gongchen Bridge and turned it into strategic fort. The Grand Canal was an artery of business for the Qing Dynasty, so the Gongchen Bridge was the most bustling station through which all loaded ships should pass before they were charged taxes. When the Taiping troops seized the Gongchen Bridge, it also seized the business along the Grand Canal. General Zuo was aware of the history of the Gongchen Bridge and the great efforts made by predecessors. He had known that the first initiator Zhu Huafeng, a Juren (a successful candidate in the imperial examinations at the provincial level), had devoted himself all into the bridge in the last days of the Ming Dynasty. He had learnt about that the previous senior officials of Zhejiang had made great efforts for the bridge. He was strongly aware of what the bridge meant.

The renovation of the Gongchen Bridge was always closely related to senior officials, who won their own reputations after the overhaul of the bridge, meanwhile they had to suffer overwhelming difficulties in finance, labours, coordination and construction.

Building a bridge was a costly project. In the reign of Emperor Kangxi, Mr Duan Zhixi, the deputy-governor of Zhejiang Province, launched the overhaul of the Gongchen Bridge. Lacking of fund and labour, the Gongchen Bridge was a simple one, though it was an effective traffic project. 12 years later the bridge was collapsed, and the tough task of renovation was passed to Governor Li Wei, who made himself an example by donating his salary in the hope of collecting fund from the common people, especially officials and businessmen.

Of course, the Gongchen Bridge was much more than an architecture or a hydraulic project. It was a symbolization of benevolence, of a practice of Confucianism that emphasized a merciful administration and advocated improving people's living conditions. It conveyed the common understandings of the universe. It bridged the ordinary people, officials and emperors.

Anyone who led the Gongchen Bridge project should be sophisticated and competent. He should be capable of not only maintaining good relations with colleagues and emperor, and also dealing with financial issues.

And this process was so long and tedious that it could last several years. Hence, some of them had sought for inner strength from a motto written by Zhuge Liang, a widely-respected strategist and the Prime Minister in the State of Shu-Han during the Three Kingdoms Period (220—280). They recited a couplet as follows:

Seeking fame and wealth, there is no way to clarify one's purpose;
Holding no inner-peace, there is no way to extend one's knowledge.

As the governor of Zhejiang Province, General Zuo, had been successfully serving the imperial court and had witnessed the tough times of those degraded officials. He sympathized to them. He also had his disappointments, failures and humiliations. It was clear to Zuo how tortuous and dangerous to be a senior official who was at the emperor's disposal. If he could not successfully suppress the Taiping troops, then Zhejiang, the major tax-paying area, would be unable to offer tribute to the imperial court as usual. Meanwhile, the honor of the Qing court would not be remained, which would shake the soldiers' morale. At this moment, the Taiping troops occupied the Gongchen Bridge — controlling the water transportation in Hangzhou City.

Although Zuo Zongtang was a senior official trusted by the emperor, his work faced many difficulties from his colleagues and subordinates: redundancy, corruption, and extravagance. All these concerns made him stressful in the fight against the Taiping troops.

General Zuo pondered when looking at the Gongchen Bridge whose elegant shape was blocked by a newly-fixed bastion by the Taiping troops. Taking the bastion on the very middle of the bridge, the Taiping troops had the military privilege over Zuo's. No commercial ships showed on the Grand Canal though the water kept flowing as usual.

Zuo Zongtang made up his mind.

According to documents, in the autumn of 1863, the Gongchen Bridge suffered serious warfare and later collapsed during the reign of Emperor Guangxu. In 1885, a Hangzhou intellectual, named Ding Bing, launched the reconstruction of the Gongchen Bridge. He made a determination to build a solid project which could stand for hundreds of years and kept benefiting people along the Grand Canal. It finally stood proudly and got its general appearance and size like it is at present.

From the end of the Ming Dynasty to the end of the Qing Dynasty, the construction, collapse and reconstruction of the Gongchen Bridge experienced for hundred years. During this period, its first and last construction was initiated by local squires, while the others were led by local officials. It was a reflection of the participation of local squires in social governance, and it was also an example of reliable local officials performing their duties to protect the safety of the people and to promote the economy of the region.

After the Sino-Japanese War, Hangzhou was listed as a trade port. Coveting the profits brought by the bustling commerce and trade of the Grand Canal, the Japanese invaders set up toll gate on the Gongchen Bridge and occupied the east of the bridge as the Japanese settlement. In the twenty-third year of Emperor Guangxu's reign (1897), the Japanese army paved a concrete slope about 2.5-meter-wide in the middle of the bridge for the driving cars. The beautiful Gongchen Bridge lost its traditional aesthetic charm, being humiliated by national disaster.

The Gongchen Bridge went through so many historical events that it was much more than a traffic project. It carried unique memories and feelings of the Hangzhou people. As a landmark of Hangzhou and the south-end of the Beijing-Hangzhou Grand Canal, the Gongchen Bridge witnessed the Qing Emperor's royal fleet, the prosperity of delivering tribute grain on the canal, and the thriving and declining of commerce. It also saw the newly-budded modern textile industry in Zhejiang Province. Modern post offices and news agencies also had a prime time around the Gonchen Bridge in 1900s.

After the People's Republic of China was established in 1949, the Gongchen Bridge began its new life. In 2005, the Gongchen Bridge was designated as a provincial cultural relic protection unit, since then its protection has been regulated by law. In the same year, Hangzhou municipal government carried out a comprehensive repair of the Gongchen Bridge, preserving the majestic and old-fashioned landscape with the principle of repairing the relics into their original forms. In this reconstruction, considering the busy navigation of the canal under the bridge and avoiding collisions, four anti-collision piers were set up beside the main arch, and each anti-collision pier was carved with a Gong Fu— a mascot that could keep away from the water disaster in ancient Chinese mythology (sea Figure 2-2).

Figure 2-2 Gong Fu Carved on Anti-Collision Pier

During the past hundred years, the Gongchen Bridge experienced many times of build, damage and reconstruction. The time changed, dynasties fell, and the shipping business went up and down. But the Gongchen Bridge stood up again and again. Its story is a reflection that the Grand Canal has been vitally important for the Chinese people's daily life and the unity of China. Today, having been presented on the World Heritage List, the Gongchen Bridge carries abundant significance of culture and tourism. It will continue its glory and legend forever.

The Xiangfu Bridge: Entertainments Along the Grand Canal

As one of the most important water route in China before the 21st century, the Grand Canal gathers dozens of branches, including brooks, creeks, pools and lakes. As a man-made waterway, the Grand Canal, from the very beginning of its birth, has positively searched for the shortcut and extremely utilized the existing natural water system. These connections led to a large quantity of bridges.

The Xiangfu Bridge (see Figure 3-1) is one of them. Located in Xiangfu Town of Hangzhou, the bridge is overlooking a brook named Huantang River which goes east to the Grand Canal. The Xiangfu Bridge is a five-hole stone girder bridge that crosses the Huantang River in the north-south direction, 28 meters long and 3.6 meters wide. The bridge rail are plain or carved with Sermuru seat pattern, with balusters bearing lotus or stone lions on the top. The area of Xiangfu Town is a water network, with the Xitang River and the Huantang River passing through the whole town. As early as in the Southern Song Dynasty, Xiangfu Town was a shipping hub where vessels were loaded with annual tribute grain from Jiangsu Province and the north of Zhejiang Province. Hence, the Xiangfu Bridge, as a main bridge in the town, had taken an important role in transportation.

Figure 3-1 The Xiangfu Bridge
(Painter: Tu Qunfeng)

Ships not only brought in a large amount of goods to Xiangfu Town, but also brought in the population growth. Merchants, hawkers, boatmen, carpenters, lacquer makers, barbers, and coolies gathered here to depend on the shipping industry for their livelihood. Most interestingly, the entertainment industry grew along with the transportation and population. In the days before electricity or internet was invented, how did people pass their spare time in an economical way? Instead of going to theater to watch plays, the Chinese people created an unique folk art called "story-telling", a performance of telling stories.

A typical story-telling performer in the Qing Dynasty and the Republic of China usually wore a gray or light blue garment with loose sleeves pulling up to reveal a white lining. In a word, he looked neat, gentle, smart and admirable.

He stood behind a simple desk, whose height was suitable for him to put his hand on. On the desk there was a rectangular wood, called Jingtang Wood, or Startling Wood[1], which was the most important tool of the story-telling performers. The little wood, plain and small, was far beyond what it looked like. Though a story-telling performer was supposed to be very good at narrating stories, it was also natural that the audience became drowsy during the long process of listening. In this case, the talk-show player would slap the little wood on the desk to produce a thunder-like sound, by which listeners would be waken up, getting their minds back and giving their attention to the hard-working story-telling performers.

A story-telling performer was a master of making hooks or creating suspense. He observed listeners' facial expressions, led them to follow the plot he described, and guided them to be indulged in a romantic or heroic story. What's more, he should use the art of making a pause. After an hour's story-telling in which listeners were all looking up at nothing but him on the stage with their stretching necks, he put forward a question like "Will the hero be assassinated?" or "Will the eloping loving couple be seized by the cruel landlord?" Then a pause. When all listeners were whole-heartedly waiting for answers, he continued, with a polite and gentle smile, "For the following story I will tell you next time." Wow! People stepped out with a mixed feeling of regret and content, exchanging their comments of the heroes in the story, in sigh or in excitement, and going back. "See you tomorrow! Be there or be square!" They made an appointment for the next day, and then the story-telling performers was pleased for he succeeded in

---

[1] A Startling Wood is initially used by an official who warns the suspects to be honest, or showing the reverence. It is borrowed by story-telling performers to get the audience's attention.

以
桥
之
名

In the Name of Bridges:
The Chinese Cultural Codes on the Grand Canal (Chinese-English Bilingual)
大运河上的中国文化密码（中英双语）

112

attracting more audience.

Story-telling performers hardly dwelled at a spot. After they had performed all stories which usually cost them a great deal of time and energy for public show, they had to leave for a new town to show (and sell) their story-telling art. They were sort of walking and telling artists, who, as lonely folk artists, would be better to find an ally, economically and socially.

Luckily it was not a tough job.

Bosses of tea houses would like to invite a story-telling performer to make performances for their customers. A tea house, according to its name, was a place where people enjoyed tea. However, drinking tea was just part of daily life at home. A tea house needed to provide an atmosphere of joy and share. Since a lot of profits came from snacks and refreshment, a tea house should keep its customers on chair as long as possible. A story-telling performer, with his tactic of language, would be of great help to tea house business. Thus, a deal would be reached between the two parties: The story-telling performer could use tea house as his performing venue, while the tea house boss would get more customers who would be addicted to the fantastic story. It's natural that both story-telling performer and tea house boss would calculate the benefits and interests. Given that story-telling performer could attract a large number of audience and make great contributions to the earnings, tea house boss would share the profit with the story-telling performer, who was now rather a partner than a linguistic artist. Story-telling performers and tea house bosses would formed a de facto symbiotic relationship, analogous to contemporary examples, like a lounge singer and a bar.

Nobles and tycoons might have their own theatrical troupes or hire famous drama players to perform in their fancy houses, while the common people could not afford it. For example, in the Chinese traditional novel *Dream of the Red Chamber*, there are a lot of chapters describing the theatrical troupe of the aristocratic Jia's Family. The aristocratic family owned a professional Kunqu Opera troupe, consisting of twelve professional actresses, a band and managers. The popularity of the Kunqu Opera has a close connection with the wealthy salt merchants of Yangzhou, a major city along the Sui-Tang Grand Canal and later the Beijing-Hangzhou Grand Canal. Unlike the upper-class, the common people preferred the entertainments that they could afford. Tea house was also a good place for businessmen to meet customers and expanded business relations with decision-makers. Tea house and the related culture like tea-ceremony, tea-feast and folk arts remain vigorous in today's China, booming in various styles.

Listening to stories hence became an ideal option of entertainment for a majority of people. The story was exciting, the atmosphere was good, and the admission ranged from economic chair to luxurious chamber. Tycoons could rent a private chamber on the second floor or buy the VIP seats, while low-income people could spend less or stand on the rear of tea house. Rich or poor, the story-telling performer offered them an equal opportunity to have a joy.

The story-telling performance was more than a popular entertainment. For people who had few accesses to the official system of education, listening to a romantic story or a historical tale was an effective and interesting way of self-learning that could dispel ignorance. An experienced story-telling performer usually gave some wise remarks, criticizing the vicious and praising the virtuous. It was by no means an over-flattery for a story-telling performer to be respected as a teacher of the ordinary people. Just like *The Romance of the Three Kingdoms, The Heroes of the Marshes, The Story of Jade Hairpin, The Romance of the Western Chamber, The Injustice to Dou E, The Plum in the Golden Vase*, and so on, these Chinese classical tales were spreading from tea houses to the whole country. Excellent tales have an effective edification function. By speaking and listening and from mouth to mouth, Chinese traditional value of morality was passed on and deeply rooted in the hearts of the people.

Just like drama was invented by ancient Greece in the crowded carnival for ode to the God of War, Chinese traditional folk arts also grew in the crowded towns. Where the water of the Grand Canal reached, there was the exciting exclamation and the thunderous applause. The entertainments along the Grand Canal were colorful. The well-dressed spectators in the gorgeous houses, the passers-by standing casually on the roadside for jugglers' play, and the audience watching intently at the magician's tricks in showroom, these people together with the performers created a symphony of the folk arts.

Booming transportation and businesses led to the booming entertainments. Story-telling was just a segment. There has always been a saying in the opera world: "Waterways are theatrical roads." "Theatrical road" refers to the performance route and activity area of theatrical troupe. "Waterway" refers to the important major traffic waterways. Waterways drive economic and cultural development, and also bring a center of theatrical activities.

"Xiangfu", in Chinese " 祥符 ", refers to the token of fortune. For the Chinese people, it's very usual to name a site, a venue, a bridge, a lane, a street or even a community for expressing their wishes. The name of the

Xiangfu Bridge is an excellent exemplification of this culture. The date of the construction of the Xiangfu Bridge is unknown. The existing Xiangfu Bridge got its appearance based on the reconstruction in the 22nd year of the reign of Emperor Jiajing of the Ming Dynasty.

Emperor Jiajing was a legendary emperor. It didn't mean that he had taken triumph great enough to be identified as a legend. The legend came from his life style as well as his control over the empire's throne for 45 years.

Emperor Jiajing sat onto the empire's chair when he was only 15, as a son of the cousin of the previous emperor. Rather than a biological son of the past emperor, he grew up as a boy far away from the throne. He had never been authorized as the crowned prince and had never been educated with the strategies and tactics that a future emperor should learn in his very early childhood. In a word, Emperor Jiajing had no adequate preparation or expectation for being the supreme leader of the giant Ming Empire. He was somehow scared of sitting on the huge golden chair engraved with holy dragons, being a sovereign taking the foremost responsibility for the whole country and the people.

This made his method of reigning quite different from most of the previous emperors in ancient China. They usually sat on the huge chair overlooking the court, waiting for their senior officials to report in their prudent voice, giving remarks, praising those who had performed excellently and punishing those who hadn't. But Emperor Jiajing didn't follow this routine during the most time of his reign.

During his reign of 45 years, for decades he did not show up in the imperial court, and did not meet officials except for a few of senior cabinet ministers. What was he doing then?

He was obsessed with Taoism. In a dark-blue garment, he unwrapped his long hair, spending days and nights in his small chamber nearby the court. Most of the time he was in his deep meditation, sitting with his legs crossed, eyes lightly closed, swallowing all his voice. Clouds of curl smoke came out of the copper incense burner, and behind the burner enshrined Taishang Laojun—the divinity of the Taoism.

Actually, beneath the surface of his "rule by doing nothing" was the pinnacle of the cabinet system. The ordinary people, however, were not aware of about the struggle in the imperial court and still simply put their hopes on the emperor for better life. They named the bridge after "Xiangfu" in the hope of heaven descending happiness and protecting all living beings.

4 The Changzheng Bridge: A Prosperous Commercial Area

Passing through the gorgeous Gongchen Bridge, the Grand Canal continues her southern journey for hundreds of meters, with rows of black-tile and white-wall houses made of wood on the west bank. The water gets obviously broader here. And it divides into two branches: the Xiaohe River and the Yuhangtang River. The Xiaohe River is actually part of the Xitang River, which was a busy assisting water lane of tribute grain in the Southern Song Dynasty. Local people prefer the name "Xiaohe", meaning a small river, which sounds more friendly.

The junction of the three rivers (sea Figure 4-1) produces a densely populated block whose prosperity had been lasting several centuries. The Kangjia Bridge, crossing over the Yuhangtang River, locates at the end of the Hushu North Road. To its northeast, a small arch stone bridge named "Hui'an" looks like an elegant eyebrow. Different from the Kangjia Bridge serving as main passage for automobiles, the Hui'an Bridge is only for pedestrians. Walking from the Hui'an Bridge and going northward through the Xiaohe Historical Block, you will come to the Changzheng Bridge over the Xiaohe River. The three bridges have different shapes and are not far apart, connecting the confluence of the three rivers and also facilitating the people's life. Leaning against the stone bridge rail, you will be impressed by the typical view of waterside residential complex in the Jiangnan Area of China.

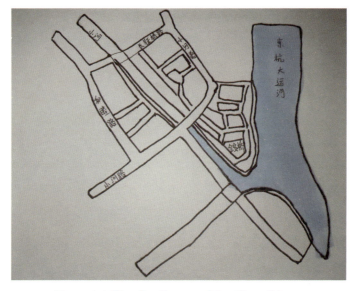

Figure 4-1 The Confluence of the Three Rivers

(Painter: Chen Xingyue)

Houses and shops stood next to each other; paper lanterns hang high under the eaves; the river ripples and sparkles in the orange-yellow light; colorful shop banners are gently waving; and the air is a delightful mixture of the aroma of flower, fresh rice and attempting dishes. The Xiaohe area looks like a traditional Chinese painting, slowly unfolding the life of the Xiaohe people living in a busy commercial port, which have been extending for hundreds of years.

Dating back to the Southern Song Dynasty, the Xiaohe area was the hub of transshipment, collection and distribution. In the middle and late years of the Qing Dynasty, the area grew into a thriving business complex crowed with restaurants, tea houses, and groceries.

People of the Xiaohe area built their houses in full consideration of the need of business activity. A typical house here was two-storied with the upper part the sleeping chamber for the owner, while the room downstairs was separated into two parts. The front part facing the main street was taken as a shop while the rear part (most of them facing the river) was a workshop as well as warehouse. In fact, such a house was a trinity of store, workshop and living place. So where did the employees sleep at night? The young men usually made a temporary bed in the shop after business, partly taking on the responsibility of security. In order to get enough daylight and catch potential customers as many as possible, the facade wall of the shop was made up of detachable wooden boards, which were lifted out in business hours and installed again when business was over. For the Xiaohe area, it was a sonata of the clicking by lifting boards with the amiable greetings among the shop fellows in the morning. And the rippling sound from washing is also part of the melody. The pale gold sunlight half casting over the black-tiled roofs, the Xiaohe area was immersed in the semi-transparent vapor rising from the water. The shops' signboards therefore, kept still like a young man who was not waken up until the sunlight drove the moisture away. Sometimes the morning tune of the Xiaohe area had other players—vendors. They used bamboo shoulder poles to carry a couple of large bamboo baskets on their shoulders and shouted as they walked: crystal home-made snacks, sweet seedpods of the lotus without huge lotus-leaves, fuchsia water chestnuts just picked up from the ponds... Among the noisy markets and the bustling streets, no sound was more appealing than the calling of a snack-seller. Sweet-rice-wine, a traditional sweet and sour drink, was an ideal refreshment for the workers of quays and crew as the special taste, offering a source of energy as well as satisfaction.

Sometimes snack-seller would come with tofu. A wooden box sat on a bamboo basket, and white tofu is spread all over it. Someone raised his hand and beckoned: A piece of tofu! Then he handed over the change, and more often handed over a coarse porcelain bowl containing half a bowl of soybeans. Tofu was probably the low-threshold barter cargo remaining for the long time. However, in the commercial street of the Xiaohe area, the most common are loquats. Taking a boat from the river port and going north along the canal for about half an hour, it was Tangqi Town. Tangqi Town is rich in loquat. When loquats ripened in early June, the peasants would take a boat to the bustling commercial port of the Xiaohe area. Here, loquats could be sold for a good price.

The Xiaohe area was much busier when temple fair was held, people from afar coming here to pray for happy life. During temple fair days, Xiaohe block woke up as early as the first light of the dawn. A shopkeeper put the first batch of fried stuffed buns one by one into the large pan, covered it with a wooden lid; after a few minutes he opened the lid and added half a spoonful of water along the edge of the pan. Instantly, a piece of water vapor rose up from the pan, and the fried stuffed buns puffed up their faces in the water vapor. The shopkeeper quickly sprinkled a handful of black sesame seeds and then a handful of chopped scallion, whose mixed rich fragrance allured passers-by to stop: Come to eat! Come to eat! In the next door, the wonton shop owner lit up the fire, put a huge soup pot, chopped pork into fine minced meat, and conjured rows of delicate wontons with flipping fingers in the blink of an eye. A sugar-painting vendor's creation attracted children's attention. He put a tiny bamboo stick into a huge bowl of syrup, used a set of special sticks and made the syrup into a vivid pattern: a cute bunny, a chubby bear face, or a sketch of Monkey King, the myth hero for all children. This sweet magic not only hooked children, but also stopped adults for appreciation. Sugar-painting, was more than a candy, indeed a wonderful folk art. The Xiaohe area was benefited from the convenience of transport, the prosperity of commerce and the natural water town scenery, so people in the Xiaohe area were lucky enough to take privilege of leading a poetically spiritual life as well as a moderately rich life.

Among dozens of timber shops, Yongda Timber Shop was quite noticeable. It was a two-storied brick building covering the construction area of about 400 square meters. Facing the Xiaohe River, Yongda Timber Shop set up its own quay for loading and unloading timbers. From the mountain the logs were delivered along the running water and assembled at the Xiaohe River. Yongda processed the logs into timbers. In addition to its own shop, Yongda Timber Shop also took the role as an agent between the log shop owners and other timber shops. Timber shops were not allowed to run business unless having the authorized license issued by the local government. In addition to its own tax, it's also the timber shop's work to supervise the buyer and the seller of the logs paying taxes.

Later Yongda Timber Shop developed into a leader in timber business by the means of "buying mountain", a jargon meaning to place an order of buying all the woods of a mountain before the business season. "Buying mountain" was not only a guarantee of high profit. Instead, it might suffer a huge risk. Paying a large deposit in prior to the business season, the shop owner, Mr Yao had to risk the loss of timber production, which was easily attacked by insects and pests. In this way, Yongda Timber Shop was rather a giant wholesaler to decide the market price than an agent merely benefited from the commission. Mr Yao, the founder of Yongda, was reckoned to be a born merchant of timber trade as his name consisting of three " 金 " (gold) and three " 水 " (water)—this was a kind-hearted explanation to his great achievements in timber business, since there was no any clue showing that he had been expected to be a tycoon of timber trade by his name-maker.

Another risk was the special way of transportation. Logs were tightly bundled together into a narrow raft, which could float down the river starting from mountains, passing through the Grand Canal to the Xiaohe area. Such an economic and genius method of log-shipment could only be possible in spring when the river lane got wider and deeper due to the abundant rainfall. Imagine the scenery! Continuous rafts, bundled with logs, found their way down the river in elbowing with the rocks or swirling with the strength of water now and then. To make the raft go smoothly, raft-man were hired. He stood concentratedly on the top of a huge rock with a long bamboo stick, watching attentively. Once the raft was about to be stuck between rocks, he dabbed or pushed the raft with the long bamboo stick, then the raft got extra help and were rescued from the dilemma and continued its journey. Floating for hundreds of miles, it finally completed its journey at Yongda Timber Shop. Only the lucky ones could reach the final line while some of them had rotted as trapped into gaps during the long water way.

The majority of trunks were cut down from the mountainous area west to Hangzhou City, floating down by the Qiantang River, the Tianmuxi River and the Tiaoxi River. When flood came (which was not rare after continuous heavy rain), the rafts would mostly be torn into pieces, as a consequence the timber shop would suffer a great loss. High profit never comes by itself alone. It is always accompanied with high risk. Experienced workers making rafts and sophisticated delivery men controlling the floating rafts took important roles in the chain of timber business.

In addition to Yongda Timber Shop, there were some other timber shops. Hence an association of timber business was organized to formulate the trade rules, to assess the quality, to coordinate the relations between the parties involved (including the association of workers), and to endorse for collective benefits. This association was indeed one of the non-governmental autonomous bodies and was boosted by the business along the Xiaohe River. It was also an evidence of the business civilization in the Xiaohe area.

Today we can find the former site of the Association of Timber Business in the Qiaoxi Historical and Cultural Block.

5. The Dengyun Bridge: A Torturous Road to the Imperial Examination

There was a long road in the imperial examination in ancient China, but the success in the imperial examination was as great as riding and flying on the clouds. An intellectual named Xia Shizheng in the Ming Dynasty passed the final imperial examination for selecting elites and was granted with the highest title of Jinshi, an officially acknowledged scholar, who was ranked at the top level that an intellectual could reach in ancient China. After that, he became an honest official and was loved by the people. His path to the imperial examination began near the Dengyun Bridge, beside which his statue stood. Xia Shizheng's imperial examination road and the name of the Dengyun Bridge can be regarded as a microcosm of the imperial examination system in ancient China.

The way to be a Jinshi was so long, tedious, time-consuming and energy-consuming that only a few of candidates could cross the finishing line. It was indeed a marathon demanding time, money, and the strong will.

A candidate following this educational system had to be deeply involved in studying classics, writing papers and attending exams organized by the local to the national authorities. He started this one-way journey when he was a little boy about 7 years old and spent day and night on exam-oriented study. However, the great deal of time and money he had spent on the long journey was not a guarantee to his qualification of attending the final competition—the national exam in the royal court with emperor as the chief examine.

The Chinese imperial examination system could be traced back to the Sui Dynasty. Emperor Wen of the Sui began to recruit talents from the common people in addition to recommendation from nobles who could be powerful enough to be his political opponents. In fact, Yang Jian was from a powerful family before he took the throne, and as a successful leader, he did not want to become an example of his former peers. In the first year of the Daye (605), the Emperor Yang of the Sui initiated the Jinshike, which was regarded as the beginning of the imperial examination system.This innovative talent-selecting approach later developed into a quite complicated system in Tang, Song, Yuan dynasties. It reached its peak in the Ming and the early Qing dynasties, then went down until it was in the year of 1905. This system, running for more than 1,300 years, was undoubtedly an overwhelmingly important institution that influenced the Chinese people and the whole country. Brief table on the imperial examination of the Ming Dynasty is shown as the Table 5-1.

Table 5-1 Brief Table on the Imperial Examination of the Ming Dynasty

Exam Item	Tongzi Test /Shi	Yuan Test/ Shi	Xiang Test/ Shi(Qiuwei)	Hui Test /Shi (Chunwei)	Dian Test/Shi
Nature	Preparatory test	Screening test	Screening test	Screening test	Honorary title test
Examinee	Tongsheng	Shengyuan (Xiucai)	Keju Shengyuan (qualified candidate)	Juren	Gongshi
Chief Examiner	Head officer of a county/city	Education administrator of province	Senior education administrator or scholar assigned by the central government	Officer of the Ministry of Rites	Emperor

Site	County/city school	City school	Capital city of province	Capital city of country	Royal Palace
Title of the passer	Shengyuan (Xiucai)	Keju Shengyuan (qualified candidate)	Juren	Gongshi	Jinshi - Jinshi Jidi - Jinshi Chushen -Tong Jinshi Chushen
Time	Every year	Twice in three years	the 8th lunar month (Once every three years)	the 2nd lunar month (Next spring of the Xiangshi)	the 3rd lunar month (After the Huishi)

Note: 1. August and February fell respectively into autumn and spring in Chinese Lunar Calendar;

2. The author draw the table according to the comprehensive data.

Now let's go back to the Ming Dynasty and follow Xia Shizheng to understand the far-reaching and difficult system.

Young Xia Shizheng completed the pre-school education in the village and came to the county school to participate in the admission exam for getting the title of Tongsheng. He was intelligent, prepared early, and passed the test. After attending the Tongzishi, another exam held by the county, he won the first place. At a young age, he had the title of Xiucai.

His academic excellence was a great news for his mother. "Born in the peasant family and being an official in the imperial court later" carried the huge dream of obtaining the class transition through the imperial examination. The imperial examination system in ancient China was the country's talent selection system, and the children of poor families who studied well not only meant that they could get the chance to be selected, but also meant that they contributed to the family economy.

Passing the Tongzi Shi was just one step in the imperial examination system. The provincial education administration would organize a knockout academic examination, Yuanshi, which would select candidates for Xiangshi. Xia Shizheng once again ranked at the top and was granted with the qualification of Linsheng, in Chinese "廪生". "廪" means "rice warehouse". As the name suggested, their food and clothing were afforded by provincial government. The Qing Dynasty generally followed the imperial examination system of the Ming Dynasty. A stone tablet engraved *Notifying Shengyuan by Imperial Order* in the ninth year of the reign of Emperor Shunzhi (1652), at the beginning of the Qing Dynasty, recorded the subsidies and expectations: "...offer adequate food and lodge ... All government officials should treat Shengyuan with courtesy, and let them to be talents for the imperial court..." The less excellent or average Shengyuan were called "Fusheng", meaning the students of provincial schools, who paid for their own food and lodging. It could be seen that the term "scholarship" was not unique to western universities, but already existed in junior high school education in ancient China. In general, all boys who passed the entrance exams of the local official school were smart enough. With the official title — Keju Shengyuan, they got the official candidate's qualification of this comprehensive royal education system. It was also the starting point of the road for the ordinary people to the upper class of the society.

Yuanshi selecting Keju Shengyuan was just the preparatory test. From then on, there're three more important exams ahead of Xia and his peers, of whom a few could enter the final court.

The first one was called Xiangshi, or provincial union test. It was organized every three years by several provinces covering the northern area, the southern area and other areas. Usually it was held in the 8th month of the lunar calendar, so it had another name "Qiuwei" . "Qiu" means the season of autumn, and "wei", the small door of imperial palace. So "wei" was borrowed to refer to the booth in which candidates taking examination.

"Wei" also implied the rare chance to the imperial's hall where only high-ranked officials were allowed to participate in discussing national issues in front of the emperor and the glory.

Now Xia Shizheng, a teenager, was whole-heartedly preparing for the Xiangshi. Compared to his fellows, he seemed not to be in great pressure. He was so young while most candidates were in their 20s' and some of them were even older because they had failed the exam several times. Xiangshi was a watershed. The ones who failed were called Xiucai, which means talents with potential. Those who passed were called Juren, meaning that they were qualified to be recommended as officials. "Learning to be excellent and then be an official" was from Juren. Since Juren had the qualification to be an official, Xiangshi was the most competitive and arduous part in the Ming imperial examination.

Xiangshi was a threshold that keep the common people away from those who enjoyed higher social status. A rich man could not gain real respect if he had no academic fame. Even in terms of marriage, he had less advantages than one from a reputable scholar's family. While a poor man could receive that as long as he succeeded in latter imperial examinations. There was indeed a prestige attached to the title of Juren, because the title was the first threshold on the road to official career. The idiom "yiju gaozhong" (一举高中) gave the connections between "Juren" and "ascending" or "high ranks".

What's Xiucai's life then? It was sort of a tragedy to be frank. Year after year they trapped themselves in shabby rooms in the hope of passing the Xiangshi, but the light was dimming out. Therefore, they were often ridiculed as "Xiucai is not useful at all".

Wu Jingzi was a failed candidate of Juren but a great litterateur in the mid-term of the Qing Dynasty. His novel *The Scholars*, ruthlessly lashed the decadent nature of the imperial examination system that hurt a great number of intellectuals. It portrayed a series of pedantic readers and hypocritical pseudonyms who were deeply poisoned by the imperial examination. In the novel, the famous one was *Fan Jin Becoming an Juren*, telling the story of a Xiucai named Fan Jin encountered a series of over-flattering after he finally passed the Xiangshi. The ecstasy passing the Xiangshi after long-term failures drove him insane. Novels were originated from the reality. Wu Jingzi was able to describe the great changes happening to Fan Jin, precisely because he himself had suffered from the failures in the imperial examination for many years. Although he was talented, he led a poor life because he could never pass the threshold of the Xiangshi.

Coincidentally, Cao Xueqin, the author of the greatest Chinese classical novel—*Dream of the Red Chamber*, was also a victim of the imperial examination system. The imperial examination turned into a very strict and stiff system that it finally prevented many talents from fulfilling their ambitions and devoting themselves into the country. It was a real misfortune for Wu Jingzi, Cao Xueqin and their families, but the hardships and discouragements on the road of the imperial examination made them turn to literary creation that was more suitable of showing their talents. Their works are the permanent treasures for the classical literature of China, leaving valuable spiritual wealth for future generations.

Let's go back to Xia Shizheng. Xia Shizheng failed when he took part in the Xiangshi. But he did not lose his faith. He was encouraged by a message that a twelve-year-old boy had successfully passed the Xiangshi and won the title of Juren. This meant that the twelve-year-old boy was qualified to be an official in the provinces. Continuing studying and taking exams was the right way to the ones in the world.

Hard work pays off to those who wait. In the season of osmanthus fragrance, good news of the enrollment announcement of the Xiangshi came when he was 32. We can imagine how tortuous the way was for him! The list of the newly-selected Jurens, coming with the aroma of osmanthus, was also called the Osmanthus Bulletin. And the lucky candidates on the bulletin were described as the ones who held a bough of osmanthus in their hands. It is quite similar to the honorable title of Poet Laureate, isn't it?

Xia Shizheng had no much time to celebrate his victory in the Xiangshi because he must devote himself into the next imperial test—Huishi in the coming spring. Huishi, organized by the Ministry of Rites[①], was a national examination taken by Jurens from all provinces, in which the successors would have the academic title of Jinshi, or Presented Scholar, who would have the chance to be the middle or senior officials. Huishi was held in the empire's capital city, therefore, candidates had to get prepared financially for the long journey to capital. Some Jurens in a poor financial situation (which was easily inferred from the reality that they had endured the long-time study with little income) would have to accept the contributions. This was reflected in many literary works. For example, Jia Yucun, an important figure in the *Dream of the Red Chamber*, couldn't go to the capital for the Huishi before he got the financial support from a wealthy gentleman Zhen Shiyin, who gave him the fund as much as the living expenses of an ordinary peasant family for two years, which implied the huge cost of participating the Huishi. Granting funds was certainly an act of kindness, but it also could be seen as an investment in human resource. After all, as soon as Juren passed the Huishi and entitled with Jinshi, famous gate would open widely in front of him, welcoming a

---

① The Ministry of Rites: a ministry in charge of academic affairs and disciplines.

new elite with brilliant future.

It was on a morning of the early winter in 1445 that Xia Shizheng was ready for the fate-deciding journey to the capital. Xia, at a dock along the Grand Canal, said goodbye to his wife, children and mother. He could not stay at home for the New Year Eve and the Spring Festival, the most important festival for the Chinese people, because the journey would cost him no less than two and a half months. He boarded a ship in Hangzhou and went north along the Grand Canal.

It was quite natural for Xia to Beijing by ship. Cruising down the canal was slower than riding horse or taking carriage, but it was much more economic. Riding horse and taking carriage had always been the exclusive of the rich. The construction of the Grand Canal and the convenience of traveling by boat made it convenient for ordinary people to travel, study and work. The Grand Canal developed into a very busy shipping channel for China in the Ming Dynasty. Grain, silk, clothes, tea and precious ornaments were carried from Hangzhou and others in the southeast to the capital and the central court, the latter would distribute them to the army and the administration, including senior officials in Beijing for the operation of the country.

Xia Shizheng arrived in Beijing in the late of the first month of Chinese lunar calendar. The capital city was in an exciting and merry atmosphere for the coming new year, and Xia Shizheng could not help missing his families. Although mail-delivery was not efficient, he wrote a letter with his brush-pen to tell his safety arrival. The whole family, as well as his relatives, close or far, were praying for his luck in the destiny-determining exam—Huishi. Later he attended the first session. In the low-roof booth separated for each candidate in the examination, Xia sat on the stool for a whole day and wrote. Occasionally he stopped to rub his

hands for warmth while profoundly thinking over the testing question. It was extremely cold in winter in Beijing, and the booth had no door. It was widely agreed that exam-booth should not be equipped with any door nor a curtain so that it would be convenient for the imperial guards to monitor candidates' minor behaviors. Cheating was dangerous, but the "rewards" could be huge therefore strict monitoring was essential. This test, which was only organized every three years, was so important that once someone passed, it would be of great significance not only to the examinee himself, but also to his whole family and even to the whole village and county. In the villages where "Jinshi" came out, the family ancestral hall was built in a grand manner, which not only showed that the family had good manners and had talents, but also meant that there were disciples in the court as officials, telling the neighbors: "We are a respected family, and can not to be underestimated."

On the 12th and 15th of the second month in the lunar calendar, Xia Shizheng attended the next two sessions of the examination. He did well. Now he had a new academic title "Gongshi". But he couldn't return home to tell his family the good news, because there was another exam waiting for him, which was called Dianshi.

Dianshi, as the name suggested, was hosted honorably and ceremonially by emperor. The test, was set on the royal court, where the empire and his senior officials discussed major issues of the country. Hence the site of this test was granted a sense of honor: Candidates were no longer the ordinary people, but the students selected by emperor, the elite of the country, shouldering the future of the country.

This pride occupied every contestant's mind and some of them were strongly motivated while some did not perform well as they were supposed to be.

Xia Shizheng, again, was proved to be a one-of-ten-thousand intellectual: He ranked the 12th in the final exam. He was honorably bestowed the academic title Jinshi Chushen. Some of the new recruits were assigned to be magistrates, while others were incorporated into the Hanlin Academy, the national highest academic institute, as reserve talents. In short, Xia Shizheng began to step onto the road to the imperial examination in his childhood and ended more than twenty years at his middle age. He was already one of the luckiest winners.

On the long journey, he was one of the few people who stepped into the final game field and crossed the finishing line. It was a great triumph. A triumph admired by all the intellectuals. It was the fortuitous triumph of the necessity of years of hard work.

The good news was spread to his hometown. Xia Shizheng was assigned as a senior official in the Ministry of Justice by the emperor. As a responsible supreme judge of the Ming Dynasty, Xia Shizheng worked diligently and won reputation around the country.

To memorize and praise him, also to show the origin of the prestige official, the local people built a bridge nearby the dock where he went on board for Beijing. The bridge was named "Dengyun", which meant riding and flying on the clouds—a sincere wish that he could start his promising and lofty journey of life. The Dengyun Bridge also carried the common people's wish for being protected by more qualified officials who could lead the city or country into prosperity and harmony, because it was not only the emperor who could really bring them prosperity and peace, but also the local rulers. From this aspect, the imperial examination system was quite an effective mechanism to select elites to be the backbones of the giant empire.

6 The Maiyu Bridge: Fish Fair and Fish Culture

Suppose you lived in Lin'an (today's Hangzhou) in the Southern Song Dynasty when there were no smart phones that could locate a specific site and guide you. When you needed some daily necessities, how could you get them without wasting much time in searching for shops and stores on narrow lanes and allies hidden in crowded complex? The smart Hangzhou people at that time found an easy way by naming sites and locations according to the types of the business, which was a great invention that tremendously helped people's daily life in the era devoid of intelligent communication equipment.

For example, Maiyu, in Chinese "卖鱼", meaning "selling fish", indicates that there is a fish-mall around the corner. The Mishi Lane, tells you that grain trades here. There're many other examples, like the Pishi Lane, the Caishi Bridge, the Mashi Street[①] … "Shi", as a noun in Chinese, means a mall or a fair, a place where people sell and buy the things they need; or as a verb, is to buy and sell something. So the Pishi Lane was the place for leather trade; the Caishi Bridge was the vegetable and groceries

---

① Pishi, means leather fair; Caishi, means vegetable fair; Mashi, means horse fair.

market; and on the Mashi Street you could buy a horse and dressed it with a beautiful saddle and horseshoes... Guess where you could meet the senior officials of the Southern Song Dynasty in the early morning? Just went straight to the southern area of the city and waited at a place named "Guanxiang Kou", meaning lane of official residence (similar to the Downing Street in the UK), where the route to the emperor's court was within a walking distance.

The area around the Maiyu Bridge was a flourishing fish fair, where fishing boats from the upper stream north of the Grand Canal, departing from water-side villages and flowing on brooks in counties, all gathered here to sell fish.

Let's get back to a summer day of 1163, when the Southern Song Dynasty started a new reign of Emperor Zhao Shen. The emperor, who was full of ambition to reform the administration, promoted Lu You[1], as a middle official and granted him with "Jinshi Chushen" title. The good news flied into Lu You's house, his cook, Xia Ma[2] got to the Maiyu Bridge to buy fresh fish for a good meal. In China, a great news is usually followed by a feast, and a feast without fish is unqualified. Fish was not rare in the Jiangnan Area which was due to the abundant rain and rivers. However, it was a scorching day and Xia Ma had to go to the big fish fair for the best fish.

Dozens of fishing boats stopped near the Maiyu Bridge; some fishmen sold fish to the local people while most of them made a whole sale to the local fish stores.

---

[1] Lu You: is a famous poet in the Southern Song Dynasty. He lived in Lin'an (today's Hangzhou) in most of his life.

[2] Ma: referring to an ordinary married woman in her middle age, especially those who were employed as servants in officials' family or the house of the rich in the past.

Xia Ma firstly walked towards to vendors who put the dried fish and dried shrimp on bamboo trays. On their feet, stood a couple of buckets in which several grass carps and river eels were pushing with each other. These fishes were hooked from sub-streams but seldom from the Grand Canal—the Great Canal was such a busy waterway that no fishman could find a calm water area waiting for sensitive fish being caught.

Neither the dried shrimp nor the small fresh fish was to Xia Ma's satisfaction. Knowing the disappointment of solicitous vendors, she declined their offers by a consoling response of "well, well, maybe next time" and stepped towards a bigger fish-dealer's store. As soon as she stood in front of the shop, she got a very enthusiastic greeting from a young shop assistant. "How are you! Aunt Xia! How gorgeous you look! I dare say you have definitely great news! Aha, your master, Mr Lu, got the title of Jinshi! How wonderful! Isn't it definitely worthy of a big feast?" After a bundle of joyful small talks, the young man put forward what he really meant to ask: "Can I help you? Look! Fresh fish!"

He looked so zealous that Xia Ma could hardly decline anymore. "Harmony generating wealth" is a practical truth that Chinese businessmen believe.

The young man was called A Hui, an ordinary name for ordinary young men in China. He had been working in the fish shop owned by one of his relatives for five years. The first three years of his working was not paid off, and this was a widely established rule of apprenticeship: free food and accommodation, but offering security and miscellaneous work. It sounded like a drudgery to be exploited, but it was much more profiting in business than farming. Since Hangzhou was designated as the national capital by Zhao Gou, commerce flourished more. Although Emperor Gaozong of the

Southern Song Dynasty was criticized by historians in resisting invasion of the Jin, his awareness and policy of advocating "city commerce" laid a good foundation for the prosperity of the southeastern provinces.

At 13, A Hui left his parents in a waterside town to be an apprentice. China was an agriculture-based country, and the emperor followed the practice of ploughing the field in spring as a ceremony to encourage farmers and peasants, but A Hui's parents believed that it would be easier to make a fortune in business in the metropolis crowded with senior officials, reputable intellectuals, and rich merchants. After 3-years' apprenticeship, his rewarding consisted of a monthly-based subsidiary, which was a small figure, and a bonus given at the end of year. The owner of the store, like any other smart businessmen, would distribute bonuses according to the performance of the staff. Of course, the bonus was supposed to be much more significant than the fixed daily-life subsidiary. Bosses might be generous or thrifty, merciful or greedy, but all of them were aware of the value of a good employee. In order to reduce the turnover of employees and reduce the cost of employment, bosses usually did not give employees long vacation, because long holidays meant increased possibilities for employees to change jobs in addition to the coordination of employment. So, until the end of the year, when everyone went home for reunion, the guys did not get bonuses.

The coming new year would witness A Hui's 19th birthday. And the coming Spring Festival was more than an annual vacation for family reunion. Actually, he would marry his 16-year-old fiancé. The engagement wedding was held two years ago. It was a popular consensus that it took a lot of money to get married. Saving money to marry and have children were the major events that young men had to complete. Therefore, after

以
桥
之
名

In the Name of Bridges:
The Chinese Cultural Codes on the Grand Canal（Chinese-English Bilingual）
大运河上的中国文化密码（中英双语）

138

the engagement, A Hui had always been diligent—having a bride was his biggest motivation, and this motivation also made his diligence joyful.

His sincerity and joy from the bottom of heart was of greatly positive infection. Xia Ma, in a good mood, finally picked and chose a couple of reddish carps. In Chinese culture, a reddish carp has always been the totem of fortune and luck, particularly meaning a big leap from the lower class to the higher one. Getting the title of Jinshi was widely believed to be a guarantee for such a soar among the Chinese people. Carp tastes not so delicious but is still necessary today just because it is the wish for good destiny. Today, carp remains a popular element on New-Year Painting, on which a chubby boy is holding a big and glorious carp in his arms, laughing to bare his teeth. Such a boy-and-carp painting is a direct wish for fortune, hanging on the most prominent place in the guest hall. This is the power of the traditional culture.

Fish, in Chinese pronounced "yu", is a homophone of the Chinese character "余", meaning abundance or more than enough, hence it is taken to be a metaphor. That is why there must be a fish-dish of the feast on New Year' Eve. In some areas, there is a fish-dish kept as a whole without being touched a bit. Now, dear readers, can you understand why Xia Ma bought two fish?

The Beixin Pass: A Major Tax Bureau Seeing the Prosperity of the Grand Canal

With the Grand Canal being the economic artery of the empire, the Ming Dynasty set up 7 official tax bureaus along the canal, and the tax from shipments became the main resource of the state coffers. The Qing Dynasty followed the system. Since ships couldn't pass through the sluice or the water gate before paying tax, tax bureaus along the Grand Canal was called "Pass". The Beixin Pass, a tax bureau located in Hangzhou, was a typical one from which we can get a glimpse of the operation of tax affairs in the Ming and Qing dynasties.

The Beixin Pass was recorded to collect annually more than 10,000 taels of silver in the 25th year of the reign of Emperor Kangxi in the Qing Dynasty, which was about 8.8% in the national revenue. It climbed up to 123,053 taels in the reign of Emperor Guangxu. It meant that the Beixin Pass was more and more important.

The Beixin Pass, located about 5 kilometers north to the center of Hangzhou, was built in 1450, the 1st year of the Jingtai period of the Ming Dynasty. The Beixin Pass was actually a complex consisting of a bridge, an official mansion, and a couple of water gates. Vendors and merchants had to pay the toll fee for crossing the bridge, while ships were required to go through the water gates set for levying tax. Ships, boats and sampans crowded on the Grand Canal and congested around the pass, so it gradually became a breeding ground for corruption as well as a vital business spot. Time was money; and money made time run faster. Impatient ship-owners and merchants knew this very well, and they, of their own accord or not, bribed the pass officials to expedite the proceeding of formalities. In particular, the river fresh fish, vegetables, and fruits produced in the Jiangnan Area couldn't resist hot or rainy weather, and a slow process would cause considerable losses to owners. The Ming empire set up seven main passes along the Grand Canal, and the bribery was almost filled in every pass. Ironically, officials in charge of pass were, at least at their early ages, the disciples of Confucianism, so they were supposed to be upright, uncorrupted and should refuse dirty money. The vendors and merchants knew what the officials worried about, so they sent them calligraphies, paintings, porcelains, instead of money.

Grain and goods were taxed according to their quality. This rule sounded reasonable, however, it was deflected in practice and led to corruption. Tax rules were exquisitely worked out, at the very beginning, to seek the fundamental fortune for huge empire, but the prudent rule-makers might not foresee that the leaking of great profit was made by sophisticated watch-dogs themselves. The secret of being an unknown thief of the empire was hidden in the process of grading grain and goods. Unlike modern quality control system like "ISO 9000" or other benchmarks, the Ming and Qing dynasties established quality criteria which was most likely to be dependent on the integrity of the inspector officials, however, they were not so loyal to the oaths they had pledged in their early days when entering the official circles and following Confucianism principles of morality and probity.

The officials in charge of tax affairs could milk the rewards by degrading the grain and goods, postponing, or even asserting the shortage of the amount. Where's the benchmark? It's on their tongues. What's the measurement instrument? It's their eyes. Once the scale of their heart lost balance, there was no justice for the taxpayers.

Another resource of corruption lied in the types of ships. According to the Ming Dynasty's law, the Grand Canal was mainly serving as the national shipping of tribute grain—Caoyun, i.e. tribute grain delivery ships enjoying privilege when going through the passes. In busy days of levying tax, the private ships had to give way to the official ships. Besides, the official ships could enjoy preferential tax rate, even tax-free. This was not a secret to merchants, so some of them managed to hire official ships for Caoyun with official flags waving arrogantly in the air, claiming their privileges. Naturally, the merchants got the benefit at some cost.

Merchants were not the only people who had to bribe the pass officials. In fact, some local officials who undertook the task of collecting tribute grain (Caoliang) were involved in the disgrace, though they might not mean to do so at the beginning.

Grain piled on ships, being exposed to moisture from continuous rains, could easily go rotten, like color-fading, sprouting, turning rotten, or losing weight. Either the shortage in amount or flaw in quality would lead to political risk for the officials in charge, such as severe condemn, deposition, or losing their lives as the worst. In order to protect themselves from such tragedies, those officials took a wrong but accessible approach: buying the privilege of levying tax and getting high-rank in grading the grain.

Hence a net of corruption was knitted, including the directors of ships for Caoyun, the local officials, the pass officials. None of them was innocent and none of them was of strong guilty.

Even the emperor had a blind eye to these under-table deal. It was recorded that Emperor Kangxi once enquired the minister of the Yellow River and the Grand Canal Administration who had sophisticatedly conducted the tribute grain shipments and the maintenance project on the Grand Canal. Satisfied with the minister's performance, the emperor, who looked in amiable mood, put forward a question out of sudden: "Have you ever embezzled funds? Have you made a fake account?" With a subtle smile and a sharp light in his eyes, the emperor was staring at his subordinate, to whom the emperor distributed a huge portion of national revenue at his disposal.

The national defense at boundaries, the hydraulic maintenance project, and the tribute grain delivery, were the three utmost concerns of Emperor Kangxi. As a daily reminding he even wrote the three problems on the pillars of the administration hall. Despite he had the powerful commanding over the troops and got the military triumph in defeating the rebellions in remote southwest area or the ambitious aggressors on the northwest border line, Emperor Kangxi, a leader growing up as a son of a nomadic tribe on the vast prairie, had no experience living by the riverside nor self-confidence in controlling the national river affairs. Though he was reckoned as a mighty emperor, he was not sure whether his decrees had been sincerely abided with. He was not sure whether his power was far-reaching as it supposed to be; in other words, he was not sure of his ministers' faith and integrity.

Scared when hearing the emperor's inquiry, the minister made a bold decision instantly and instinctively. He confessed with his knees knelt down: "Your Majesty, Your Great Majesty, I confess, I have done some fake accounts." Not daring looking up, he crouched on the black brick ground, waiting for Emperor Kangxi's fury. A dead silence. Being sweating, he managed to control his shivering, and added: "I make some fake accounts to process the delivery of the tribute grain."

His strategy proved his sophistication in serving the emperor. Pleased with his frankness, Emperor Kangxi was convinced with his minister's loyalty instead of fooling him. This short conversation ended up with the emperor's laughter showing the solicitude and gentle warning to those officials. After all, the emperor was aware of the fact that he was not absolutely free from the disgrace and the corruption in the tribute grain delivery.

During the Daoguang period of the Qing Dynasty, the transportation of grain withered for many reasons. After several disputes, with the rise of sea transportation, Emperor Guangxu issued an edict in 1901 to officially abolish the Caoyun.

Today, the present Beixin Pass site can give us a glimpse to the tax along the Grand Canal more than 500 years ago, but the detailed structure of the Beixin Pass can only be found in the papers of scholars. In the Ming and Qing Dynasty, the building complex of the Beixin Pass was arranged symmetrically, with five entrances along the central axis, and ancillary facilities such as the offices of the staff and the inner studies on both sides. At the very front of the Beixin Pass stood a ten-meter-high drum tower. Behind the rail was tax bureau, facing the canal, indicating that this was the boundary. The vestibule was divided into three chambers, and when you entered, you could see the main hall, which were also three chambers. There was a small hall behind the main hall that served as a reception room. Next to the reception room were study room and library. There were five lofts behind the main hall, overlooking the small pond. The left of the main hall was the living room of the chief officer, as well as the rooms of the assistants and servants. On the right side of the main hall was a warehouse, which was used to store grain that hadn't been taxed, as well as five offices; and officials who had not yet completed their work were not allowed to leave the offices at will. There were two offices where clerks handled the grain tax registration, called Wufang, meaning the rooms surrounding the main hall.

It was interesting that outside the ritual gate there was a temple for the local God of Grain, sitting in the light incense and enjoying worship from the bureau officials with fruit and delicacies. Officials in the Ming and Qing dynasties, as we learnt from the precious chapter "The Dengyun Bridge", usually were successful candidates in the imperial examination which advocated Confucianism study. Although the officials were educated in Confucianism and were familiar with the teachings of Confucius — "Confucius dismissed the discussion of the odd", they bent deeply in front of the idealistic Grain God made of clay and openly prayed for good luck. The public worship was not a belief contrary to the Confucian teachings, but as a flexible adaptation under the pressure of the great reality. Food production in underdeveloped agricultural societies was largely dependent on the climate, and the grain harvested after hard work were expropriated as the Caoliang and became national strategic materials. It was important for officials who handled the tax on the Caoliang. Improper storage or unfavorable weather would cause significant losses of the Caoliang. Therefore, officials openly held worship ceremonies, not only as a manifestation of the simple desire to be protected by the immortals, but also as a way to warn all the officials of the importance of tax. In a sense, the belief in immortals and the fear of the law are the two sides of the same management system.

The Fuyi Granary: Remains of Food Reservoir System

Let's leave the Beixin Pass and continue going south along the Grand Canal, and soon a special white cylindrical building appears on the east side of the wide river, with two recognizable Chinese characters " 富义 " on the wall. This is the Fuyi Granary, which has the reputation of "the granary of the country", and is an important relic of the grain transportation and storage system of the Grand Canal.

As a man-made river, the Grand Canal was from the very beginning designed to undertake the delivery of the grain from the south where rice-production was abundant to the north where the imperial court dwelled. In ancient China, imperial power emerged originally in the north, with its capital on the plains nearby or along the Yellow River. Main feudal sovereignty, from the earliest Qin Empire to the final Qing Dynasty, situated the capital in the vast northern land. Xianyang of the Qin Dynasty, Daxing and Luoyang of the Sui Dynasty, Chang'an of the Tang Dynasty, Bianjing of the Song Dynasty, Dadu of the Yuan Dynasty and Beijing of the Ming Dynasty and Qing Dynasty, all of these metropolises were typical northern cities both in geography and in culture.

This tradition of establishing the capital city in the north helped the north grow gradually into the political center of the country, hence the huge imperial administration were set up in the northern cities, and later more huge auxiliary bodies were established. As a result, the people who operated the giant mechanism, including the emperor and his ministers, officials and servants who served for the imperial family, as well as the staff of the central government at all levels, the royal troops, and all kinds of people, needed a lot of food. Food also serves as the ministers' salaries. During the Warring States Period, all countries generally adopted the system of taking grain as official salary and subsequent dynasties continued and developed this tradition.

Though the north area enjoyed the political advantage, the country had to rely on the south for the grain. As an old saying goes, "Food is the paramount necessity of people, and grain is the basis of a state." The increasing demand for grain became the utmost concern of the empire. How and where could the empire get adequate grain? The two emperors of the Sui Dynasty, Yang Jian and his son, Yang Guang, casted their eyesight to the vast places south to the Yangtze River. Thanks to the abundant rainfall and the fertile earth, the south area had become the dense-inhabitant area, where people developed a grain-based agriculture as well as fishing and silk-weaving.

The great project of building a canal hence came to the mind of Yang Jian, the initial emperor of the Sui Dynasty. No sooner than he set up the Sui Dynasty, he asked his talent minister Yuwen Kai to preside and design a canal connecting the natural rivers and brooks between the capital Daxing and Tongguan (an important military fortress). This canal, named the Guangtong Qu (the Guangtong Ditch), was built to improve the production of grain, as well as reduce the negative impact of the drought.

The second (also the last) emperor of the Sui Dynasty, Yang Guang, continued his father's scheme to build a thorough in-land water transportation system. The young and ambitious emperor, who once had governed a rich city Jiangdu (now known as Yangzhou), a harbor on the Yangtze River for ten years, and governed its neighbouring area for another nine years. His wife, a princess of the previous dynasty growing up in the Jiangnan Area, influenced him with the Jiangnan culture. Yang Guang appreciated the culture and civilization of the Jiangnan, and had an intuitive understanding of the production capacity in this area. Jiangnan's richness impressed Yang Guang so much that in the year of 605 when he held the imperial throne, he decreed to build a southward canal connecting the Yangtze River with the Qiantang River, from Jiangdu to Hangzhou, which was call the Jiangnan. Thus the Sui-Tang Grand Canal was basically formed.

The Sui-Tang Grand Canal was centered with Luoyang, the east capital city of the Sui Dynasty. Hence, bulk shipments including the tribute grain from the south to the north became reality. The Sui Dynasty completed the water transportation system connecting the north with the south in the vast country, but the great project didn't promise the longevity of the empire, and the Sui did not fully enjoyed the fruits of this artificial water conservancy project. The Tang Dynasty, which replaced the Sui Dynasty, continued the canal excavation project and developed it into a nationwide water transportation system. Pi Rixiu, a poet in the late Tang Dynasty, once made a fair assessment of the Grand Canal in the Sui Dynasty. On one hand, the excavation of the canal was so costly that it even expedited the collapse of the Sui; on the other hand, the Tang

Dynasty's thousands of miles of water commerce depended on the smooth flow of the canal. Pi Rixiu even compared Yang Guang's construction of the canal to the feat of the ancient Chinese water-control sage Dayu.

In the middle period of the Tang Dynasty, the Sui-Tang Grand Canal carried grain utmost to 3 million dans[①] a year from the south to the capital city of Chang'an. This grain was specially called the Caoliang referring to the shipment of grain via water route to the capital.

The amount of Caoliang continued to increase, and the construction of the canal was further developed. Around the Grand Canal, small canals were constantly being made, gradually connecting sections of the canal. The Yuan Dynasty shorten the Grand Canal by dispelling Luoyang as the center so that the length of the canal reduced to about 1,800 km from about 2,700 km in the Sui and Tang Dynasty. The around 1,800-km-long canal was later called the Beijing-Hangzhou Grand Canal, the Grand Canal for short. By the end of the Yuan Dynasty, the Beijing-Hangzhou Grand Canal finally became a complete system of water transportation flowing through most of the eastern land in the country. Later generations of the Ming and Qing dynasties, as the population grew, relied more on the Grand Canal for grain transportation.

During the Ming Dynasty, the average amount of grain transported through the Grand Canal was about four million dans per year. Before Emperor Guangxu of the Qing Dynasty abolished the Caoyun in 1901, the Beijing-Hangzhou Grand Canal was undoubtedly the economic artery of this vast empire.

Along the around 1800-kilometer Grand Canal, a variety of barns

---

① dan, a volume unit for grain in ancient China. In the Tang Dynasty, 1 dan is equal to 79.32 kg.

were set up to store grain. These barns, differing from size and functions, were the important grain reservoir and adjustment system in ancient China.

The Chinese government set up the grain storage system to regulate grain price, relieve people in famine, prepare for natural disasters and keep the country running stably. Marco Polo praised this system: The emperor would collect grain and store grain in large granaries for three or four years at the time when the grain was too much and the price was low. When the price of grain went too high, the stored grain would be sold to people at a lower price.

For thousands of years, people have been prayed for favorable weather and abundant harvest. The granary preparing for disasters could date back to the Spring and Autumn Period at first, then appeared officially in the Western Han Dynasty. This granary system reached to grand scale in the Sui Dynasty and the Tang Dynasty, which was described as the "storage covering the whole nation". According to different locations and functions, it consisted of a series of granaries, including Zheng Cang (the Main Granary), Zhuanyun Cang (the Transfer Granary), Tai Cang (the Royal Granary), Changping Cang (the Balance Granary) , Yi Cang (the Charity Granary), etc. The Main Granary was the most important grain granary; the Transfer Granary was a temporary storage granary for grain transshipment; the Royal Granary was specially used for the royal; the Balance Granary was used to store grain to adjust grain prices; and the Charity Granary was usually built and maintained with donations from the local gentry, while the other granaries were built and managed by the central or local government.

The efficient operation of the imperial granary system was helpful for the government to effectively run the state by relieving the starvation and seasonal famine as well as supporting the national troops and officials.

How was the whole barn system operated?

The Main Granary was the central warehouse of the country, which was usually set up in the main grain-producing areas, and assumed the function of the strategic grain. The Transfer Granary, as the name suggests, was used to transport grain. The Transfer granary was usually built along the Grand Canal. The Royal Granary, located in the capital, was for royal storage of grain. The Balance Granary was a remarkable initiative. The Western Han Dynasty set up balance granaries to achieve a balance between supply and demand by adjusting grain price. When the production was more than demand and the price went down, the Balance Granary purchased grains to store. When the natural disaster resulted in poor production, the stored grain went into the market to lower the price. By means of storing abundant grain, the Balance Granary benefited the peasants and the stability of the society.

The Charity Granary could be dated back to the Sui Dynasty. Floods made people suffer from famine frequently, which led to the emergence of charitable warehouses. The Charity Granary was not set up by the government, but was donated by the people. The grain in the charity warehouse was only distributed to the local people when there was a famine, especially caused by the extreme weather. In the Southern Song Dynasty, Zhu Xi, the leader of the national scholars at that time, proposed the establishment of charity granary in the countryside. This attempt proved successful, and as a result, charity granaries spread throughout the country, saving poor people in remote villages from starvation.

In the Ming Dynasty, there were five major transfer granaries respectively in Tianjin, Linqing, Dezhou, Xuzhou and Huai'an. By the

Qing Dynasty, the transfer granaries in Linqing and Dezhou were the most durable and effective ones. The transportation of grain on the canal was closely related to the development of city. In the case of Linqing, its prosperity depended to a large extent on the transportation and storage of grain. At that time, when the Linqing Gate and Huitong Gate in Linqing were opened or closed, some grain ships unloaded grain and stored it in Linqing. Most of the grain from Henan that was transported through the Weihe River while the grain of Jiangsu and Zhejiang transported through the Huitong River were stored in the warehouse of Linqing for the capital. In addition to transporting grain, grain ships also carry beans for horses, as well as special products called "Tu Yi"(local specialties), which was arranged by the imperial court to increase income of the Caojun, the army protecting the Caoliang, who were equipped to guard long-distance grain transportation, and this arrangement also promoted the exchange and circulation of materials between the north and the south.

During the period from Yongle to Xuande period (1403–1435) of the Ming Dynasty, the granary of Linqing reached its peak, with the reputation "the first granary in China". The cargo throughput, transportation volume and strategic position of the warehouse were much higher than other barns along the Grand Canal. With the increasing storage and transshipment of grain, Linqing had also developed from a small town to a prosperous city. A new class of citizens emerged, and their spiritual and cultural needs contributed to the prosperity of the cultural and entertainment industry. Many famous novels and operas have rich Linqing elements, such as *The Plum in the Golden Vase*, a large number of storyline with the background of Linqing. *The Legend of Awakening Marriage, Liao Zhai Zhi Yi, The Travels of Lao Can* and so on, have a large number of characters from

以
桥
之
名

In the Name of Bridges:
The Chinese Cultural Codes on the Grand Canal（Chinese-English Bilingual）
大运河上的中国文化密码（中英双语）

152

Linqing, in which the vivid scenes are from Linqing. From singers to merchants, from wine stores to shops, from knights who are eager for justice and righteousness to the richmen who seek to raise money, all of these show the prospering Linqing because of the canal. The corruption and helplessness of grassroots of warehouse presented in works also show the diversity of human nature in the pursuit of interests.

There was a famous granary complex along the Grand Canal in Hangzhou, between the Jiangzhang Bridge to its south and the Gongchen Bridge to its north. The granary was built in the reign of Emperor Guangxu in the late years of the Qing Dynasty. Being sponsored by the local celebrities and generous business men, the construction of the granary was presided by Tan Zhonglin, the governor of Zhejiang. It was named "Fuyi", meaning richness and righteousness, conveyed the Confucian morality that "being rich and being merciful". Covering an area about 8,000 square-meter and a total construction area about 3,000 square-meter, the Fuyi Granary was a complex of barns; its affiliated constructions included a greeting hall, a grain-sunning ground, rooms for clerks and meetings, over 50 barns about 20 square-meter laid in four rows, and several rooms for processing grain into rice.

Granaries were not made for canals. However, after the Grand Canal was successfully made and took the utmost role of delivering grain, granaries became the important facilities for people's living and social stability. The Grand Canal gave granary a special strategic position, and the granary became an integral part of the development of the Grand Canal. Without granary system, the transshipment and storage of grain would be impossible. In addition, the efficient storage of food set people free from the fields where they worked, allowing them to engage in other livelihood.

Granaries brought in delivery and distribution center, and administration body, then towns came into being. Gradually, more people came here and commercial activities occurred, and then urban agglomerations and citizen classes emerged. It's appropriate to say that the granaries gave birth to the colorful and splendid flower of the human civilization.

The Jiangzhang Bridge: Secrets of Emperors' Visits to the Jiangnan Area

The Jiangzhang Bridge, meaning that the river water is climbing as high as the bridge, is located at the center of the Grand Canal in Hangzhou. With a span of about 95 meters in length and about 20 meters in width, the bridge links the Dadou Road on the east bank and the Hushu North Road and the Xinyi Fang on the west bank. There were tales that the tide of the Qiantang River could reached here, and it was the origination of the name "Jiangzhang".

The supporting walls of the bridge (abutments) on the left and right sides are carved with relief sculptures of Emperor Kangxi and his grandson—Emperor Qianlong. Both are by far the most familiar emperors for the Chinese people. Their legendary stories have been written into many novels and adapted into hit films and television dramas.

Before 1911, there were 494 emperors in China; and most of them for the ordinary people were strangers who only existed in the historic archives, why were the two emperors mostly known to the public? Kangxi and Qianlong were not just the names of two great emperors, the supreme commanders of the army and the supreme leaders of the state; they were not just symbols of the imperial power in the solemn imperial court in the huge Forbidden City. They have been living in the vivid stories passed down by the common people, who even added imaginary details, when pointing proudly at a rock carved with several characters and the author's name, Kangxi or Qianlong.

In Hangzhou there are a large number of calligraphic works made by the two emperors in the form of poem, essay and motto. Their works were engraved into distinguishingly huge characters painted in golden ink on big plaques hanging on pavilions, attics, temples, or on rocks in gardens, woods, hills, or alongside small springs. Were their works of great artistic or aesthetic value? It didn't matter whether the answer was yes or no, because an emperor's hand writing was usually respected for their supreme status, and as a royal member he was undoubtedly educated strictly including being endowed with good aesthetic and literary appreciation. It was said that Emperor Qianlong wrote more than 40,000 poems during his lifetime, some of which were related to Hangzhou.

Local senior officials were eager for the emperor's hand writing, long or short, poem or character, because the hand writing was from the emperor was a manifesto from the emperor was a manifesto of great appreciation, which would somehow turn into a legend through tales in the common people.

The emperor knew well of the value of his writing. Compared to jewelry, land, house and gold, his hand writing cost him least. In terms of honor and glory, however, the emperor's hand writing was of eternal value for an official and his whole family who would pass it down from generation to generation.

Why did the two emperors, Kangxi and Qianlong, leave so many writings in Hangzhou? The answer was closely related to the extraordinary fact: their 12-time visits to the Jiangnan Area.

Today we can get a brief description of their stay in Hangzhou by viewing the story-and-poem walls when going through the Jiangzhang Bridge by boat along the Grand Canal. The west wall is lightly-carved with a five-character poem composed by Emperor Kangxi who expressed his appreciation for the impressive landscape of Zhejiang Province and his satisfaction with the worship that he received from the common people. In front of the wall sits a bust of the emperor, in his imperial gown, looking at the opposite wall which bears the story of his grandson, Emperor Qianlong's 6 exploratory trips along the Grand Canal from Beijing, the capital, to the south-end of the canal, Hangzhou. The architect and designer of the Jiangzhang Bridge must have read Kangxi's mind. It was said that Qianlong was believed to be potentially assigned as a successor of the emperor in his childhood by Kangxi.

Why did the two emperors make so many exploratory tours along the Grand Canal despite of the long distance, long time and high cost? Emperor Qianlong, who made 6 southern tours from Beijing to Hangzhou, recalled: "In my 50 years of being the emperor, there are two triumphs I have made—one is the military expedition to the western area of the country, and the other is the exploratory tour to the south..."

It is partly true that Qianlong sometimes relaxes himself in the beauty and prosperity of the Jiangnan Area, but it is quite unfair to say that the emperor is indulged in luxury and leisure. As recorded in historical documents, Qianlong practiced improving the administration of the giant empire, namely, to decrease local taxes and tributes, to inspect hydraulic engineering constructions, to learn about people's living conditions and look into local officials' performance, to show mercy and appreciation to reputable celebrities and intellectuals, to inspect troops, and to attend the sacrificial ceremony worshiping the common ancestor of the Han people though the emperor himself was one from the Man people. Interestingly, quite a lot of his mercy and appreciation for those celebrities and intellectuals showed by his creative poems and four-character-mottos. Well, these celebrities were not lacking in fortune, and what they wanted was prestige. Writing some calligraphy and poems was the elegant recreation for an emperor, however, it was more a job when he left the central court.

Maybe you are curious why the emperor writes so many.

In a long feudal society, the Han people established themselves as the masters of the vast territories. "It's easy to win the world, but it's hard to win people's hearts." The Qing emperors took large territory of the country from the previous Ming Dynasty, a total regime of the Han people. The new comer realized that they had to learn the lessons from the Yuan Dynasty, also a regime of the non-Han people, which was overturned by the Han people not before long. The Yuan Dynasty's short sovereignty was partly because the Mongol emperors disdained the culture of the Han people and Confucianism, which had been the dominant culture since Qin Shihuang. The intellectuals in the Jiangnan Area deeply practiced Confucianism, and most of the gentry insisted that the superiority of the culture of the Han people was incomparable. They denounced the rule of the Qing Dynasty over China as the absurd and complete betrayal of Confucianism—Chinese ideological core.

Of course, the articles and views of these clans would shake the stability of the central court. What did Confucian believers value the most? Not wealth, but fame—the reputation of upholding Confucianism, the reputation valued and respected by emperor, and the reputation relied on by emperor. Therefore, the emperor found the most effective and economical way to appease the clans: giving his hand-writing to a few highly anticipated clans. They might immediately engrave the emperor's personal hand-writing on a plaque and hang it high. For the emperor, this method was simple, but it was very witty, wasn't it? But now, there is a bit of irony.

Kangxi and Qianlong's trips to the Jiangnan Area was far more than sightseeing tours. As one of the giant empires in the world at that time, the Qing Dynasty was on its way to the prosperity during the reign of Emperor Kangxi, and his grandson, Emperor Qianlong, managed to continue this great glory that a feudalism country could reach. Their 12-time visits to the Jiangnan Area, made an irreplaceable role in improving the administration of the country, the whole integration of culture of the Han and the Man people, and people's living condition and in controlling over the empire.

However, The southern tours costed a great deal of money and labour: Emperor Qianlong made a self-criticism in recalling his 6 trips to the Jiangnan Area: "My 6 southern exploratory tours cost extremely high both in economy and people's energy. This is the only misbehavior in my 60-year as an emperor... " He demanded his ministers and senior officials: If you couldn't prevent my successors from the tour to the Jiangnan Area, you would be too ashamed to meet me after death. Actually, his final words were abided by his senior officials and his heirs: Since his resignation in 1795, none of the 6 successive emperors had the long tour in the following years of the Qing Dynasty.

Usually a trip to the Jiangnan Area lasted 3—5 months. Archives recorded one trip: An enormous royal fleet consisting of about 500 ships, about 6,000 horses and 3,000 soldiers, departed from Beijing in the middle days of the first month in lunar calendar and went down the Grand Canal. In the early days of the third month, the royal fleet arrived at the south end of the Grand Canal, Hangzhou, where the royal fleet made a detour and finally returned Beijing after a few months. Such a long and luxurious journey was undoubtedly a heavy burden for the central court, and it's more overwhelming for the local officials, who spared no efforts competing with each other in offering auspicious signs as the token of the emperor's longevity and the stability of the country. And out of question the officials' ambition would be an heavier burden on the local people.

An emperor managing a great country well deserves the reputation of "Wise Emperor" both on people's tongues and historical archives. What is more worth recording, however, in my opinion, is his spirit of self-criticism.

The Desheng Bridge: A Legend of Love and Triumph

"Desheng" means virtue and victory. Its homophone meaning getting triumph. The name of the Desheng Bridge reminds people of the legendary battle between government and rebel in the early days of the Southern Song Dynasty.

In ancient China, the abnormal substitution of regime mainly occurred in two cases: One is the rebellion of powerful politicians of own country; the other is the invasion of opponents from non-Han people or sovereignty. The establishment of the Southern Song Dynasty was due to the latter.

The Southern Song Dynasty was a passive remedy when the original Song Dynasty lost most of its northern territory to the Jurchen people, a regime established in the southern area of the Song Empire. After Emperor Qinzong and his father had been put into jail for months by the Kin, the Jurchens intended to take them as a bargaining chip in exchange for vast land and enormous fortune. The war party objected to surrender. Their proposal to crowning a brother of Emperor Qinzong was accepted, so Zhao Gou stepped onto the golden dragon chair as Emperor Gaozong (1127 — 1162).

Fearing of the invasion of the Jurchens and the humiliation of being a prisoner like his father and brother, Emperor Gaozong removed the capital from Bianjing (today's Kaifeng in Henan Province) to Lin'an (today's Hangzhou in Zhejiang Province), which was in the southeastern area of China. Therefore this regime was historically named as the Southern Song Dynasty.

The legitimacy of Emperor Gaozong was still in doubt since Emperor Qinzong was still alive.

Zhao Gou's justification being the heir to the imperial throne was doubted openly in his third year (1129) as the emperor. He was criticized of being lack of ambition as a qualified emperor should be. He didn't care about leadership and military strategies, instead, he overindulged in magnificence. Trusting eunuchs and authorizing them with confidential administration power, he hurt some loyal generals who had guarded the emperor's families at the risk of their own lives. General Miao Fu and General Liu Yanzheng, who were in charge of the troop safeguarding the capital city, were two of those senior officials.

General Miao and General Liu launched a military campaign. They besieged Zhao Gou, demanding him to hand over the imperial throne to his nephew, a 3-year-old son of Emperor Qinzong. Zhao Gou, now afraid of being beheaded by the furious generals, responded in a very humble way: It is true that I am not qualified for sitting on the golden dragon chair.

Nevertheless, Miao and Liu did not brutally execute the emperor. "What we do is a justice revolution, not a rebellion," they argued. And they were scared of being attacked by other generals, especially the honorable General Han Shizhong. The Prime Minister, Zhu Shengfei, who had yielded to Miao and Liu, strongly suggested that they should persuade

General Han to join in their team.

General Han was born in a village in Shaanxi Province, a northwestern province of China. Joining the army since he was a teenager, he had grown up to be a brave solider and made a great contribution to triumph of battles. To his disappointment, however, he was only granted with a junior title. At the celebrating banquet afterward, Han was attracted by a young woman called Liang Hongyu who was dancing and singing for the entertainment. She expressed her admiration for him and her assurance of his great success. Nothing could be of a great comfort for the frustrated young man but the admiration from a pretty young woman. He fell in love. He learnt that she was an offspring of a general who had been sentenced to death due to a failure in a battle, which overturned her destiny from a darling daughter of a prestigious family to a low social butterfly in the army. Heroism and love coming together, Han took her home as a concubine, regardless of the malicious comments about her previous life. They loved each other deeply. Later, Liang Hongyu gave birth to a son, and both of them were the apples of Han Shizhong's eyes.

Miao and Liu also heard about the romance and believed that General Han would be persuaded by this woman. What did Liang Hongyu do? Hearing this plan, she hugged her son tightly and whole-heartedly, but finally left the boy as a hostage. She went forward to Han's military camp.

She spent a whole night riding a horse towards her husband's camp located in Xiuzhou (today's Jiaxing), about 90 kilometers north to Lin'an. However, she didn't follow Miao's instruction. Nor did she persuade Han to take side with the rebellion troop. Actually she had learnt the Prime Minister Zhu's real intention. She freed Han from hesitation to fight with the rebels. Han's loyal choice led to the failure of Miao and Liu's military campaign near the Desheng Bridge. The Southern Song Dynasty went through a serious crisis which made a foundation of peace and prosperity of the people.

Han Shizhong, for his feat in the counter insurgency, was endowed with "Zhong Yong" (loyalty and bravery) by Emperor Gaozong. As for Liang Hongyu, she was bestowed as "Anguo Furen", meaning the lady safeguarding the nation, which was an peerlessly extraordinary honor for a woman.

Later, Liang Hongyu joined in the army led by her husband. The year of 1130 recorded her another bravery by bumping the drum to encourage General Han's troop to defeat the enemy. During the 48-day battle taking place about 200 kilometers north to Hangzhou, Liang Hongyu, in her armour, jumped onto the high platform, stretched her arms to full length, beaten the huge fighting drum again and again, motivating the soldiers and her husband. After the victory, the emperor awarded her the title of "Lady of Yang Guo". Her image was just like the Joan of Arc in France, or the Nike in Greece.

It is worth noticing that Liang Hongyu was honored as an independent female warrior, instead of the wife in the shadow of her successful husband. In a patriarchal culture that devalued women for many years, Liang Hongyu's efforts and achievements broke the boundary of perception of women and shaped a female legend in ancient China.

For General Han, Liang Hongyu was much more than a woman or a wife. She was his partner, who shared the same value, discussed the plan, risked being wounded and fights together until the last minute. They were soulmates indeed. Growing up in an official's family, Liang Hongyu had received good education both in martial arts and loyalty to the country.

Having suffered the catastrophe in her life, Liang Hongyu developed herself into a strong woman both physically and mentally.

Another interesting issue to discuss is the loyalty to emperor that the officials and generals hold.

The U-turning plan offered by Prime Minister Zhu proved that his yield to the rebellion troop was a fake one, of which only he himself was aware. In the time of crisis, he would rather risk his life supporting the trapped emperor than a 3-year-old puppet emperor held by Miao and Liu. He was also assure of Liang and Han's loyalty to the Song as well as to the emperor.

"Shizhong" means being loyal for generations, and Han Shizhong is a commander loved by tens of thousands of soldiers. He would rather risk losing his son than betray the emperor, although Zhao Gou was not so competent to be a responsible emperor.

In fact, Zhao Gou was not worth his salt since the day when he put on the crown. In the crisis of the Song Dynasty, Zhao Gou was in great fear at the very beginning of being an emperor. The invaders had captured his father and brother, and even insulted his mother and sisters, but they were not satisfied. The invaders did not stop their horses and did not pack their spears. When the loyal generals and ministers were racking their brains in every minute to resist, Zhao Gou, the supreme, was indulged in feasts day and night with his concubines and maidens to relieve himself from the huge terror. Though the discontent was growing among his loyal followers, his luxurious living style was still tolerable because of their simple belief that an emperor was the Son of Heaven, and his privilege was part of the imperial power over all the people.

Obsessed with entertainment and having no interest in political affairs, Zhao Gou handed over the imperial administration to an eunuch Wang.

On the way to the south, the eunuch looted huge quantities of treasures and antiques, and dozens of ships to carry them, while turning a deaf ear to the cries of the people who could not get on board, leaving them to fall into fear of being killed and humiliated by the increasingly approaching invaders.

Miao and Liu declared that the purpose of their military campaign was not to overturn the royal Zhao's reigning over the country but only to give the throne to "real inheritor, the Son of Heaven". It's also necessary to point out that the two generals had never tried to seize the emperor's throne.

The ancient historical documents remarked Miao and Liu's military campaign as a "rebellion to the emperor and his court", regardless of the incompetence and the devilry of the emperor. For most of the officials, it was a prevailing belief to be loyal to emperor, no matter how incompetent he was. They quoted Confucius's teaching, "The emperor is the emperor, and the courtier is the courtier." But Mencius, another famous philosopher in ancient China, took the opposite view, arguing that the common people should be prioritized over emperor, and the interests of the common people should come before the interests of emperor. Of course, for the representatives of the ruling class — the emperor and the king, It was not conducive to their rule. But Mencius had his follower. One of the most successful believer was Wei Zheng, the Prime Minister of the Tang Dynasty, who compared people as water and emperor as boat, and he thought the water could either carry a boat or overturn it. This idea was accepted by Emperor Taizong who created a super flourishing era of the Tang Dynasty with great efforts.

Miao and Liu's challenge to Zhao Gou did not gain support from the ministers and senior generals. Their failure was a consequence of the rigid loyalty to emperor who was treated as the supremacy of the empire.

　　Liang Hongyu and Han Shizhong, brave and faithful, remain alive in popular legends and dramas, and the name of the Desheng Bridge is a practical token to honor their virtue and triumph.

The Chaowang Bridge: A Folk Hero Controlling Flood

"Chaowang", King of Tide, was an honorary title awarded by an emperor of the Tang Dynasty to a man who sacrificed in flood-fighting by the Grand Canal. Like the queens of the Great Britain bestowed her brave and sincere ministers with aristocratic titles, the emperors in ancient China entitled his close relatives and high officials with title of nobility. "King" had the highest position in a fief, but was second to the emperor. In addition to approving suggestions and proposals on people's daily life and agricultural production, the king was also the general commander of the troop protecting the people in his fief. In a word, the king was expected by the common people to protect their lives. Considering the great contributions and taxes devoted to the king, it was full of rationality for common people to bear such an expectation.

Unfortunately, the king was not the Mighty. When the flood comes, the king was no better capable of than a passer-by in the street or a peasant working in the fields. His wealth and power couldn't give him supernatural power.

Fortunately, this was not a secret to his obedient people. Even the Son of Heaven, the emperor, could do little when flood took away everything. Hence, both the king and his people were in urgent need of a hero who could control and conquer the flood, preventing the flood from taking away people's food and life. And this hero, much more mighty than a king or an emperor, was believed to be a divinity, like Poseidon, the God of the Sea in Greek myths.

Well, we've talked enough before introducing Chaowang, the King of Tide.

The King of Tide was honorably and virtually crowned by an emperor, despite that the hero had no any blue blood of a noble family. Indeed, he was not bestowed as the King of Tide until he had sacrificed himself in the roaring flood after continuous efforts to rescue the drowning people. So this is the hero's story.

The hero's name was Shi Kui, a strong and warm-hearted man, good at swimming. When the flood was roaring, he always jumped into the furious river to rescue people with no hesitation. Finally, out of strength, he was swallowed by the flood, leaving even no body. Local people who witnessed his efforts were deeply touched, and reported his bravery deeds to local administration. His story was finally reported to emperor. The emperor, eager for an inspiring model to alleviate the flood problem, which was a very difficult task that few senior officials were willing or dare to undertake, was very pleased to see that the common people themselves had found an epitome. Hence, the emperor entitled the hero as "the King of Tide" and called on people to show their respect for him as far and wide as possible.

And I suppose, by granting the greatest honor that the ordinary people could never dreamed of, the emperor was actually encouraging his officials and people to learn from Shi Kui: You should try to protect yourselves from the flood instead of just relying on the court or the emperor.

Please note that Shi Kui was entitled only after his death. People in ancient China had unanimously belief in gods, divinities, and fairies, and some believed the existence of supernatural power. That's why people built memorial halls for mighty ones, like the utmost valiant and loyal general Guan Yu in the Three Kingdoms Period. But if we take a second thought, we would be a little confused that why the hero was not greatly praised when he was alive.

Well, this could be another secret of the emperor: Only he should be the person in the real world respected and worshiped by the common people. The difference between the emperor and the King of Tide laid in the nature of their power: Emperor possessed the real power in his realm, while the King of Tide received offerings like pork and fruit. "Chaowang", as a clay statue, obviously couldn't taste any bite of the food. Where did all these delicacies go? Some might be kept in the pottery plate in front of the statue of "Chaowang", while others were eaten by bats, crows, and even creatures such as wild cats and weasels. The starving people also took away the offerings, risking being punished by the God of Heaven. In the face of unbearable hunger, it is better to grab real food rather than relying on gods.

Dear friends, do you think that these bold people whose stomachs were stuffed with the offerings dedicated to "Chaowang" could gain the strength to resist the flood?

The Chengdong Bridge: Hearing the Looms' Rolling

The Beijing-Hangzhou Grand Canal runs from Beijing to the south—Hangzhou. At the Wulinmen Dock, the canal turns left. Hence it goes from west to east. Above this section of the Grand Canal, several modern bridges have been built, one of which is the Chengdong Bridge. At first sight, the Chengdong Bridge looks simple and unremarkable, just similar to the common contemporary road bridges. This bridge actually has a unique aesthetic charm. People who cross the bridge by car will not find its creative design, but those by ship will never miss the colorful patterns on the bridge rails (see Figure12-1). The large characters on the bridge rails are eye-catching, though this early ancient Chinese font — Zhuanti is difficult to figure out for the modern people. For people growing up in Hangzhou and the northeast of Zhejiang, these big characters are familiar old friends and can be recognized at sight. Why? Because these characters are all related to silk, which has been an important specialty of Hangzhou over 1,700 years.

Hangzhou has a long history of silk and textile production. Relevant studies state that as early as the Spring and Autumn Period, Hangzhou's sericulture has been vigorously developed. With the migration during the Yongjia period in the late Western Jin Dynasty (265–317), A large number of skilled craftsmen moved to the south area, the sericulture in Hangzhou had been qualitatively improved. Marco Polo described in his travel book that the citizens of Hangzhou enjoyed the convenience of wearing exquisite silk clothes, no need to import like the West. The artistic design of the Chengdong Bridge shows the deep connection between Chengdong and silk weaving of Hangzhou.

Figure 12-1 The Colorful Patterns on Rail of the Chengdong Bridge (2021)

Near the Chengdong Bridge there is a community called the Jishen New Village, which was named after the once largest Jishen Temple in Hangzhou. The Jishen Temple was actually the guild of private silk weaving workshops in Hangzhou, enshrining three major immortals of loom: Emperor Xuanyuan, who received silk from the silkworm goddess; Boyu, the god of skillfully tailored clothes; and Chu Zai, a famous official of the Tang Dynasty who taught the craftsmanship of operating looms. Looking back, looms developed in the east of the city due to the two large rivers — the Qiantang River and the Grand Canal. The calcium-rich soil brought by the Qiantang River was beneficial to the sericulture. In the Sanbao Lock (see Figure 12-2), the Grand Canal connects the Qiantang River, which flows eastward to the East Sea. Hence, the comprehensive water transportation, consisting of the Grand Canal, the Qiantang River, and the East Sea, provides efficient delivery for domestic and foreign trade of silk and silk products.

Figure 12-2 The Sanbao Lock

In the Tang Dynasty, a well-known poet Bai Juyi, who once taking the position of the mayor of Hangzhou, recorded vividly that the young silk-weavers in Hangzhou displayed their crafts and appreciated exquisite designs. As early as in the late years of the Tang Dynasty Hangzhou's silk weaving had been quite developed. During the period of the Wuyue Kingdom (907—978) with Hangzhou as its' capital city, King Qian Liu encouraged sericulture and set up sewing and weaving workshops, which was the initial silk production organization administrated by the government in Hangzhou. In the Northern Song Dynasty, official silk weaving workshops kept growing. A special bureau in charge of foreign trade was set up, and Hangzhou-based silk products took an important role in exportation, selling well as far as to the Southeast Asia and the Arab region. After Hangzhou became the empire's capital of the Southern Song Dynasty, numerous craftsmen and skillful weavers moved here so that the silk-related techniques widely spread. Hangzhou silk became the staple commodity of export in the Yuan Dynasty. The Ming Dynasty witnessed another peak of Hangzhou silk weaving, when a verse described: "Silk-related techniques are remarkable and silk fabrics are popular in the world." The Qing Dynasty set up three Jiangnan Weaving Bureau (Nanjing, Suzhou, and Hangzhou) in the country, of which 4,683 bolts of silk fabrics were produced by the Hangzhou Bureau during the Qianlong period, accounting for 40.4% of the three bureaus', as the first in the country.

The development of the silk weaving techniques in Hangzhou since ancient times could be seen from the Jishen temples in many places in the city. *The Miscellaneous Notes of Dongshe* records: "Hangzhou ranks the first with the quantity and quality of looms in the country." Private silk weaving workshops in Hangzhou were gathered near the Dongyuan Lane and the Genshan Gate, where the rolling of looms could be heard in every family.

On June 1, 1926, the World Expo was held in Philadelphia. What would this dragged-out oriental country—China show at the World Expo that was a fair gathering the most advanced products in the world? What kind of product could this former giant, who had been eroded since the late nineteenth century and was too weak to ride the wave of the Industrial Revolution, present to match this shining world event?

This doubt was proved unnecessary when Du Jinsheng's selection of antique brocade painting Night Tour of Concubines won the gold medal. His landscape-pattern brocades also caught people's eyesight. Among them, there was one showed a vast area of calm water with gentle ripples reflecting the light shadows of soft branches of willow trees and peach trees in blossom along a long causeway, which found its way into the continuous greenery mountains with a splendid pagoda erecting atop one of them. The picture epitomized a vivid and elaborate general view of Hangzhou as a capital of a prosperous ancient empire over 800 years ago and revealed its beauty in the early years of the 20th century with its perfect blend of modern crafts and traditional skills.

Du Jinsheng (1897— 1943) founded Du Jinsheng Silk Weaving Factory. In 1926, Du Jinsheng Silk Weaving Factory had 100 manpower silk looms, 5 spinning machines, and 134 employees. Du Jinsheng even paid costly salary to employ 8 Italians as silk weaving experts, who indeed contributed to the improvement of silk products. It can be said that Du Jinsheng Silk Weaving Factory was a flagship of the silk industry in the 1920s in China.

The success of Du Jinsheng in the silk industry was the fruit of combination: The traditional Huzhou sericulture provided high-quality raw materials; the traditional Hangzhou silk weaving production provided experienced technicians; and Du Jinsheng got modern education of silk production. Du Jinsheng majored in weaving project in the Jiazhong Industrial School of Zhejiang Province, and continued staying at the school as a teacher with his honorary academic achievements. Three years later, in 1922, Du Jinsheng set up a silk weaving factory. His first brocade product was worked out in his teaching practice.

Before the establishment of the modern industrial school, Hangzhou established a sericulture school for women in 1907, where women could learn the techniques of scientific cultivation and weaving, and this school was also managed by women. The students who walked out of the school would become the modern professional women, who were respected by others in that era.

The Bazi Bridge: Chinese People's Totems of Dragon and Phoenix

The sunset casts her final glance at the water of the Donghe Brook, leaving a vast golden veil to shake the reflection of the Bazi Bridge (see Figure 13-1), which is a unique one with a pavilion among all arch bridges stand on the tributaries of the Grand Canal in Hangzhou.

Figure 13-1 The Bazi Bridge
（Painter： Tu Qunfeng）

The Bazi Bridge originally got its name because there was a dike on the Donghe Brook next to it in the east area of Hangzhou. "Bazi" means dike. Though the Gongchen Bridge is unanimously regarded as the symbolic building of the south terminal of the Grand Canal, it is not the final stop on the huge man-made canal. The canal continues its way and meets some other bridges, smaller but helpful. The Bazi Bridge on the Donghe Brook, a branch of the Grand Canal, is one of them.

The earliest archive about the Bazi Bridge was taken in the Chunyou period (1241—1252) of the Southern Song Dynasty, recording that there was a bridge near the dike to adjust the volume of water over 100 years ago. The bridge was called "the Bazi Bridge" at the beginning, then had changed the name several times and finalized as its original name.

Though the history about 1000 years adds glory to the bridge, it is the bridge-pavilion that really enriches its aesthetic value.

In the western legends, Athena bears a crown; Muses have their instruments; Satyr carries deer's horn; Venus is rising from a huge marble-white seashell in the sea. One of the reasons that the goddesses impress their admirers is their particular ornaments with practical function. So does the Bazi Bridge, which makes itself remarkable by bearing a beautiful pavilion.

The pavilion is established in the typical Chinese traditional aesthetic mode: Eight pillars prop up from the four sides of the roof that go up to the main center ridge winding up two dragons on its right and left ends. Four eave-corners erect in a slight arc line, with a bronze bell under each eave ringing liquidly in the gentle breeze. The side-part of the roof looks like the hieroglyphic Chinese character " 山 ", which is borrowed to name the roof as "Xie Shan Ding". The whole pavilion looks light and graceful, with the roof facilitating drainage. It is innovative design suitable for the humid and rainy climate in the Jiangnan Area.

On the center beneath the eave, there hangs a plaque inscribed with Chinese calligraphy " 凤凰亭 ", meaning the Phoenix Pavilion. It is somehow interesting that two dragons, instead of phoenixes, as the name declaring, are occupying on the top of the pavilion.

Dragon is not strange to people who are familiar with the Chinese culture, in which dragon has been the most important totem from the first dawn of the Chinese civilization. They get increasingly familiar with the image of dragon, which can be found as the exclusive embroidery patterns on the emperor's garments, engraved on the huge white marble pillars standing tall and upright in front of the main hall of the Forbidden City, painted lively in black ink on white walls of an ancestral hall in worship of divinities, and winded on the middle-ridge of some temples' halls. Dragon, with its big and round eyes, tremendous and wiggly body covered with squama, and huge and sharp claws stretching in the air, looks mighty enough to be capable of protecting the common people.

In ancient times, dragon appeared in primitive myths as the mighty creature in charge of rain, thunder, water and sea, just like Poseidon in Greek mythology but enjoyed much higher status. Bearing extraordinary expectations, dragon is comprehended as the holy symbol of the emperor, who highlights his supremacy with ornaments of dragon on his garments, daily utensils and his golden chair in the imperial court.

None of the Chinese people have witnessed the dragon in the real life, but the totem of dragon or dragon-worship has been passing down through generations. Dragon-related culture is sort of the mother-theme in the Chinese culture.

To this day, "龙" ("long" in Chinese Pinyin, meaning dragon) is one of the most common characters when naming boys, expressing parents' hope for their son's outstanding ability and bright future. During the 32nd Olympic Games in Tokyo, the captain who led the Chinese table tennis team to achieve excellent results was called "Ma Long". While, women's names and titles often have the character " 凤 "("feng" in Chinese Pinyin, meaning phoenix), such as Wang Xifeng, an important figure in the *Dream of the Red Chamber*, also known as "Sister Feng". For another example, the eldest daughter of the Jia's Family was elected as an imperial concubine, with the title of "Minister of Fengzao Palace", implying her talents superior to that of phoenix. In Chinese traditional culture, phoenix is the highest appraisal and admiration for women.

Phoenix is believed a mythical bird with its three splendid long tail-feathers waving in the air. Crowned with three plumes, adding a peacock-like body, phoenix looks extremely gorgeous and acts in a decent style. Phoenix is an exaggerated model created by the common people learning from the image of bird, which had been long worshipped in many areas in ancient China. As to the reason that phoenix and dragon are matched as a holy couple remains unexplained; maybe, it's just because both of them can fly high in the sky.

Another reason is that they are subtly equal in their social identity. Although they all have supernatural powers, they are not high-level immortals who are in the appearance of human beings. The ones with animal form can only be the servants of human-like immortals. This rule was completely reflected in the mythic fiction *Journey to the West*. After all, myths and legends are mirrors of the real world. The rules governing the real world on earth are the same in the world of immortals. Based on their own experience of their secular life, the ancestors believed that the dragon, as a male, should have a wife, a female.

Phoenix, with its gorgeous appearance and its competence of flying high, became an ideal spouse of dragon. When talking about the marriage, it's funny: Why can't a dragon have a female dragon as its mate? Female dragons must exist. And it is more interesting that the dragon and phoenix couple never give birth to any heirs. I guess phoenix is just the soulmate of dragon!

Well, let's get back to the Phoenix Pavilion on the Bazi Bridge. Like the feminine role phoenix carries, the Phoenix Pavilion has a lady-like style. She stands on the middle of the Bazi Bridge, swiftly and elegantly, and offers an ideal place for people to enjoy their leisure time. Especially on summer nights, amateur singers come to the Phoenix Pavilion to sing songs, sometimes in bel canto-style. Now and then, a mini-band can give a small outdoor concert, and the band members are usually the retired. People will always have artistic pursuits with the improvement of the material life.

There are no walls on all sides of the pavilion on the Bazi Bridge, and under the bridge the Donghe Brook flows quietly. Performing in the pavilion, the melody of the singers and bands sounds more intoxicating. The Phoenix Pavilion in the early morning is a nice venue for tai chi players, who escape from the crowds and vehicles shuttling in the rush hour to seek for the calmness in the mind. Occasionally the tranquility is interrupted by the trumpet of ships or the engine of motorized-vessels, but it would never be deprived of. It is the noise and chaos that will finally vanish.

Legend has it that the pavilion of the Bazi Bridge got its name

"Phoenix" because a flock of the legendary holy birds had been seen assembling and relaxing on the bridge. This is, of course, an imaginary scene. However, in today's spring and autumn, the pavilion often welcomes enthusiastic visitors with huge wings and beautiful white feathers, sometimes gently skimming the water, sometimes freestanding by the brook. They have a beautiful and authentic name—egret.

Compared with the mythical bird phoenix, egrets are the messengers of the beautiful environment and the true friend of human beings in the real world.

The Taiping Bridge: A Manifestation of Traditional Stone Carving

The Beijing-Hangzhou Grand Canal connects the Qiangtang River at Hangzhou. Crossing the Qiantang River, the transportation of water system is called the East Zhejiang Canal, making the East Zhejiang Canal de facto part of the Grand Canal of China. Unlike several world-famous bridges along the Grand Canal, the bridges on the East Zhejiang Canal are not so well known to the world, but they are also of high value in transportation, architecture and aesthetic.

The East Zhejiang Canal flows mainly through Shaoxing and Ningbo. Different from the geographic feature Ningbo bearing as a harbor facing the East China Sea, Shaoxing is a distinctive water town of Jiangnan inner-linked with comprehensive water system, consisting of rivers, lakes, ponds, bays, as well as ports, wharves, dikes, etc. In such a prosperous city that had become a kingdom's capital earlier than Hangzhou, traffic highly relied on boats and bridges. From ancient times to the end of the Qing Dynasty, the construction of bridges had not stopped. According to the local documents, in the end of 1993, there were 10,610 bridges in

Shaoxing. The continuous repair and construction have greatly improved the craft level and aesthetic value of bridges.

The glory of Shaoxing as a capital city could be dated back to more than 2,500 years ago. As early as 490 BC, the capital of the State of Yue in the Spring and Autumn Period, was Shaoxing (then known as Kuaiji). The legendary king, Gou Jian, recovered the prime time of the State of Yue as an independent sovereignty after the slavery life in the stable of the conqueror of the Wu Kingdom. It was an impressive legend full of heroism, iron will and persistence, and even the endless humiliation and desperation would not hinder his ambition to rebuild the State of Yue. Over 1,300 years later, when Qian Liu established a completely new state, he used "Yue" as part of the new name "the Wuyue State" to salute the ancient state. During Qian Liu's reign, Shaoxing gradually developed into a prosperous city with dense population and advanced culture. When the royal family of Song Dynasty escaped from the invasion of the Jin Kindom, the fugitive emperor Zhao Gou at first appointed Shaoxing instead of Hangzhou to set up his temporary palace.

Plenty of experienced craftsmen, workers and literati moved to Shaoxing along with the fleet of Zhao Gou, who in return enriched the city with the diversity of constructions and buildings. Bridges, common hydraulic projects in daily life of a water town, became ideal carriers of their aesthetic thought. The Taiping Bridge is an example displaying the exquisite stone-carving art and the sophisticated construction techniques as well.

The Taiping (meaning the thorough peace) Bridge was initially built in the Song Dynasty, in which Chinese art in painting and engraving had reached a peak. This was quite natural, and a few emperors became talented artists. Emperor Song Huizong was so gifted that he created a new style of calligraphy called "the Thin Gold Style", which combined elegance and power with thin and strong strokes. He was obsessed with painting and had a high taste in Chinese painting. The flowers and birds in his paintings were delicate, and the petals of peonies were overlapped and lifelike. Appreciating paintings requires a lot of patience, sufficient prudence, peace of mind, and considerable technique. An art masterpiece is a miracle invented by genius during the long endurance of loneliness.

Unlike the common single-hole or three-hole arch bridges, the Taiping Bridge (see Figure 14-1) is an outstanding example of multi-span-bridge that combines arch bridge and girder bridge. It is about 50 meters long with one single-hole stone arch bridge and one long stone girder bridge divided into eight section with eight holes. The big ships go though the high arch, while the small sampans use the low girder bridge. The Taiping Bridge, providing efficient traffic with the genius design, was a great multi-functional water conservancy facility. Inside the bridge arch, a narrow pavement was made for ship trackers. With pedestrians on the bridge, ships under the bridge, and ship trackers walking the pavement, it looks like an ancient overpass on the canal. From south to north, from the high arch bridge to the girder bridge gradually descending toward the water, the whole shape of the Taiping Bridge looks like a dragon just diving into the water.

Figure 14-1 The Taiping Bridge
(Painter: Tu Qunfeng)

The Taiping Bridge shows the superb art of the traditional Chinese stone carving. Before carefully appreciating the architectural beauty of the Taiping Bridge, it is necessary to have a general view of Chinese arch bridge at first.

A typical Chinese arch bridge usually consists of four parts: the flat core plate in the center of the bridge, the symmetrical side rails of the bridge, the stone step slopes on both sides, and the arch on the water surface (see Figure 14-2). Among them, the side rails of the bridge are smooth and in a certain width, which has become exhibition panels to display the carving skills of carvers.

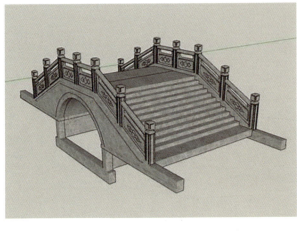

Figure 14-2 The Chinese Arch Bridge

The longest side plate of the Taiping Bridge is richly patterned, as shown in Figure 14-3. The main body of the composition bears relief of elephant with an immortal sitting on it (the upper part of the immortal has gone), surrounded by green pines; and in front of it there is a plant called Wannianqing (meaning evergreen). Above the head of the elephant, there is a large lotus flower in full bloom. The whole pattern is hexagonal, with two lines carved, like lotus petals. The background of the pattern is continuous swastika patterns, which in Buddhism means the eternal life.

Figure 14-3 The Stone Carvings on Side Slate

The stone carvings on the slate directly opposite are generally similar, except that in front of the elephant there is not Wannianqing but auspicious clouds, as shown in Figure 14-4. Another notable detail is that bats are hovering in auspicious clouds. Unfortunately, the upper of this engraved elephant rider turns illegible too.

Figure 14-4   The Stone Carvings on the Slate Opposite

The carvings of both main side slates are rich in Buddhist elements: lotus flowers, continuous swastika patterns, the frame of lotus petals. "Fu" in the "bianfu" (bat), is homonymous with the Chinese characters " 福 " and " 富 " meaning fortune and property. The pine tree and wannianqing symbolize health and longevity. The stone carvings of the pair of main side slates on the Taiping Bridge express the hope of the common people in the world for prosperity and longevity.

On the slates fixed on the side slopes, we can find out simple but graceful engravings. One of the patterns displays a long ribbon, which winds into three ovals and makes the whole pattern an obvious Chinese knot. On the middle of each oval engraved four petals looking like a cruciferous blossom. It is hard to name because of its ordinary shape, and may be osmanthus, which is rich in the Jiangnan Area and conveys good news of imperial examination (as we have read in "The Dengyun Bridge"), as shown in Figure 14-5.

Another side slate bears a pattern of five connecting and crossing circles, with the fifth bigger than the other four and occupying the very center of the pattern. The five-circle pattern resemble ancient bronze coins of China, as shown in Figure 14-6.

Figure 14-5 The Stone Carvings on the Slate of the Side Slope

Figure 14-6 The Stone Carvings on the Other Side Slate

Now we know that the stone carvings of the Taiping Bridge are the combination of Buddhist motifs and secular aspirations. Let's take a look the balusters standing between side slates. At the top of each baluster, each side bears very exquisite relief sculptures, as shown in Figure 14-7. They deserve a closer look, for a cursory glance will overlook the subtle beauty of these stone carvings. Although they look similar at the first glance, they are actually

Figure 14-7 The Stone Carvings on the Baluster

different. These stone carvings include folk musical instruments such as pipa, flute, and sheng instrument; two scrolls; a pair of proposal strips used by officials in the imperial court; large flower baskets carrying lotus flowers; and bells. These seemed no connection. Why did they appear together? Did cavers make them by accident or on purpose? Why are these unrelated patterns carved on the bridge? What did a craftsman bear in his mind when he conceived the pattern?

We may find clues from the Taoism. Unlike the Buddhism that was "imported" from ancient India, the Taoism is more a Chinese local belief. Being invented by Chinese common people, the divinity of the Taoism were from the real world and for the real world. Naturally, their personal belongings have the counterparts in the real world. The widely known group is "the Eight Immortals"(see Figure 14-8), led by Tieguai Li, a cripple who can cure the sickness with an iron stick. The other seven immortals are: Lyu Dongbin, a Taoist priest holding a horsetail whisk; Han Xiangzi, a gentleman playing bamboo flute; Zhang Guolao, a senior riding on a donkey; Cao Guojiu, brother-in-law of emperor in official's garment; Han Zhongli, a heavy-bearded man with his hair pulled up into two buns; He Xian'gu, a beautiful woman carrying a huge lotus; and Lancaihe, a teenager singing and carrying a basket full of flower.

Figure 14-8 The Eight Immortals (Part)

(Painter: Chen Xingyue)

Stories about the eight immortals are very popular, providing rich resource for Chinese folk art like paper-cutting, local opera, stone-carving and new year painting. It is reasonable to say that the handymen and engravers were fond of these modest and good-hearted immortals so that they chiseled the immortals' identity-related-items on the Taiping Bridge, protecting people and ships from misfortune and disaster.

In 2013, the Taiping Bridge was enrolled as an important protective cultural relic unit nationally.

⑮ The Tishan Bridge: Glamour of the Chinese Calligraphy

Located in the Jishan Street of Shaoxing City, Zhejiang Province, the Tishan Bridge (see Figure 15-1) is a single-hole stone arch bridge. The bridge has a total length of 18.5 meters, a height of 3.8 meters, a width of 4.3 meters, and a slope about 20 steps on the bridge body. It remains its appearance when it was rebuilt in 1828. In the imperial examination reference book *Cefu Tongzong*, published during the Guangxu period of the Qing Dynasty, the Tishan Bridge was enrolled as the only representative of the ancient bridge of Shaoxing.

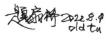

Figure 15-1 Tishan Qiao
(Painter: Tu Qunfeng)

This bridge is said to be related to the great calligrapher Wang Xizhi in the Eastern Jin Dynasty (317 — 420). Wang Xizhi's house was in the Jishan Street. When he crossed the bridge in front of his house, he always saw an old woman selling handmade fans. Having no customers, she looked hopelessly sad. One day Wang Xizhi went across the bridge and saw her again. Having strong sympathy, Wang Xizhi, without asking for permission, grabbed a brush pen and wrote immediately several characters on fans. Seeing her fans stained by this man, the poor old woman was very annoyed and more desperate. However, Wang Xizhi gave her a comforting and confident smile, and said: "Just tell passers-by that your fans are bearing Wang Xizhi's calligraphy and the fans will be sold well at a high price." Half in doubt, the old woman followed Wang Xizhi's suggestion. For her surprise, people gathered soon and her fans were sold out. Since then, the bridge has been known as the Tishan Bridge, in which "ti" means writing characters and "shan" means fan.

An ordinary fan becomes valuable as soon as Wang Xizhi inscribes on it, because Wang Xizhi is a famous calligrapher whose work is precious and hard to acquire.

Chinese calligraphy is integral part of the Chinese culture, and calligraphy is one of the four basic skills and disciplines of Chinese literati, together with stringed musical instrument (qin) , chess (qi) and painting (hua). In imperial examination, Candidates' handwriting was a significant factor when ranking their answering paper. The dashing and beautiful calligraphy would highlight the cultural accomplishment of the writer as well as his thought.

Chinese characters have changed through the centuries and are mainly divided into five categories today: the Zhuan Style used on the seal-carving, the Li Style mainly used on the official documents, the Kai

Style looked regular and square, the Xing Style with smooth script and popular in daily life, and the Cao Style featured with cursive strokes.[①] The Zhuan Style undertakes the standardization of characters of the whole nation in the Qin Dynasty. The Zhuan Style is very elegant with lots of curving strokes and tight-laid frames, but it is too complicated and alike to be distinguished. The Li Style is invented as a simplified style easier to write and read, especially popular in officials who dealt with a lot with documents. The Li Style leads to the emergence of the Kai Style, which looks regular and square in form and lack of change in strokes in the third century. An extremely opposition to the Kai Style is named the Cao Style, which is quite difficult to recognize because the Cao Style breaks the restriction of traditional strokes and layout, showing a challenging charm of writing. In the Cao Style, the last stroke of the first character usually merges into the initial stroke of the next character, which made the writing process much faster. "Cao" in Chinese means "in hurry and hush, no time to write each stroke in a serious and prudent way", so the Cao Style has a lot of cursive strokes that are hard to recognize. The Xing Style hence is invented. The Xing Style, which combines the beautiful precision of the Kai Style with the efficiency of writing of the Cao Style, is widely used by officials and literati and later popular among the common people.

Preface to the Poems Composed at the Orchid Pavilion (*Lanting Ji Xu*), which has been unanimously regarded as the most precious calligraphic work in China, is written by Wang Xizhi in the Xing Style. This great episode is related to the ancient festival named the Shangsi Day, which falls on the third day of the third month of the lunar calendar every

---

① The five categories are also translated as the Seal Script, the Official Script, the Regular Script, the Walking Script, and the Cursive Script.

year. From the imperial court to the people, all gathered to the waterfront to play and wash in order to remove the ominous and seek blessing. Later, the festival became a good day for spring outing.

On the Shangsi Festival in the ninth year of the Yonghe period in the Eastern Jin Dynasty (353), Wang Xizhi, who was the governor of Kuaiji (now known as Shaoxing), and his friends, sons and nephews, a total of forty-one people, gathered at the Orchid Pavilion (the Lanting Pavilion), along a clear stream winding down. They sit casually alongside the stream, watching a cup with rice wine (a specialty of Kuaiji) floating down stream. When the cup was approaching, the nearest man was the one selected by nature. He fetched the cup, drank the rice wine, and then composed a verse. Someone rose to his feet and took a stroll for inspiration. Someone read loudly his verse line by line, pondering while walking. And when he finalized his work, some of his friends would give favorable remarks, others listening and nodding. The pleased author would said "well, well, I'm over flatted" and drank one more rice wine to say "thank you". Then a new round would begin. Such an entertainment became the challenge to one's smartness in thinking, the testimony to one's accumulation in literature, and the amusement in the nature of the early spring. It's also a good opportunity for literati, most of them taking administrative positions, to express their political attitudes as well as literary accomplishments so that they could find out their close friends in literature and allies in the royal court.

When the party was coming to its end that dozens of poems had been composed and many cups of rice wine had been empty, Wang Xizhi, the governor and the highest administrator of Kuaiji, in his delightfulness and great pleasure, worked out a preface to the collection of poems in the Xing

Style.

It was called *Preface to the Poems Composed at the Orchid Pavilion* (see Figure 15-2) . The greatest Chinese calligraphy work was created.

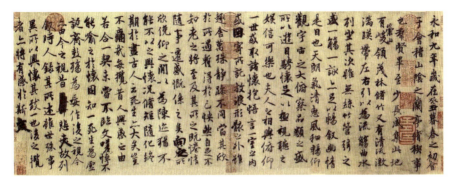

Figure 15-2 *Preface to the Poems Composed at the Orchid Pavilion*

Consisting of 324 characters in 28 columns, this improvisational work demonstrates Wang Xizhi's extraordinary calligraphy art with elegant and fluent strokes. Wang Xizhi also showed his uniqueness and creativity by writing the same character " 之 " more than twenty written in different calligraphy appearance. What's more, the work as a verse itself is also an outstanding one. With selected words and beautiful rhythms, he gave readers a very vivid description of the tasteful cultural occasion.

The story of the Tishan Bridge is widely known, but it does not end. There is a rock near the bridge called "the Duopo Rock", meaning getting hidden from the old woman, and an alley called "the Bifei Lane", meaning throwing out brush pen. After the old woman knew the magical power of Wang Xizhi's calligraphy, she made more fans and waited by the bridge for Wang Xizhi's calligraphy. Wang Xizhi knew that and as soon as he saw her, he hid himself behind a rock and threw his brush pen into a nearby alley.

The anecdote of the fans can be found in *The Book of the Jin*, but the stories of "the Duopo Rock" and "the Bifei Lane" are folk tales. However, the two interesting place names add literary interest to the story of the Tishan Bridge, making people not only feel the charm of Wang Xizhi's calligraphy, but also get a subtle sense of human nature.

The Bridge-Related Folklore: Modest Wishes of the People

It seems to be an universal faith for people around the world, the West and the East, that there are three zones for human beings, namely, earth for the living people, heaven for the holy and hell for the dead. It is interesting that people accept the fact that many of them could only go to hell instead of heaven though they always pray for going to the holy paradise. Yes, it is also a pragmatical thought of the Chinese people.

In Chinese tales, a person can go through the gate to hell only after crossing a special bridge named "Naihe". This bridge is very special, and there is an old woman named Mengpo on the bridge. After drinking her soup, people's souls are no longer bound in the real world, and can be unencumbered to go to hell. "Naihe" refers to a sigh of helpless meaning "I have to convince myself to accept what given to me and I have nothing to do" and it is also a live-with-what-I-have attitude of accepting the inherent destiny. During the Republic of China, Gu Hongming (1857 — 1928), a scholar proficient in both Chinese and Western studies, stated in his famous book *The Spirit of the Chinese People*[①] that Chinese people lead a polite, optimistic and poetic life. The tales of "Crossing the Naihe Bridge" and "Drink Mengpo's Soup" could be considered as examples of Chinese people's spirit.

In the Jiangnan Area of China, there was a custom that women walked through three bridges on the 15th night of the first lunar month. In feudal society, women walked through three bridges to pray for pregnancy. Unlike Britain, where eldest sons and daughters could be family heirs, in ancient China, only sons enjoyed the privilege of inheriting family property and strengthening the family. Therefore, a woman who did not give birth to a son would take great pressure, being regarded as an unqualified wife. What's more, she might be repudiated by her husband. It was a great shame for herself and her parents and brothers.

As a symbol of leading people to communicate with the immortals, the bridge became a messenger for women to pray for having a son. On the night of the Lantern Festival, women dressed up and made appointments with female companions, or simply accompanied by mothers-in-law and sisters-in-law, stepped out of the courtyards of the houses that trapped them day and night, and went to walk through the bridges. The bridge was bathed in the warm yellow light emitted by countless lanterns, and their hearts were lightened by hope.

They whispered to the immortals to send a son then walked devoutly through the bridges. Women certainly knew that their prayer did not guarantee a son in the coming year, but having some faith could always

---

① This book is an attempt to interpret the spirit and show the value of the Chinese civilization. Originally published in English and quickly translated into German, French, and Japanese, *The Spirit of the Chinese People* was a sensation in the West, presenting the culture and the people of China.

relieve their stress and anxiety, which was helpful for pregnancy. Even if there was no boys in the coming year, at least they had tried hard in action. And when many women walked through the bridges together to ask for sons, the tacit understanding and empathy between women was also a silent comfort. The custom of walking through three bridges in the hope of having a boy was unscientific, but it was a real comfort for women in patriarchal society who could only rely on the male members of the family. In this sense, the custom of walking though three bridges was also a special consolation.

In some places, the custom of walking through bridges had more compassionate reason: to dispel all diseases. In the classic Chinese literary masterpiece *The Plum in the Golden Vase* (considered by many researchers to be the inspiration of the *Dream of the Red Chamber*, which represents the pinnacle of Chinese classical fiction), the wives and concubines of the protagonist Ximen Qing went together on the night of the Lantern Festival to enjoy the lanterns and dispel diseases. For women who had been disciplined by the precept of "women should stay at home and should not go out" all year round, to dispel diseases was certainly an appropriate excuse, though the hidden reason probably was that they finally have the annual chance to walk out of the courtyard and breathe freely.

Today the custom of walking through three bridges on the night of the Lantern Festival has changed. It is not for women's humble and ridiculous wish for having a son, but a merry body exercise. During the Lantern Festival in the first lunar month, the water town is illuminated, and the bridge is extremely beautiful in the halo of lanterns. On the night of the Lantern Festival, after having a bowl full of high glucose dumplings (Tangyuan in Chinese), it is indeed necessary for people to do a low-intensity exercise to help digestion and avoid food accumulation. Walking through three bridges in a row ensures the distance of the walk, burns enough calories, and is also a pleasant journey to admire the lanterns, like fish, palace, rabbit, dragon, flower basket, and fairy lanterns ... Lanterns of different shapes are reflected on the water, making the night of the water town more charming. From this point of view, the folk custom of walking through three bridges on the Lantern Festival is the embodiment of the wisdom of the Chinese people: It pays attention to pragmatism as well as takes aesthetics into account; It contains both rationalism and sensibility.

For crew sailing on the Grand Canal, there's a traditional rule of keeping silent when crossing some particular bridges. Two famous of them are the Gongchen Bridge in Hangzhou and the Chaoyin Bridge in Huzhou (a city north to Hangzhou). All men on the boat were forbidden from speaking as if they were mutes so that these special bridges had the nickname as "the Mute Bridge".

Though there was a saying that crew hold their tongues in worship of the Divinity of Bridge, the real concern was for safety. The rushing water under the bridge and the busy shipping channel made chatting, talking, and joking extremely dangerous. So the boatmen must be fully focused to sail safely. Another taboo was that women were not allowed to step on the bridge when boat was going through beneath the bridge. This old custom, like walking through the bridges to pray for a boy, is discriminatory against women, but it also shows that people in the old days believe that bridges can connect heaven, earth, and hell. There is no such old custom of discriminating against women in China today.

The silkworm carnival has been popular in the sericulture area of Huzhou, a prosperous city about 90 kilometers north to Hangzhou. The top-ranked silk bears a particular collective brand as "the Hu Silk", implying the importance of the silk weaving industry in Huzhou. Though the annual carnival does not start until the night of the Tomb-Sweeping Day (usually falls on April 5th every year) , it actually commences much earlier, usually in the 2nd lunar month.

In the 3rd lunar month, creatures are awakened and refreshed after a long cold winter. Silkworm is such a tiny worm that it can only survive in a very comfortable environment. It means the suitable temperature and humidity, the dustless and stainless walls, the brisk air without a piece of stinky smell, and no insects or mosquitos. Silkworm is also a picky one in food: The fresh leaves of mulberry trees are the only food. The more it approaches to its maturity, the more fresh leaves it eats. In the late days of its life, it does nothing but chew the leaves. Partly due to this high-demanding living condition, silkworm grows like a high-demanding baby who often makes mom exhausted. Naturally, the work of attending silkworms usually goes to women who are able to devotedly take care of these delicate and magical worms, just like taking care of their own new-born babies.

Sericulture looks more profitable than farming. The Ming Empire, which was in great need of trade surplus for its huge expenditure on national defense and other vital affairs, issued a state policy to encourage sericulture in the Jiangnan Area. The policy stipulated that peasants of sericulture could pay their tax in the form of silk instead of grain. What's more, they were allowed to do other work as they like, given that they had completed the tribute of silk. This was a widely accepted regulation because it provided a chance of arranging their own work for better living conditions in most days of a year except for the sericulture season from the

3rd to 5th lunar month, no more than 100 days.

The other side of the motivating policy was that peasants who failed to perform well in the tribute of silk would be thrown into jails or even lose their life. Hence, sericulture and silkworm-feeding weighs so much for a family that the women who undertake the job must be extremely careful with silkworms.

People will always pray to a divinity for inner peace, and if the divinity does not exist, then people will create one by themselves. So does the people taking care of silkworms in the Ming and Qing dynasties. Otherwise, what else can be done?

Hence, the Goddess of Silkworm was created. The silkworm carnival was launched as a response to praying for a smooth and fruitful silkworm season. On the carnival, people from local and afar gathered to watch a particular costumed parade, led by a gang of men carving out a way from the crowds by the clangorous sound of huge drums and cymbals. The crowd took one step back and assembled within a second, not letting the most exciting scenery of the carnival slip under their noses: Who is the Silkworm Goddess of the year? Silkworm Goddess, is also called Canhua Niangniang, can be traced back to the legend of the discovery of silk by Leizu—ancestor in ancient times. According to the legend, the ancestor who rested under trees after working found that silk could be taken from cocoon. Another legend *The Horse-Head Girl* is not so softhearted. The horse-head girl is a girl who deceived a hardworking horse. When the horse was beaten to death by the girl's father, she was treacherous and did not save the horse. Suddenly the horse skin jumped up and wrapped the girl, making her become "the horse-head girl", who had to spit silk day and night until death. Apparently this is an ironic and terrifying story.

Unlike the wooden statue covered with color, the Silkworm Goddess is actually dressed up by a girl. This rare arrangement of female image rather than male image is related to the legendary female inventor. In addition to her beauty and kindness, her silkworm-raising skill is also an important factor in competing for the role of the Silkworm Goddess. People in the sericulture have combined the idealism and the pragmatism. Through the respect and praise for the fairy from the real world, people also get a chance to listen to her experience of raising silkworm face-to-face, gaining a real idol for experience. Most of the people who participate in the silkworm festival are female, because the silkworm festival is mainly used to pray for good luck of silkworm-raising.

However, there are some male participants, young or middle-aged. They come to get a glimpse of beautiful young women without risking being condemned in public as playboys. In the past, the silkworm carnival was one of the rare occasions for the young women to step out their houses and enjoyed the merry time. Today the silkworm carnival is still a public marriage-matching ceremony to some extent. Borrowing from the German Baker advertisement "How much romance starts with a glass of light beer", we can say: How much romance start with the silkworm carnival? There is no evidence on this, but there is no doubt that this annual event has contributed to the prosperity of the sericulture industry in Huzhou of Zhejiang Province. In the exhibition center located in the ancient town Xinshi in Huzhou along the Grand Canal, various customs are demonstrated in pictures, showing that women hold silkworm feast for themselves on the first day of the new year, and their work in the sericulture season.

以
桥
之
名

In the Name of Bridges:
The Chinese Cultural Codes on the Grand Canal (Chinese-English Bilingual)
大运河上的中国文化密码（中英双语）

17 The Magpie Bridge: A Popular Romance Breaking Hierarchy

In Chinese culture, bridge is far more than a sort of architecture as part of hydraulic system. In fact, it bears some mysterious belief that are prevailing in China, especially in the Jiangnan Area. Bridge is believed to connect earth and heaven.

We can find proof in a famous poem written in the Song Dynasty. The poem is called "Immortals at the Magpie Bridge". As the title suggests, magpies build a bridge connecting heaven and earth to help a couple of a fairy and an ordinary man to meet. The opening sentence depicts the splendour of the Milky Way, followed by the couple's annual intimate rendezvous. In the last sentence, the two comfort each other: "If we love each other long and deep, we wouldn't worry whether we are together day and night." This beautiful and melancholy verse passes down from generation to the next and has become the most beautiful vow between lovers, especially the long-distance lovers.

The scene depicted in this poem originated from an ancient legend. Zhinyu or the Weaving Fairy in heaven, fell in love with Dong Yong, a cattle herder on earth. She married him, and gave birth to a son and a daughter. The husband was capable to cultivate to produce grain; the wife was good at weaving to make clothes; their son and daughter were both lively and healthy. All these made up a happy model of the traditional Chinese family. However, her absence was known by the Jade Emperor, the Mighty Master of Heaven. The Jade Emperor sent guards to take her back. The Queen Mother of the West, threw out a magic hair-pin to produce a grand heaven river, preventing her escape.

The loving couple were separated. The fairy was locked into a weaving room, weeping while missing her lovely children and her husband Dong Yong. Her lament was so tragic that magpies flying by stopped to comfort her. Being touched by the extraordinary romance, these magpies determined to help her. Although the prohibition in heaven was strict and cruel, it should not forbid the true love. Why the true love could not occur between a fairy and an ordinary man?

What could they do except flying? Anyway, magpie was just a common bird without super power as that of the holy bird phoenix. Nevertheless, the profound mercy and sympathy could inspire the intelligence and strength from the common. An idea came into being.

On the 7th night of the 7th lunar month, thousands of magpies kept flapping their wings to line up as a bridge starting from the Weaving Fairy's chamber to Dong Yong's cottage.

As soon as the magpie bridge reached the ground, Dong Yong stepped onto it, with a shoulder pole carrying a couple of bamboo baskets, in which two kids were sitting. When they were running towards the sky, the Weaving Fairy fled out of her chamber and waited in the center of the Magpie Bridge. In the very center above the heaven river, the miserable, valorous and loving couple met and hugged. The family got united.

Magpies burst into merry hurray; the clouds were gone; and the moonlight was clear and gentle, as if all were wishing the lovers' meeting finally.

This magic scenario was so touching that the Queen Mother of the West persuaded the Jade Emperor to give a slice of mercy to the couple. Finally the Weaving Fairy was allowed to see her husband and kids on the evening of the 7th day of the 7th lunar month every year.

This tale has been widely accepted among the Chinese people as a symbol of romance and a symbol of crossing the pedigree barrier: The bridge of magpie stands for the sympathy to the true love and the wish of the divinity's help to the common people. Today the Magpie Bridge has become a popular metaphor meaning a chance for meeting of lovers after long departure.

Most Chinese myths follow a routine that miserable people get help from the merciful divinities or senior officials and then they have a happy ending. The Magpie Bridge, in the story of the Weaving Fairy and Dong Yong, is not an exception. Nevertheless, what makes the romantic tale particular is the close connection with the common life of the traditional agricultural society.

First, heroine is a working maiden rather than a fantastic fairy with magic power. The Weaving Fairy, as her name indicates, leads a life of weaving all day, just like an ordinary woman in the real world. Second, the Weaving Fairy fled from the magnificent heaven to earth bearing the curiosity about the common people, and this is just like a teenage girl who is longing for "the outside world". Third, Dong Yong carried a pair of large bamboo baskets (with two children sitting in the baskets) to meet his wife. This is also a true reflection of the rural fathers taking their children to distant places for fairs. Fourth, magpie is not as mysterious as the legendary phoenix; it is a common bird that the ordinary people can often see. At the same time, because its Chinese name has the meaning "joy", it also indicates good luck. Fifth, even the rulers of heaven, the Jade Emperor and the Queen Mother of the West created entirely based on imagination, also contributed to the happy ending of the story. At first their attempt to hinder the Weaving Fairy's secret marriage is also a reflection that the annoyed parents are not willing to marry their daughter to a man from the lower class. At last they agreed the Weaving Fairy to have an annual reunion with her husband and kids, just like what the ordinary parents finally accept the son-in-law and the grandchildren. It is the parental love that surpass the disgrace of being offended by the secret marriage.

Reviewing the ancient tale about the Magpies Bridge, or the romance of the Weaving Fairy and Dong Yong, we can find so many details from the common people's life in the real world. Thanks to the close connection with the reality, this tale is most popular and told by grannies no matter in the rural or in the urban. Actually, this story is an evergreen legend passing through hundreds of years, forming part of the foundation of the Chinese spiritual life. In addition to kindness, loyalty and reunion, the tale also conveys the common people's wish for bridging the deep gap between the high and the low social classes. The wish for true love and the persistence for pursuing true love will never cease, no matter how modern and smart the world is and how it will change in the future.

Bamboo: A Cultural Bearing of Handicrafts

China is rich in bamboo. This plant carries a variety of virtues, slender but strong, leafy but light, easy to bend but still beautiful, vigorous though tender. Traditional Chinese intellectuals love bamboo, because bamboo's natural properties are the direct reflection of gentlemen's characters, like modesty (bamboo is hollow in its middle), flexibility (bamboo will bend but not break), strong-will (bamboo can survive the coldest winter with its root keeps growing under the earth), and good-manner (bamboo is elegant with its shape and leaves).

Chinese intellectuals are fond of bamboo. They have bamboo printed onto their stationeries or engraved on their study desks. They depict bamboo in their paintings and lyrics, and entitle bamboo together with plum and pine as "the three close friends in winter". Bamboo pattern can be inscribed on the decorative plaques of stone bridges, and as the elegant accessories of clothes. Sitting in the bamboo grove, they enjoy tea, meditate, or play the seven-stringed instrument… Bamboo is the soulmate of the traditional Chinese literati.

Bamboo is an everlasting theme in masterpieces created by Chinese scholars and artists. A famous poem *In a Retreat Among Bamboos* written by Wang Wei in the Tang Dynasty, describing the ideal life of an intellectual:

In quiet bamboos I'm sitting alone.

Lute I play, verse I intone,

In the deep I'm known to nobody,

Only the clear moon as my company.

For the majority of the common people, bamboo is not a spiritual companion. It is more an economical tool, a hardworking servant, and a tolerant friend. Bamboo requires less to grow well. It weighs little, and is not an intractable plant to be cut down. It is a wonderful material to be made into utensils for people's daily life.

As Hangzhou (Lin'an at that time) was the capital city of the Southern Song Dynasty (1127—1279), the handmade bamboo ware had been quite developed. The collection of memory for the capital city Lin'an of the Southern Song Dynasty, *Mengliang Lu* written by Wu Zimu, recorded that bamboo workshops in Hangzhou could produce a variety of bamboo ware, ranging from bamboo broom, bamboo chair, bamboo curtain, bamboo summer pillow as household articles to bamboo case, bamboo hat, and bamboo carrying pole for outdoor work. Bamboo was also the main material for lodge and hut in the Jiangnan Area due to its flexibility, tenacity and low cost. It also inspires architects.

In the early autumn, peasants in the hilly west area of Hangzhou go to the bamboo grove, cut down some bamboos and dragged them through the narrow path of the village. The lush bamboo leaves sweep the group,

以桥之名
——大运河上的中国文化密码（中英双语）
In the Name of Bridges:
The Chinese Cultural Codes on the Grand Canal（Chinese-English Bilingual）

210

kicking up dust all the way. A man steps into house, drops the long plants on the ground, which is immediately full of immense greenery. After a tedious journey from the mountain to the peasant's house, bamboos gently bounce up and down a couple of times, for their hollow stem are always getting accustomed to the surroundings.

For a skillful craftsman, every part of bamboo is lovely and useful. The stem, bolder and harder at the bottom while thinner and softer at the top, can be made into different products. The hollow and long stem bottom is a ready-to-use tube for rain reservoir or carrying mountain water. The middle part of stem is a natural container for cooking rice. Cut a section of stem, put in some rice and water, cover the bamboo joint as the lid. Make an oven with rocks, ignite some tiny bamboo branches and then add some for more fire. Hang the bamboo tube stuffed with rice over the bamboo fire, and wait. When the half transparent steam is releasing, and the appetizing aroma is rising, you should persuade yourself not to remove the lid at once. Put out the fire and wait for another several minutes or so. When the steam disperses, you may taste the bamboo-tube rice. The white rice is magically glimmering with the very modest green—it's the gift of the bamboo. If you are thirsty, just grasp a bamboo bowl to get mountainous spring flowing in the bamboo tube. And of course, you can easily make a pair of bamboo chopsticks. The tiny boughs of bamboo are easily to be made into chopsticks, which are necessities for local people's daily life and also the cheap souvenir for travelers.

The fresh leave of bamboo can be used as the economical herbal medicine healing cough. The newly buds smells fresh and clear, so it is also a good type of tea. And the tiny root of bamboo, tasting very delicious, is the key ingredient in several famous Hangzhou cuisine. Even the internal coating of bamboo has its value. The extremely thin and half-transparent bamboo membrane can be processed into fabric, which is an ideal material for clothes in hot and humid summer in the Jiangnan Area.

Now let's go back to the courtyard of the peasant. We'll call him Lao Wang, and "Wang" is a common surname in China. The Chinese people like to call each other by his surname and plus a "Lao"—meaning senior or old, to express courtesy and friendliness as well.

How will Lao Wang deal with the bamboo? Lao Wang starts his work by cutting off the tiny boughs bearing lots of leaves, which can be bundled into big broom. The long straight bamboo stem is cut and separated into two piles: One pile is pliable and slender, and the other hard. He then takes out a stem and divides it into several strips. Bending the bamboo strip over fire, Lao Wang makes some clothes hangers. Now he will make a set of bamboo rack. First he selects one stem, making it into a smooth stick without any leaves or small twigs. Then he selects two other stems, on which he will leave several twigs. These twigs will serve as the holders on which hanger-sticks can be put on. The best part of the man-made bamboo rack is that it can be adjusted to the suitable height, higher for drying the sheets and lower for small items. The rack can also serve well in winter for hanging the salty pork, the dried fish and the preserved duck, which are the favourite food during the Spring Festival for every family in the Jiangnan Area. With clothes waving on the bamboo rack, or special food releasing the smell of meat in a line on it, the simple yard is valuable for families.

Lao Wang's wife is satisfied with his husband's work. But what would be done for their beloved son? The boy is in 5 years old, and is eager for toys. A peasant-father can hardly offer extra coins for toys from market, but a handy father will manage to make a basket of bamboo toys.

Lao Wang selects a branch, tests its pliability, then cut it into a bundle of extremely thin sticks with a special bamboo knife. He is going to make a bamboo dragonfly. It consists of two parts, the handle and the wings, and the whole one imitates the shape of a dragonfly. It also looks like a capital letter "T". Lao Wang firstly prepares a bamboo chip with a length of his hand, then drills a small hole in the very center. Symmetrically he cut off a small section of the chip into bevel so that it becomes the dragonfly's wing. The final step is to put a stick into the hole, working as the handle, or the body of dragonfly. When he is doing the job patiently, his boy crouches beside him, starring at him with great curiosity. He holds his breath in fear of disturbing his father's work. In the little boy's eyes, his father, who is always working but seldom talking with him, is now as mighty as a magician. He is too eager to join the bamboo dragonfly contest with his peers.

Now the boy has a bamboo dragonfly in his hands, but can it fly in the sky like a real dragonfly? The boy holds the handle with his two palms, rub it fast, and then loose his hands—in a sudden the little bamboo dragonfly soars! It is flying! It even rotates for a while before falling down. Can't wait for another trial fly, the proud boy rushes merrily out of the yard, upholding the bamboo dragonfly above his head. He will have an exciting game with other boys!

Bamboo dragonfly was invented by the ancient Chinese and introduced to Europe in 1700s. It was a simple but magic toy for boys, and it amazed missionaries, who called it the Chinese spiral. An English man named George Cayley, the father of aerodynamics, inspired by the Chinese bamboo dragonfly and started his research on helicopter propeller.

The kid has run out with his new bamboo dragonfly. Lao Wang and his wife will continue their work with bamboo. Among the many bamboo products, Hangzhou basket is very popular. It is the time for Lao Wang's wife to show her craft. Hangzhou bamboo basket (see Figure 18-1) sells well not only in Hangzhou City but also in the districts nearby. Lao Wang cuts bamboo stem into many pieces of slender strips which are soft enough to be knitted by hand. His wife takes

Figure 18-1 Hangzhou Bamboo Basket
(Painter: Chen Xingyue)

two strips to make a cross-knot, and adds another strip to enlarge the knot; then one more strip joins in and the knot bigger. With her nimble knitting, the knot is getting larger into a small round, which is the bottom plate of a basket. Then she locks the bottom plate with harder bamboo strips. For the main body of the basket, she needs to put tens of thinner strips into the edge of the bottom plate, and then connects them with each other. After several hours, she completes the main body of the basket. And then it's Lao Wang's job to fix handle of the basket. A pair of strips are put into the basket body with their four ends, then are tied together with soft bamboo skin into one handle. This is not the final step of making basket. Lao Wang examines the basket to make sure there's no bamboo thorns. This is the responsibility of a craftsman, and also the resource of his pride.

They will make a dozen of baskets, because Hangzhou bamboo basket is not only a daily utensil but also a souvenir for visitors, especially popular among the women pilgrims. Most of them are from the neighboring counties, taking boats along the Grand Canal to have a sightseeing in the name of praying for fortune in some famous temples in Hangzhou. They are willing to buy a Hangzhou basket as a testimony to her Hangzhou trip. A Hangzhou basket is light and durable, simple and graceful, exquisite and economical. Who can refuse such a basket?

The Qiaoxi Straight Street Block: Aroma of the Chinese Herbal Medicine

With the Qiaoxi Straight Street as the main body, the Qiaoxi Historical and Cultural Block west to the Gongchen Bridge, now is a complex featured with the Chinese herbal medicine culture. Along the stone-paved alley stand several reputable Chinese herbal clinics, solemn for the white-walls and the black-roofs and the soothing herbal medicine aroma.

These clinics' names are full of interest. Fanghuichun Hall, literally means "going back to spring", also a metaphor of recovery from illness, just like the weather getting warmer from the freezing winter to spring. Tianlu Clinic meaning "heaven brings fortune", seems to have a secret power bestowed from heaven so that the common people should trust the clinic.

The mystery of the name of the Traditional Chinese Medicine (TCM) clinics is part of the culture of Chinese herbal medicine. Stepping into the spacious medical hall, you are greeted by a large cabinet with numerous small drawers. All the drawers are in the same appearance, neatly and silently arranged, like unsmiling guards in a palace. However, these drawers also release a sense of humor through the labels attached. Look at their Chinese names: Dang Gui (It's time to go home), Wang Bu Liu Xing (the emperor can't keep you stay here), Shi Da Gong Lao (top 10 achievements). Some names sound precious like jewelry but you can't help bursting into laughter when you get to know their real ingredients: Ye Ming Sha (bright night grit), actually the excretion of bats. Wang Yue Sha (watching-moon grit), the waste of rabbits. That's right. Is there a rabbit in the legendary Moon Palace, isn't it? Bai Ding Xiang (white lilac), you think it is a white lilac but actually it's sparrows' droppings. Think about it, a flock of sparrows flying over your head, poof, bird droppings, oh no, white lilac falls. Long Xian Xiang, is it the aromatic fluid from dragon's mouth? No, it's ambergris — sperm whale intestinal secretion. It is said that the ambergris contributes to the alluring Chanel No. 5—the classical, expensive, and most favorite perfume for ladies. Similarly ambergris showed up in mysterious tales of luxurious imperial palace in ancient China—both for its rarity and its name showing it is from a dragon — as the token of emperor. Interesting, isn't it?

The name-givers clearly know that people dislike those waste from animals, but Chinese herbal doctors hold that these waste from animals, usual or rare, are magically effective ingredients in some prescriptions for some symptoms, so that they, the name-givers and doctors, also become masters of language and rhetoric. We should appreciate the art of naming Chinese herbal medicine instead of scolding them for cheating. After all, comforting patients is part of medicine and language is part of the art of prescribing. Just like the Civet Coffee, made from the excretion of civets at high price, we can easily get a better understanding of the name trick of Chinese herbal medicine.

Different from modern western medicine, Chinese herbal medicine has been developed for more than 5,000 years, and its efficacy is increasingly being discovered and recognized by the world. In the pandemic COVID-19, the traditional Chinese medicine has been shown to have a positive effect. TCM theories can be difficult to understand, partly because of ancient words such as acupuncture points and meridians, but it is also an indisputable fact that Chinese managed to survive for thousands of years before the appearance of the modern western medicine. Traditional Chinese herbal medicine is respectful of nature. The ancient Chinese doctors believed that each plant and animal, tiny or immense, weak or strong, beautiful or ugly, rare or common, bore its own inner-value and therefore had its own place in nature. They held a simple but sincere worship to nature, so they tried to seek out the essence and utilize it to cure the sick people. To some extents, the traditional Chinese herbal medicine is a philosophy — to respect nature and to take advantage of the beings in nature. In short, Chinese traditional philosophy — following nature, just like the spirit of the Taoism.

Here we should spend several minutes learning about the Taoism, which is an important stream of Chinese culture. Taoism, or "Dao" in Chinese pinyin, is one of those philosophical concepts. It connotes a kind of natural rightness, but not mandatory. When "Dao" serves as a verb, it means "to lead, or to guide". There is no need to be compulsive: A person following the "Dao" should not constrain himself or to struggle for what he wants, because that will happen to him naturally as a sort of destiny prescribed in nature.

What is the "Tao"? Laozi, the proponent of the Taoism, explained the "Tao"ha by comparing it to water. He said, "The best is like water."

Water can give form, but also can attach form, according to the situation naturally. This is the core of the "Tao".

In Chinese folk tales, Zhang Sanfeng, a man living in the late Yuan Dynasty to the early years of the Ming Dynasty, is believed to be the most well-known master of the Taoism. He even founded a type of Chinese kung fu and the Wudang School, named after the Wudang Mountain in Hubei Province where he took daily body exercise and meditation. He was more popular when he became an impressive character in a series of best-selling kung fu novels written by some talent novelists, who combined the legends of kung fu masters with the destiny of nation in turbulent times.

Among the novelists, Jin Yong is the best-known one. He has greatly developed the art of martial art novels and made great achievements in literature. Millions of readers are deeply touched by the conflicts rising from the strong emotions in his novels: the patriotism vs the nationalism, the true love vs the family hatred, the benevolence vs the hypothesis, the desire for power based on slaughter vs the humanism deprived from cruelty. By reading his martial art novels, boys get the first lesson of heroism; girls cast the first glimpse of love; the middle-aged get an echo in their hearts on the struggle between family responsibility and personal freedom; and the old fall into their nostalgia when they read the poems and lyrics. Jin Yong's martial art novels are rather the traditional Chinese culture encyclopedia featured with exquisite literary expressions, comparing with the shallow popular stories. Moreover, his novels are appealed to a great deal of readers outside China. His novels has being interpreted into English or other foreign languages, and has being moved on TV screens. When Zhang Sanfeng founded the Wudang School, he could never imagine that his pursuit for longevity would develop into a dreaming martial school that bore profound wish for harmonious society and strong country.

That might be the reason that another Mr Zhang was remembered by the common people in an honorable and unusual way: A memorial Taoist temple named after him was set up near the Gongchen Bridge. This man, who followed the exercise of the Taoism and cured many patients with the traditional Chinese herbal medicine without taking any money. In fact, Mr Zhang's name was Zhang Shenggui and he was a real person. He lived at the end of the Qing Dynasty. On a night of 1878, he was sitting on the top of the Gongchen Bridge to practice his routine exercise when he saw a woman falling into the Grand Canal. Without any hesitation he jumped into the river to rescue her. The woman was rescued but Zhang Shenggui was drowned. At this moment an eagle dived to drag him towards the river bank by seizing his long hair. He had no breath, while his face remained fresh. This incredible sight led people to believe that he had attained nirvana and become an immortal. He was buried beside the Gongchen Bridge with the statue of eagle on his grave. Next year, a petition of building a memorial temple in honor of Zhang Shenggui was approved by Emperor Guangxu to praise his sacrifice and benevolence. Since then, Zhang Shenggui, known as Zhang Daxian, had been worshipped in Taoist temples in the image of a kind-looking old man with silver beard.

Today we will find the Temple of Zhang Daxian next to the famous TCM clinic "Fanghuichun Hall" in the Qiaoxi Straight Street.

Many Taoists are good at keeping themselves in good health and even longevity. Some of them, with the knowledge of picking up wild herbal medicines, become famous doctors. To a certain extent, the Taoism has a close relation with the TCM. Therefore it is natural that there stands a Taoist temple among the TCM clinics. The inner peace of mind and the good condition of body make up the human's health and Zhang Daxian's temple neighboring the TCM clinic can be another example of the Chinese spirit of pragmatism.

参考文献

［1］PICKUS D. Postcards from China: travels along the Grand Canal［M］. Syracuse, NY: New Classic Press, 2020

［2］BALL P. The water kingdom［M］. London: Penguin Random House, 2016.

［3］POLO M, DA RUSTICIANO P. The travels of Marco Polo (volume 2)［M］. SIR YULE H, trans. New York: Signet Cliassics, 2004.

［4］马应心，孟丽莉 . 中国传统文化英语阅读教程 2［M］. 上海：上海交通大学出版社 , 2019.

［5］叶朗，朱良志 . 中国文化英语教程［M］. 北京：外语教学与研究出版社 , 2010.

［6］周家华 . 京杭运河［M］. 武汉：长江出版社 , 2019.

［7］陈述 . 杭州运河风俗［M］. 杭州：杭州出版社 , 2006.

［8］王国平 . 杭州运河遗韵［M］. 杭州：杭州出版社 , 2006.

［9］大河报社 . 行走大运河［M］. 郑州：大象出版社 , 2014.

［10］张翠英 . 大运河文化［M］. 北京：首都经济贸易大学出版社 , 2019.

［11］邱志荣，陈鹏儿 . 浙东运河史［M］. 北京：中国文史出版社 , 2014.

以
桥
之
名

In the Name of Bridges:
The Chinese Cultural Codes on the Grand Canal（Chinese-English Bilingual）
——大运河上的中国文化密码（中英双语）

222

［12］吴齐正.江南大运河古桥［M］.北京：人民交通出版社，2020.

［13］薛家柱.杭州运河新貌［M］.杭州：杭州出版社，2013.

［14］徐吉军.杭州运河史话［M］.杭州：杭州出版社，2013.

［15］陈述.杭州运河历史研究［M］.杭州：杭州出版社，2006.

［16］董桂萍，韩一飞.杭州运河旧影［M］.杭州：杭州出版社，
2017.

［17］赵怡，冯倩，项隆元.杭州运河桥梁［M］.杭州：杭州出版社，
2013.

［18］陈述.杭州运河桥船码头［M］.杭州：杭州出版社，2006.

［19］朱惠勇.杭州运河船［M］.杭州：杭州出版社，2015.

［20］俞燕君，卫军英.大运河城市文化书系 运河南端文化剪影［M］.
北京：首都经济贸易大学出版社有限责任公司，2021.

［21］吴顺鸣.大运河［M］.合肥：黄山书社，2014.

［22］姜师立.运河王朝 从东周到明清［M］.北京：中国地图出版社，
2021.

［23］王英翔.杭州运河文化之旅［M］.杭州：浙江人民美术出版社，
2017.

［24］张环宙，沈旭炜.外国人眼中的大运河［M］.杭州：杭州出版社，
2013.

［25］顾希佳.杭州运河非物质文化遗产［M］.杭州：杭州出版社，
2013.

［26］李泉.运河学研究 第1辑［M］.北京：社会科学文献出版社，
2018.

［27］李泉.运河学研究 第5辑［M］.北京：社会科学文献出版社，
2020.

［28］任轩.遇见：一个人的大运河［M］.杭州：杭州出版社，2019.

［29］郑民德.明清京杭运河沿线漕运仓储系统研究［M］.北京：中

国社会科学出版社, 2015.

［30］王国平. 运河名城：杭州［M］. 北京：中国文史出版社, 2009.

［31］董文虎, 等. 京杭大运河的历史与未来［M］. 北京：社会科学文献出版社, 2008.02.

［32］魏向清, 邓清, 郭启新, 等. 世界运河名录 英汉对照 简明版［M］. 南京：南京大学出版社, 2017.

［33］顾志兴. 运河文化名镇塘栖［M］. 杭州：杭州出版社, 2015.

［34］蔡禹龙, 汪林茂. 运河边的租界：拱宸桥［M］. 杭州：杭州出版社, 2015.

［35］顾希佳, 袁瑾, 丰国需. 运河村落的蚕丝情结［M］. 杭州：杭州出版社, 2019.

［36］仲向平, 陈钦周. 口述杭州河道历史［M］. 杭州：杭州出版社, 2013.

［37］徐则臣. 北上［M］. 北京：北京十月文艺出版社, 2018.

［38］吴齐正. 浙江古桥与古寺［M］. 北京：人民交通出版社, 2016.

［39］罗关洲. 绍兴古桥掇英［M］. 杭州：浙江人民出版社, 2006.

［40］拱墅区档案局. 拱宸桥杂记［M］. 杭州：浙江摄影出版社, 2015.

［41］肖芃. 中国传统文化［M］. 大连：大连理工大学出版社, 2008.

［42］《中国传统文化教程》编写组. 中国传统文化教程［M］. 北京：中国人民大学出版社, 2020.

［43］张芹玲. 新编中国传统文化［M］. 北京：高等教育出版社, 2015.

［44］崔刚, 莫嘉琳. 中国传统文化英文入门教程［M］. 北京：清华大学出版社, 2015.

［45］常宗林, 李旭奎. 中国文化导读［M］. 北京：清华大学出版社, 2006.

［46］王宁．文化翻译与经典阐释 增订本［M］．南京：译林出版社，2022.

［47］金惠康．跨文化旅游翻译［M］．北京：中国对外翻译出版公司，2006.

［48］顾建国．运河名物与区域文化考论［M］．上海：上海三联书店，2014.

［49］朱秋枫．杭州运河歌谣［M］．杭州：杭州出版社，2013.

［50］应志良，赵小珍．杭州运河戏曲［M］．杭州：杭州出版社，2013.

［51］顾希佳．杭州运河非物质文化遗产［M］．杭州：杭州出版社，2013.

［52］朱惠勇．中国古船与吴越古桥［M］．杭州：浙江大学出版社，2000.

［53］袁飞．困境中的挣扎［M］．北京：中国社会科学出版社，2018.

［54］佟洵，王云松．国家宝藏博物馆里的中国史 第1卷［M］．北京：石油工业出版社，2020.

［55］徐珺．汉文化经典外译理论与实践 ［M］．北京：北京大学出版社，2014.

［56］王琴玲，黄勤．中国文化英译教程［M］．北京：清华大学出版社，2015.

［57］中共拱墅区委宣传部．运河家书［M］．杭州：杭州出版社，2019.

［58］墨川．南宋大航海时代 中国第1部大宋航海史诗［M］．北京：经济管理出版社，2008.

［59］姚迪．基于多维价值的大运河遗产保护规划理论与方法研究［M］．南京东南大学出版社，2020.

［60］洪艳，朱明德．京杭大运河沿线历史建筑的现代适应性研究

［M］．杭州：浙江大学出版社，2020.

［61］张强．运河城市与明清通俗小说［J］．江苏社会科学，2014(3): 176–184.

［62］钟行明．明清大运河北新关关署空间及其管理活动［J］．山西建筑，2017(4): 1–2.

［63］胡梦飞．明代淮安的常盈仓［J］．江苏地方志，2012(6): 26–28.

［64］虞云国．南渡君臣：宋高宗及其时代［M］．上海：上海人民出版社，2019.

［65］邓广铭．宋史十讲［M］．北京：中华书局，2008.

［66］任轩．运河的指纹［M］．杭州：杭州出版社，2022.

［67］徐铮，袁宣萍．杭州丝绸史［M］．北京：中国社会科学出版社，2011.

［68］魏向清，邓清，郭启新．世界运河名录 简明版［M］．南京：南京大学出版社，2017.

［69］刘海峰，李兵．中国科举史［M］．上海：东方出版中心，2004.

［70］赵怡，冯倩，项隆元．杭州运河桥梁［M］．杭州：杭州出版社，2013.

［71］《CCTV–10中国记忆》摄制组．中国大运河［M］．上海：上海科学技术文献出版社，2010.

［72］邱志荣，陈鹏儿．浙东运河史（上卷）．北京：中国文史出版社，2014.

后　记

终于。

终于！

2019 年 5 月的一个夜晚，当我在学校图书馆打开笔记本电脑，敲下 "The Dengyun Bridge"，我绝不会想到，这本意在为中西文化交流搭建一座桥梁的小书，会耗费我整整 4 年的时间。

毕竟，动笔之前，我已经在京杭大运河拱宸桥畔住了 9 年。我无数次走过运河两岸，无数次看着货船、游船推开运河波浪，熟悉那一桥一河一亭一台，熟悉运河边的多个文化遗产点。我骑车或者步行从运河杭州城区段最北边的北星桥一路向南、向东再向南，一直到达三堡，亲眼看到运河在这里挽起了钱塘江——浙江的母亲河。我自驾去过湖州的德清、新市、潞村、和孚，桐乡的崇福、屠甸，海宁的盐官、长安，绍兴的安昌、柯桥，杭州的博陆、临平、塘栖、西兴，寻找运河与江南水乡唇齿相依的交集，抚摸古镇人文与运河深深相融的痕迹，追溯运河作为经济大河、文化大河与民生大河的源流。

我细细探访过京杭大运河沿岸古镇上与蚕桑、谷仓、古桥等相关的博物馆、展览馆及名人纪念馆，亲手触摸过古桥上布满岁月包浆的石狮子，端详过桥栏和望柱上雕刻的各种图案，用脚丈量过古桥斑驳的石阶。我在西兴为百岁老人的绿植浇过水，在德清拜访过双目几乎失明而坚持写地方志的作家，与大运河专题纪录片的总撰稿人、绘画工作室的青年画家等都有过有关运河文化的交流。我也为拱宸桥畔的历史文化馆、民俗记忆馆等做过文本翻译，了解了历史深处的运河变迁，也了解了中华人民共和国成立后特别是中国大运河申遗以来政府与相关管理机构为保护运河和传承运河文化付出的巨大努力。

我还看了学校图书馆能借阅到的所有与运河、桥梁相关的图书，翻阅了与中国传统文化相关的图书，细读了与中国文化对外交流相关的图书，领会了"讲好中国故事"的精神，研读了有关中国文化的翻译理论。

由此，写作思路逐渐成形——面向中外读者尤其是外国读者，以运河上的桥梁为线，讲述中国传统文化。

所以，我以为，我已经胸有成竹，只需要把所见所思诉诸笔端，一行一行地，把这座文化交流之桥构建起来。

万万没想到，这个我以为做了充足准备的构建文化交流之桥的工程，竟然如此艰难。

第一个难处在于史实的把握。大运河悠悠千年，年代的久远和流域的辽阔，以及列入世界文化遗产之后取得的巨大关注，都使得相关资料汗牛充栋。而信息众多会造成甄别的困难，文化学者和地理、水利学者的研究重点不同，对同一个对象的结论也不尽相同。同时，作为一条"活着的"大河，大运河本身也在发生变化，单是京杭大运河的长度，究竟是不是 1794 千米就有不同的说法。大运河的概念也是多维的，中国大运河、隋唐大运河、京杭大运河、浙东运河，这几个"运河"彼此之间是什么关系？常常见诸报端或人们口口相传的运河，是哪一个？运河上的古桥，长宽高、台阶数，不同的资料给出的说法不同，应当采信哪一种？

第二个难处在于文化的生发。这本书的初衷是让外国友人更好地了解大运河，了解大运河串起的中国传统文化。但是中华文明五千年，选取什么样的传统文化进行讲述，才能塑造"可亲、可敬、可爱"的中国形象？从什么角度进行讲述，才能在众多对外的中国传统文化读本中独树一帜？非虚构写作要求事实清楚、文风朴实，在事实和想象之间，怎样行文才能有一定的文学性，有未来的传播性？

第三个难处在于非母语写作。母语写作我已经坚持了多年，从事英语教学和应用翻译也有了不短的年头，但是用英文进行大篇幅的含有创意性的写作，则实实在在是另一个"频道"。英语和汉语分属不同的语系，其逻辑思维存在差异。除此之外，对英语词汇的选择也大费周章，绝不是翻阅词典就可以轻易落笔的。中国传统文化是中国特有的，如何表达文化词（culture-loaded words）才能让外国读者顺畅地理解？从翻译的角度来说，又该怎样处理好"归化"与"异化"的关系以达到"功能对等"？何时何处需要进行"文化补偿"？除考虑词汇的准确性之外，还需要考虑词汇以及表达会不会有"大国的傲慢"？在此基础上，能不能带有一点生动和幽默，从而更符合外国读者的喜好，达到文化交流的目的？

这些问题，如果说动笔之初还没有充分预计到，那么在写完数篇之后，就越来越成为萦绕心头的问题。出于某种文化自觉，我必须有所努力。仅举数例：

"进士"，这个在中国科举制度中特有的称号怎么用英文表述？词典给出的英文是"Scholar"。尽管首字母"S"大写，但是"scholar"这一单词本身十分常见，意为"学者"。而"学者"是十分宽泛的概念，与"进士"中"学而优则仕"的内涵相去甚远。那么，是不是可以借鉴英国的皇家学会院士（Fellow of the Royal Society）、美国科学院院士（Fellow of the National Academy of Science）的译文呢？不行。"进士"虽然是指在科举考试中最高一级殿试的胜出者，但不代表其有相当高的学术成就，而且从人数上来看也远远少于上述英美院士（"翰林"倒是相对接近），因而，从荣誉性上来看也要远远低于

"院士"。另外，"进士"是中国传统文化中的核心词之一，与它相关的一系列名称，自成体系。那么，"进士"一词就可以本着"让译入语读者了解译出语文化"的原则，采用汉语拼音"Jinshi"，而书稿中对科举制度的详细解释能够让英文读者理解"Jinshi"的内涵。毕竟，有"kung fu"（功夫）这样的珠玉在前，"Jinshi"承载的中国传统文化也应当走向世界。

又比如，中医药文化怎样激发读者的兴趣？五行经络虽然有其奥妙，但是诉诸英文，很难从科学实证的角度进行阐释，强行论证"气""穴"恐怕只会适得其反。那么，就从中药的名称入手。我选取了"当归""夜明砂""白丁香"等药材名称，在给出拼音之外，还进行了汉语字面意义上的解释，使得意象与事实之间发生断裂（如"白丁香，是洁白的丁香花吗？不不不，它是麻雀的粪便"），这种断裂产生了修辞上的效果，让人忍俊不禁之余加深了印象。

再比如，如何让英文读者更好地走近中国传统文化？讲到运河边的说书艺术时，我论及了英国的戏剧；讲到抗金女将梁红玉时，我引入了古希腊的胜利女神和法国的圣女贞德；讲到"道"时，我引入了英国小说家毛姆的理解。《红楼梦》是在海外广泛流传的中国古典文学经典。在本书中，我多次引入了《红楼梦》的相关内容，一方面是为了自证本书所写的中国传统文化并非虚言，另一方面也是希望进一步宣传《红楼梦》这部集中国传统文化之大成的经典名著。由此，可能会使更多的读者有兴趣进一步了解中国。聚沙成塔、集腋成裘，讲好中国故事、传播中国文化，是一项综合性工程。

在行文的文学性上，我也做了努力。这里摘取一段对金庸的武侠小说的介绍：

Millions of readers are deeply touched by the conflicts rising from the strong emotions in his novels: the patriotism vs the nationalism, the true love vs the family hatred, the benevolence vs the hypothetic, the desire for power based on slaughter vs the humanism deprived from cruelty. By reading his martial arts novels, boys get the first lesson of heroism; girls cast the first glimpse of love; the middle-aged get an echo in their hearts on the struggle between family responsibility and individual freedom; and the old fall into their nostalgia when they read the poems and lyrics. Jin Yong's martial arts novels are rather the traditional Chinese culture encyclopedia featured with exquisite literary expressions, comparing with the shallow popular stories.

译文：

　　成千上万的读者被小说中激烈的情感冲突深深地感动：爱国主义与民族主义、真爱至上与家族世仇、仁义道德与虚伪背叛、为争名逐利而进行的嗜血屠杀与远离残暴的人文精神。通过阅读他的武侠小说，少年获得了英雄主义的第一课，少女投去了第一次爱恋的目光，中年人的心中响起了在团队责任和个人自由之间挣扎的共鸣，老年人则在传统诗词中陷入了遥远的乡愁。金庸的武侠小说，不是读罢就扔的浅薄之作，而是某种意义上的中国传统文化百科全书。

　　好事多磨。出版社十分严谨，要求我对书中所涉事实与数据提供出处。就在昨天，因为一张照片，我惊出一身冷汗。书稿第 12 篇写的是城东桥与杭州的丝织业，配图是我实地考察时拍摄的城东桥的照片，其栏杆上有丝帛元素的彩绘，在运河上的桥梁中独一无二。但是昨天下午我骑车再去看城东桥的时候发现，丝帛彩绘竟然消失了！丝帛彩绘是这一篇的写作基础，没有丝帛彩绘，就无法将城东桥与杭州丝织业联系在一起；拿掉该篇，书稿大缺；放着不管，则是谬误。一夜未能安睡。情急之下，我咨询了运河专家任轩老师，他明确地告诉我他曾经设计过这座桥的文化元素，丝帛彩绘正是考虑了附近集镇的丝织传统。可是，眼前的城东桥没有了丝帛彩绘，到底是哪一座桥呢？焦急之中，我拜托住在那一带的朋友亲临现场，把就近的三座桥都看一看。对着朋友发来的同角度拍摄的照片，我们反复比较，方才恍然大悟：原来，确实是城东桥，只是桥栏上的彩绘不知何时被抹去了。这一发现，让我赶紧对书稿中的配图照片做了说明，心里的石头才落了地。类似的求证，在本书的写作过程中是时时发生的。

年少时读到贾岛"推敲"的典故和"捻断数茎须"的诗句，总觉得那是文人夸大其词的自我感动，甚至是自我标榜。而今，经过长达数年的中英文双语写作，不计其数的斟酌修改，甚至几次沮丧、逃避，我才知道"文责自负"这 4 个字背后所蕴含的辛劳。在这漫长的过程中，我像是走在一条隧道里，一开始为隧道外美丽的山坡所吸引，觉得不过如此而已，往前走就是了；走着走着，往来汽车的嘈杂、走不到尽头的慌乱、压在心头的沉闷，都让我不止一次怨恨自己当初的不自量力。动笔写这本书时，既没有科研项目资助，也不是岗位职责，何必如此自苦呢？但是，脱离隧道困境的唯一办法就是继续走，往前走，放弃大步流星、脚底生风的幻想，耐心地、安静地，挑着担子，小步向前。毕竟，半途而废，我丢不起这人。而且，我曾对我 70 多岁的母亲夸口：上一本书献给父亲，这一本，要献给您。老母亲当时"哦"了一声再无其余的淡然平静的态度，对我是一种特殊的心理解压。何况，还有关注此书的朋友的支持与鼓励。正如深耕运河文化 20 年、为大运河申遗工作及"后申遗"做出过诸多贡献的任轩老师所激励的：这件事情是有功德的，是真正为"擦亮大运河这张中国文化金名片"而踏踏实实地做事情。现在，我已经到了隧道的出口，世界光明，空气清新！心头重负虽已卸下，但是这燕子衔泥般构建的"桥梁"，究竟能不能入行家法眼，能不能让外国读者喜爱，能不能真正助力中外文化交流，需使用者评判。

靡不有初，鲜克有终。溯洄从之，道阻且长。作为住在运河边的一个普通的中国人，我看到运河静水流深，看到运河流淌的时间力量；作为一名多年从事英语教学的高校教师和一个写作与交流的爱好者，我也看到在运河文化的国际化推广和对外交流上，还有可以补充和完善的地方。这本 26 万多字的《以桥之名——大运河上的中国文化密码（中英双语）》，是我的一次努力和尝试，是对心中"讲好中国故事"的召唤的回答，也承载着从手绘画者到运河学者到英语学者再到出版社诸君的襄助。从这个意义上说，这本小书有其文本之外的宝贵之处，它见证了人与人之间的真诚。自勉，亦与读者诸君共勉。

王雅平

于杭州流云轩

2023 年 5 月